PRAISE FOR
My Money Journey

"*My Money Journey* is a must read for people—of any age or experience—who want to be better at managing their financial lives. It is chock full of real-world stories of financial and investing success, and challenge, from people 'just like us.' There's no better way to learn. Those stories, and the summary lessons from each contributor, provide a great road map for readers as they chart their own course to financial well-being."

—Jack Brennan
Author of **More Straight Talk on Investing** *and the former CEO and Chairman of Vanguard Group*

"I loved every bit of this wise book. Its financial success stories don't owe to towering salaries or complicated investment strategies. Instead, the contributors chalk up their financial freedom and peace of mind to more relatable factors: healthy savings habits, common sense, and a dash of good luck. I saw a bit of my own story reflected in its pages, and it's a good bet that you will, too."

—Christine Benz
Morningstar's director of personal finance

"A real-life look at how messy, complex—but ultimately rewarding—a personal relationship with money can be."

—Morgan Housel
Bestselling author of **The Psychology of Money**

"Any book can talk about the blocking and tackling involved in personal finance. What I love here are the stories of the stops and starts, the successes and the oops through the decades of a personal journey. No one's life is a predictable straight line. It is how we navigate the unexpected that gives us the foundations for financial independence and security."

—Clark Howard
Renowned consumer advocate and founder of Clark.com

"These 30 deeply personal essays on achieving financial goals are inspiring and instructive. Great reading for all who want to achieve lifetime financial security."

—Consuelo Mack
Anchor and Managing Editor, Consuelo Mack WealthTrack

"Embedded in the unique and delightful financial life stories of 30 individuals are the most important lessons investors must learn. Financial security requires disciplined, regular saving and investing, minimizing costs (as through indexing) and taxes (as through Roth IRAs), and avoiding common blunders. Perhaps even more important than financial health, loving your work and having a genuine interest in others leads to a fulfilling life."

—Burton G. Malkiel
Author of **A Random Walk Down Wall Street**
(50th anniversary edition)

My Money Journey

My Money Journey

HOW 30 PEOPLE FOUND FINANCIAL FREEDOM —AND YOU CAN TOO

EDITED BY **JONATHAN CLEMENTS**

Harriman House

HARRIMAN HOUSE LTD
3 Viceroy Court
Bedford Road
Petersfield
Hampshire
GU32 3LJ
GREAT BRITAIN
Tel: +44 (0)1730 233870

Email: enquiries@harriman-house.com
Website: harriman.house

First published in 2023.
Copyright © Jonathan Clements

The right of Jonathan Clements to be identified as the Author has been asserted in accordance with the Copyright, Design and Patents Act 1988.

Paperback ISBN: 978-0-85719-986-7
eBook ISBN: 978-0-85719-987-4

British Library Cataloguing in Publication Data
A CIP catalogue record for this book can be obtained from the British Library.

CONTENTS

WINDING PATHS

RISK AND RETURN

INTRODUCTION:

Your Journey Starts Here

BY
JONATHAN CLEMENTS

IMAGINE YOU TOOK a group of folks—mostly male, mostly older, mostly upper-middle class, mostly well-educated—and had them describe their financial journey. They'd all be pretty similar, right? You might be surprised. I was.

When I asked 29 writers for *HumbleDollar's* website to join me in contributing essays to this book, I wasn't quite sure what I'd get. But as the last few essays trickled in and I looked over the submissions, what struck me most was the diversity of the stories. There are many paths to the top of the mountain. Most journeys start haphazardly, trying one route and then another. But eventually, successful investors settle down and do mostly the right thing for many years, and they end up with surprising wealth—and nobody's more surprised than the investors themselves, who discover that a huge pile of dollars has resulted from decades of prosaic prudence.

While each journey described here is unique, you'll likely notice that certain themes crop up again and again. Here are the eight themes that struck me:

Our parents mold our financial beliefs. This comes shining through in almost every essay. Trust me: If you're a parent, it's scary to realize how much influence you have on your children. Really scary. What beliefs from our parents should we hang on to, and which should we discard? For some contributors to this book, it's been a lifelong struggle.

The key to financial freedom is good savings habits. It's banal to say it, and yet it can't be said enough. The virtue of thrift is a theme that runs through almost all 30 essays.

Complexity is unnecessary. Again and again, you'll hear mention of the same simple strategies. Dollar-cost averaging. Extra-principal payments on a mortgage. Maxing out retirement plan contributions. Indexing. To the uninitiated, the world of personal finance can seem baffling. But once you dig into the details, you'll discover that complexity is usually the route to high costs and mediocre returns, while simplicity offers not just better financial results, but also a comforting sense of control.

We don't need to be great investors. That's just as well, because most of us aren't. In fact, most folks end up with investment results that trail the market averages, which is why indexing—humbly accepting the results of the market averages—is a strategy embraced by virtually all contributors to this volume.

Success is apparent only in retrospect. It usually takes decades to achieve financial independence, and, along the way, progress often seems grudgingly slow. And then one day, we look back and realize how far we've come—and how all those small, sensible decisions have compounded one upon another to ensure a comfortable future. Are you early in your financial journey and saving regularly, but it feels like a game of inches? For inspiration, look no farther than the stories in the pages ahead.

Don't discount the role of luck. Our financial success often hinges on things beyond our control. Does our boss take a shine to us—or instead favor others for no apparent good reason? Does our employer prosper, or do we find ourselves struggling to survive in an organization beset by red ink and constant layoffs? Once we have a healthy sum invested, does a booming stock market fatten our nest egg even further—or are we hit by a vicious downdraft?

It seems almost all of us get dealt a bad financial hand at some point in our life. The wound might be self-inflicted, or it may come out of the blue—a major medical bill, a bad investment, a family member needs our help, unemployment, divorce. Such financial hits may set us back, but—as you'll learn from some of the essays—the damage doesn't have to be permanent.

We infuse money with meaning. Money is just money in the same way that a Maserati is just a car and the silver cutlery we inherited from our parents is just flatware. My point: These inanimate objects hold meaning far beyond their objective attributes—and how I feel about such things will likely differ from the sentiments you harbor.

It's worth spending serious time pondering the meaning we attach to money and its many uses. Are we buying the Maserati because we love finely engineered automobiles—or because we want to impress the neighbors? Are we saving diligently because we want the financial freedom to pursue activities we find fulfilling—or are we over-saving because we're terrified that we'll end up destitute? In the essays that follow, many of the writers discuss their relationship with money and their efforts to make their peace with the almighty dollar.

At its best, money is a tool that delivers a sense of security, lets us devote our days to activities we're passionate about, allows us to have special times with loved ones, and lets us help those around us, not just family and friends, but also those we'll never know personally. How should we divvy up our money among these possible uses? It comes down to our values—to what each of us believes is meaningful and finds fulfilling.

At some point, we need to declare "enough." Then comes the next hard task: learning to be satisfied with what we have—and enjoying the money we've accumulated. This may be the destination we've long had in mind, yet most of us find that the journey never quite ends and contentment remains elusive. That isn't so terrible. We humans are built not to rest and relax, but to dream and strive. There's great satisfaction to be had from that striving.

Everybody who contributed to this volume has also written for *HumbleDollar*, the website I launched at year-end 2016. One thing you might notice: Just five of the 30 contributors are women. Despite the many great female personal-finance writers over the years—think Sylvia Porter and Jane Bryant Quinn—it seems that, in many households, money management remains a largely male preserve. I wish it were otherwise.

For the writers involved in this book, the essays often didn't come easily. It's hard to step back from your life and write with some objectivity, being neither falsely modest nor excessively self-congratulatory. Money, I believe, is the last great taboo. Most of us are reluctant to reveal the details of our financial life, and yet the contributors to this volume did just that.

And once they did, they were tortured by me.

Many of the 30 essays received an initial edit from Greg Spears, *HumbleDollar*'s deputy editor. Retired newspaperman Joe Kiefer also pitched in. Many thanks to both of you. Once Greg and Joe were done, I would wade in, sometimes playing the heavy. In every instance, the writers dealt with my questions and comments with great patience.

Among the writers, Adam Grossman deserves a special mention. Not only has Adam been *HumbleDollar*'s most prolific contributor, but also he set this project in motion in late 2021, when he shot me an email suggesting that *HumbleDollar* put out a book.

This is the second project I've worked on with Harriman House editor Christopher Parker. As with the vast majority of *HumbleDollar*'s writers, I've never met Christopher in person. But if that ever happens, I imagine we'd have a good time—because working with him has always been great fun.

Last but far from least, there's the lovely Elaine, who has heard so much about *My Money Journey* that she's well-acquainted with every writer and knows the pertinent details of all their financial journeys. Thank you for your willingness to listen to me ramble—and for your wise counsel. No, I don't mention you in my essay. But you are, without a doubt, my story's unexpectedly happy ending.

JONATHAN CLEMENTS

FIERCE FRUGALITY

If there's one financial virtue that trumps all others, it's the discipline required to save great gobs of money. No matter how much you earn, if you don't take a slice of those earnings and set it aside for your future self, you'll never achieve financial freedom. Saving diligently is a theme in almost every essay in this book. The six writers in this section have turned frugality into a fine art—though sometimes the personal cost has been higher than they would have liked.

ROAD TO RETIREMENT by Dennis Friedman

SAVING MYSELF by Kristine Hayes

FREED BY FRUGALITY by Sanjib Saha

EARLY AND OFTEN by Mike Zaccardi

TAKING CONTROL by Jiab Wasserman

NOW AND THEN by Jonathan Clements

ROAD TO RETIREMENT

BY
DENNIS FRIEDMAN

Dennis Friedman retired from Boeing Satellite Systems after a 30-year career in manufacturing. Born in Ohio, Dennis is a California transplant with a bachelor's degree in history and an MBA. A self-described "humble investor," he likes reading historical novels and about personal finance.

WHEN I WAS in my early 20s, many of my friends wanted to buy expensive new cars. But I wanted to save money. In fact, I was probably too thrifty. Some people wear their frugalness as a badge of honor. But I was sometimes embarrassed by my spartan lifestyle.

I was a college graduate with a history degree. There weren't too many jobs for someone like me. That could be the reason I was squirreling away so much money. Later, I did get an MBA, but that insecure feeling never went away.

Most of the homes I lived in were small apartments without the standard conveniences you would expect when renting or buying a home. Some of my apartments were so terrible I was embarrassed to invite friends over. In 1980, I was looking for an apartment to rent. I walked by an older building that had two vacancies.

One was a studio apartment located on an alley above a garage. The rent was $300. The other apartment was a one-bedroom with a long and narrow floorplan facing the street. It reminded me of a bowling alley lane. The rent was $500. I chose the studio apartment because it was cheaper and I could save more money. I was making decent money at the time, working as a production control planner, but I was determined to live well below my means.

It wasn't the safest place to live. A drug dealer lived in the apartment next to me. My car was broken into more than once. One day, someone stole my clothes from the laundry room. But none of that fazed me—until the new owner raised my rent to $390. At that moment, I realized I needed my housing costs to be more stable and predictable if I was ever to reach financial freedom. I knew if I kept renting, my landlord could increase my rent at any time. I'd have no control over one of my biggest expenses—my home.

MY FIRST BIG INVESTMENT

In 1985, I found a small 789-square-foot, one-bedroom condominium for sale in Long Beach, California. It was on the top floor of a nice-looking, secure, three-story building and overlooked the street. It felt like you were in a treehouse because the top of a big tree was hanging over the front of the unit. It was within walking distance of the beach and plenty of good restaurants. It seemed like the ideal place to settle down. The owner was asking $102,000, but I was able to negotiate the price down to $91,000.

The next morning, I woke up with buyer's remorse. I felt anxious about being a first-time homeowner. I'd never purchased anything that expensive before. The only other thing I'd bought of any real value was a new 1976 Mercury Capri, and that cost just $4,500. I went to work that day thinking about all the things that could go wrong with owning that condo: What happens if I lose my job? What happens if I can't get a home loan? Is that big tree out front going to be a problem? Is it going to be too noisy facing the street?

I was sitting in my boss's office at Hughes Electronics discussing some manufacturing issue, when he asked, "Is there something bothering you?" I guess my demeanor revealed the uncertainty I felt about the purchase.

I told him I'd put a deposit down on a condo, but I was thinking about canceling the transaction. I said, "I don't know if it's a good deal for me." Cliff was reassuring. He pointed out the upsides of being a homeowner. It could increase my net worth because I would build equity if the condominium rose in value. I could also deduct the interest on the home loan and the property taxes on my tax return. It started to sound like a pretty good deal, after all. It was what I needed to hear.

The condo was one of the best investments I ever made. My mortgage payment was only about $150 a month more than the rent I'd paid for that crummy studio apartment. Later, I refinanced at a lower interest rate and my mortgage payment was even less. I eventually paid off the mortgage in 14 years.

The condo purchase put me on the road to financial security. Because of my low and stable housing costs, I was able to save a lot of money during the 35 years I lived there. I maxed out my 401(k) plan contributions. When I reached age 50, I added regular catchup contributions to the plan. Any other extra money I had left over I invested in a taxable account at Vanguard Group. My salary kept going up and my housing costs were going down. It was a perfect scenario for someone who's an avid saver. I thought I'd reached nirvana.

When I sold my condo in 2020 for $380,000, my old studio apartment on the alley above the garage was renting for $1,564. If I'd stayed there, or rented another apartment, I never could have saved the amount of money I did. At the time I sold the condo, my housing costs were approximately $600 a month. That included homeowners' association fees, property taxes, insurance and utilities. I rarely had any out-of-pocket expenses for repairs.

A MISTAKE PAYS DIVIDENDS

While I was doing a good job of saving money, I wasn't doing a very good job of investing it. I was constantly jumping in and out of different mutual funds and stocks, trying to find the right investment—until the day I got some fatherly advice.

I used to call my mother every day just before I left work. If I didn't call her, she would think something was wrong. One day, I called and my father picked up the phone. He started talking about this guy on the radio who was giving out investment advice. He encouraged me to listen to his show at the weekend. I was skeptical, but I gave it a try.

It was the early 1990s. The host started talking about something called Spiders—otherwise known as Standard & Poor's Depository Receipts—and about a Vanguard 500 index fund. At first, I had no clue what the guy was talking about. I didn't know you could buy a mutual fund or an exchange-traded fund that tries to match the performance of an index, such as the Standard & Poor's 500. But the more I heard him talk about how these types of investments cost less, generated less taxable income and were highly diversified, the more I liked what I heard.

The one thing he said that really caught my attention was this: If you invest in an index fund, you take away one of the biggest risks in investing—underperforming the stock market. After all the years of unsuccessfully trying to beat the market by investing in actively managed funds and individual stocks, this statement rang true. I began to make low-cost, broad-based index funds the core holdings in my investment portfolio.

Unfortunately, I also listened to something else the radio show host said—and that advice cost me money and sleep. He was a market-timer. He issued a major buy signal for the Nasdaq Composite index and suggested buying an exchange-traded index fund that's now known as Invesco QQQ Trust. I bought QQQ at $70 a share and watched it fall to $20. I found myself invested in the most volatile part of the stock market during a savage bear market. As the share price plunged, I felt like I had jumped out of an airplane without a parachute. And I wasn't the only one. I had talked my sister into it. Then my dad jumped in. He didn't want to miss out on the opportunity. I felt terrible for sucking them into this mess.

It took many years before QQQ reached my breakeven share price. I learned an important lesson about trying to time the market: It's extremely difficult to predict what the stock market is going to do in the short run. After that financial fiasco, I decided to keep it simple and become a long-term investor. When I retired, almost all my money was in just three funds. I had roughly 35% in Vanguard Total Stock Market Index Fund, 20% in Vanguard Total International Index Fund and 45% in Vanguard Total Bond Market Fund. I'd learned the hard way that these three funds were all I needed to help me reach my financial goals.

A LESSON FROM MY FATHER

Although I had a fairly sizable investment portfolio when I retired, I still didn't feel financially secure, in part because of a conversation I had with my father. I received a phone call one evening from my dad. He asked if I could come over right away. I knew it must be important because I lived about 25 miles away, and the rush-hour traffic at that time was terrible.

When I got there, we went upstairs to a small room that my

parents had made into a study. He handed me a tablet and pen, and started telling me where all their money was. I knew right away what my father was doing. He was getting his affairs in order.

My father had been battling cancer for two years. He went through many rounds of chemotherapy and radiation treatment. He'd even tried experimental treatments to combat the disease. He'd finally realized he wasn't going to make it. My dad wanted to make sure I knew where every nickel and dime was located, so I could help my mother when he was gone. Most of the money was at Vanguard, but there was also money at a few banks and a brokerage house.

As I listened to my father, I realized how important it is to have sufficient guaranteed income for life. He knew it would be difficult to survive on just his Social Security benefit and their modest retirement savings. My dad had taken his Social Security at age 65. My mother also had a small pension of $495 a month from her days as a switchboard operator at a department store. They had declined the survivor's benefit option on my mother's pension, which meant my father wouldn't have received anything if she died first. They thought her pension was so small it didn't make sense to take the survivor option and get an even smaller payout, plus a woman's life expectancy is longer than a man's. It turned out to be the right decision. My mother lived until age 96, passing away seven years after my father.

When I left my parents' house that night, I knew it would be wise to delay my own Social Security benefit until age 70. I saw the worried look on my father's face, knowing that my mother's savings might run out, and that his Social Security and her small pension might not be enough for her to live on. Still, waiting until 70 to take Social Security wasn't easy. It was difficult to withdraw money from savings to cover all of our living expenses, especially after drawing a paycheck for 40 years. Knowing that all my friends and acquaintances weren't waiting until 70 also didn't help. But I kept thinking about my mother, and how a larger check would have made her life more financially secure. I wanted that for my wife.

There was another reason to delay my benefits. It lowered my taxable income. While I waited to claim Social Security, I was able to make larger Roth conversions. That means I'll have smaller required minimum distributions starting at age 72.

The wait for a larger check was well worth it. My Social Security today is over $40,000 a year. If I ever have to have a conversation with my stepson about our money, I'll be able to tell him that my larger check should be more than enough to cover our basic living expenses for as long as we live. Meanwhile, we're enjoying ourselves. We can spend more freely knowing we have a financial backstop. The experts might be right when they say retirees who have predictable income are happier. When you add together my wife's Social Security benefits and mine, they're large enough to support us during periods of market turmoil. That means we can give our portfolio time to rebound from any market hit. Maybe most important, the bigger check gives us peace of mind.

When I look back, I was obsessed with the idea of saving enough money so I could retire early. I did retire early, at age 58. Even so, I still felt financially insecure—until I started receiving my Social Security benefit.

TOMORROW IS HERE

Although I now have a financially comfortable retirement, I also have regrets. I wish I had traveled more earlier in life rather than waiting to do most of it when I retired. Instead of accumulating more wealth than I needed, I should've invested some of that money in a trip to Europe, Asia or even Australia. It doesn't seem right that a 70-year-old man, who loves to travel, has been out of the country just twice—to Canada and Mexico, and that's if you count Tijuana.

I waited until retirement to do some of the things I've always wanted to do, and that might have been a mistake. Almost immediately after retiring, I had caregiving responsibilities for my parents, and that was followed by the pandemic. Together, they've kept me from doing the things I'd planned to do in retirement. It's been 12 years and counting since I quit work, and I'm still waiting to fully experience what retirement life is supposedly all about.

I feel a sense of urgency to get on with my retirement. I don't feel like I've lived a full life yet. It's a painful feeling that no amount of money can cure. The only way to make that feeling go away is to experience life. That's what I plan to do with my remaining time.

THREE LESSONS

* If you buy a reasonably priced home and live there for the long haul, you'll lock in your housing costs and, as your income rises, you should enjoy ever more financial breathing room.

* Broad market index funds take away one of the biggest risks of investing—the risk that you'll underperform the market averages.

* Don't defer all your dreams until retirement. You may find that, when the time comes, life events or ill health prevent you from doing the things you've always wanted to do.

SAVING MYSELF

BY
KRISTINE HAYES

Kristine Hayes has a master's degree in biology and spent 24 years working as the biology departmental manager at a small, liberal arts college in Oregon. Her pastimes include dog training and competitive pistol shooting. She and her husband recently retired to Arizona.

LIKE TO THINK that what happened to me in my mid-40s wasn't a midlife crisis, but instead a midlife reinvention.

I transformed myself physically and mentally. I lost 20 pounds. I took up CrossFit. I learned how to shoot guns and began participating in—and winning—pistol competitions. I spent a considerable amount of time evaluating every aspect of my life. I thought long and hard about what made me happy and what didn't. I pledged to purge everything that no longer provided me joy. My beloved Welsh Corgis made the cut. My husband didn't.

Getting divorced after nearly 20 years of marriage wasn't as traumatic as I expected. I'd felt trapped in a loveless relationship for years. For more than a decade, my husband and I had lived like college roommates rather than life partners. We went on separate vacations. We kept our finances separate. We had few friends in common. Everything, from our taste in music to the hobbies we pursued, was completely different.

As part of the divorce settlement, we agreed to sell our home, along with almost everything we'd acquired over the previous two decades. In a matter of a few days, I went from living in a 3,000-square-foot, completely remodeled home to inhabiting a 600-square-foot apartment that hadn't been updated in at least 30 years. The few pieces of furniture I needed were purchased off Craigslist.

Even though nearly every aspect of my life had been disrupted, I found myself happier than I'd been in years. But one stress weighed heavily on my mind. Financially, I had no idea how I would negotiate the second half of my life.

In 2013, when my divorce was finalized, I'd been working for the same employer for 15 years. I was making $57,000 a year while residing in an area of the country where the cost of living was 30% higher than the national average. I knew almost nothing about managing money or investing.

I walked away from my divorce with a used car, two dogs and about $80,000 in cash from the sale of our home. I'd managed to retain the full balance of my 403(b). I did, however, forfeit half of a small state pension-plan benefit that I'd become vested in decades earlier.

I spent the better part of the next year getting comfortable juggling my day-to-day finances. I started tracking every dollar I spent, a habit that remains with me to this day. I keep a small notebook detailing my income, as well as every expenditure, no matter the size. By late 2014, I was comfortable that my income and spending habits were in equilibrium. I had more than enough each month to cover rent, utilities, insurance and food. I was able to cover any discretionary expenses that arose. I decided it was time to start educating myself about investing and retirement planning to ensure I'd continue to have a financially stable life.

I soon found myself spending all my spare time learning about personal finance. My reading list included *Women and Money* by Suze Orman and *The Millionaire Next Door* by Thomas Stanley and William Danko, as well as the annual financial guide that morphed into HumbleDollar.com. I listened to Dave Ramsey podcasts every night before bed. I read blog posts by Mr. Money Mustache. I poured over the vast amount of information posted on the Bogleheads.org forum.

It wasn't always easy to decipher the information I was taking in. I often felt overwhelmed and risked analysis paralysis. I knew I needed to develop a plan to make small, systematic changes in how I managed my finances.

MY JOURNEY BEGINS

I started 2015 with a resolution to put my financial house in order. The first step was to calculate my net worth. With no debts, the calculation wasn't difficult. The total value of my retirement accounts, my cash savings and my car came to just over $250,000. I felt good knowing that, at age 47, that figure meant that I'd exceeded the median net worth for my age group.

Next, I reviewed how my retirement funds were invested. I was vested in a TIAA 403(b) plan. Every month, my employer contributed an amount equal to 10% of my salary to the plan. Between 1998 and 2004, all my contributions were directed into a guaranteed return account. I assumed that investing my funds safely—the account was guaranteed to earn a minimum 3% annually—was the best way to ensure that I'd build a sizable nest egg.

In 2005, a TIAA representative convinced me that I was invested far too conservatively for my age. The rep suggested that I consider contributing to a mutual fund account. Starting later that year, I chose to direct new contributions into a stock index fund.

When I reviewed the performance of my 403(b) account in 2015, I wasn't unhappy with the rate of return I had been earning. My money had been growing, albeit at a slow pace, for 17 years. I was, however, convinced that I needed to invest in accounts that would deliver higher returns over the long run. I also knew I needed to start contributing a larger percentage of my salary toward my retirement savings, so my nest egg would grow faster.

The final component of my financial roadmap was to establish a specific goal. I knew that, without a target to strive for, I'd be more likely to fail. I decided to aim to have my retirement account on its own reach $250,000. I planned to get there by steadily contributing a portion of my salary to a stock-based mutual fund. Starting in 2015, I set aside $500 a month from my paycheck and invested it in a growth-stock index fund. The money my employer contributed to my account was split between a 2035 target-date retirement fund and an international growth fund.

As my account balance grew, I was motivated to save even more. Soon, I was contributing $1,000 a month. By 2016, I was setting aside almost 50% of my paycheck each month. Living frugally became a game—one I enjoyed playing. I borrowed books from the library rather than buying them from Amazon. I made my lunch every day so I wouldn't be tempted to eat out. My entertainment was limited to those shows and movies I could watch for free using my Amazon Prime membership.

I also began taking on freelance writing assignments as a way to supplement my income. The amount I earned varied wildly. Some months I brought in nothing, while other months I earned an extra $400 or $500. By late 2016, I'd achieved my first financial goal. My retirement account hit the $250,000 mark for the first time.

EYEING RETIREMENT

When I turned 50 years old, in May 2017, I began thinking seriously about how much longer I wanted to work full time. In the course of my personal finance education, I'd been introduced to the Financial Independence, Retire Early (FIRE) movement. I'd read stories of people who stopped working long before their 60s.

I began to think it might be possible for me to leave behind full-time employment when I turned 55. At that time, I'd be eligible to receive an early retiree health insurance plan through my employer. That benefit meant I'd have the freedom to take a part-time job without worrying about having access to healthcare coverage.

I felt confident I could continue the pace of my savings for another five years. Even though I didn't particularly enjoy living in an apartment, I was resigned to staying there a few more years. I didn't foresee any large expenses that would hinder my ability to keep saving a large portion of my salary. I decided my second major financial goal would be to have enough financial stability to shift to part-time work at age 55.

For the first time in my adult life, I felt like I had a solid financial plan and a lofty goal to go along with it. I took comfort in knowing that, when I turned 55, I could always reevaluate my situation. If I needed to, I could continue to work full time until I reached financial security.

A CHANGE IN PLANS

Life throws everyone curves and, for me, 2018 was a year of major upheaval. Unlike 2012—when I'd purged my life of everything that left me feeling empty—2018 was a year overflowing with happiness. I brought home a new puppy. I moved out of my run-down apartment and became a homeowner again. And the change that brought me the most happiness? I got remarried.

The financial plans I'd put in place as a single woman were suddenly no longer applicable. The flow of money previously directed to my retirement account was rerouted to a mortgage company. Overnight, I went from being a one-person, two-dog household to a member of a two-person, four-dog family. I questioned whether my goal of early retirement was still achievable.

My husband, who is 13 years older, was already retired when we married. We both looked forward to the day I could stop working. We were eager to relocate to a different part of the country, since both of us were growing weary of Pacific Northwest weather and politics.

In 2019, we visited two locations we were considering for retirement. We were priced out of the housing market at our first pick. Our second choice, a 55-plus community just outside Phoenix, Arizona, still had homes available in our price range. We put in offers on three houses before landing one. The community had everything we were looking for: multiple recreational facilities, easy access to medical care, and a thriving group of active retirees. I also felt good knowing that, if I later needed a part-time job, there were employment opportunities available in the community.

Purchasing two homes in less than a year put a serious strain on my limbic system. I took comfort in knowing that both of our homes were modest structures. Each had been built in the 1980s. Neither had been significantly updated or renovated since being constructed. As a capable do-it-yourselfer, I wasn't put off by the prospect of investing a bit of time and energy into fixing up the houses.

Buying two homes just a few months before housing values began increasing at a record pace turned out to be one of the most beneficial—and luckiest—financial moves I've ever made. Both homes appreciated handsomely between 2020 and 2022, and we walked away with a hefty gain when we sold our Portland home in early 2022. That was when I gave notice to my employer—and set off to enjoy early retirement.

WHERE I STAND

In late 2021, I transferred 40% of my total retirement portfolio into the TIAA Traditional account. Because of the way the account is structured, some of my money is guaranteed to earn just 1%. But most of it is set at a guaranteed return of 3%. The actual crediting rates are consistently higher than these minimum levels. The remainder of my TIAA account balance is invested in a couple of stock index funds. My state pension fund is guaranteed to earn 7.5% annually.

Should I choose to annuitize my TIAA Traditional account, I'll have numerous options when it comes time to draw money out. I can take interest-only payments or monthly lifetime payouts, or I could systematically withdraw all the money over ten years. While the annuity option doesn't come with a guaranteed annual cost-of-living increase, the fund has typically increased the payouts it makes to recipients, including a 5% increase for 2022.

I'm hoping I won't have to touch any of my money prior to age 65. During our initial retirement years, my husband and I plan to live on his retirement income. We also have the proceeds from the sale of our Oregon home. Should we need it, I can claim my Social Security benefit at age 62. My husband is delaying his benefit until age 70.

When I reflect on my personal finance journey, I ponder the things I would have done differently. I wish I had fought to retain my state pension rather than forfeiting half to my ex-husband. I wish I had started contributing a portion of my paycheck to my retirement plan when I was in my 20s, instead of waiting until I was in my 40s. I wish I had invested in more aggressive mutual funds at a younger age.

But I can't change the past. The roadmap that led to where I am now is filled with twists and turns I never saw coming. I also know I can't put a price on happiness. At this moment in my life, as I sit at my kitchen table writing and watching our four dogs frolic in the backyard, I'm as content as I've ever been.

THREE LESSONS

* If you set specific goals, including target dollar amounts, you're more likely to make financial progress.

* Two regrets that folks often voice: They wish they had started saving earlier in their career—and they wish they had allocated more of their savings to stocks.

* Make plans, but be prepared to remake them: Our lives are subject to frequent upheaval—sometimes good, sometimes not—and that can necessitate big financial changes.

FREED BY FRUGALITY

BY
SANJIB SAHA

Sanjib Saha is a software engineer by profession, but he's now transitioning to early retirement. Self-taught in investments, he passed the Series 65 licensing exam as a non-industry candidate. Sanjib is passionate about raising financial literacy and enjoys helping others with their finances.

WHEN I TOOK a job with a U.S.-based software company and moved to the States in 2000, I wasn't planning to live here permanently. I came under the H-1B visa program, which allows non-immigrant foreigners to obtain temporary employment. I figured I might work in the U.S. for a few years and then return to India, where I grew up.

Things didn't quite turn out that way.

I started my career as a software engineer in Kolkata, my hometown. But as a lover of travel, I seized opportunities to work abroad and get to know new cultures. My plan was to work in other countries while I was young, before heading back to Kolkata with my wife to settle down. America was on my bucket list. An opportunity came almost by accident.

While working in Ireland in the late 1990s, I returned to Kolkata to visit my parents. I bumped into an acquaintance who lived in the U.S. and worked for a software company. In those days, many software engineers regarded his employer as the premier software company. Sensing my envy, he asked for my résumé. I was skeptical about my prospects but, on his insistence, I typed up a CV.

After returning to Ireland, I forgot about the whole thing, but he didn't. A recruiter called me to set up a few phone calls to check my technical knowledge. Once I had cleared that hurdle, the recruiter offered to bring me to the U.S. headquarters for interviews. An all-expense-paid trip across the Atlantic sounded like a great deal, and I was soon on a plane heading to the Pacific Northwest.

The dozen or so interviews over two days were grueling. I was bombarded with all sorts of questions, including brainteaser puzzles and bizarre algorithmic problems. By the end, I felt I had wasted everyone's time. Demoralized, I returned to Ireland.

When the recruiter called back the next week, I was almost certain that I hadn't made the grade. But to my surprise, she offered words of congratulation: I had made it.

My coworkers and supervisor at my Irish employer advised me to accept the position. I leaned toward doing so, but there was a downside: Taking another foreign job in my early 30s would delay my eventual return to India.

On the other hand, the upsides were too attractive to ignore. The chance to be part of a transformative company might never come my way again, I'd get to explore a beautiful country full of natural wonders, and the job might be my ticket to financial freedom—for two reasons.

First was the promising math of working in a high-income country before returning to one that has a low cost of living. Even modest savings would go far in my hometown. I'd already saved a bit from my previous overseas jobs. A few years of saving in U.S. dollars would mean increased financial security.

Second, my pay package included stock options—a benefit I'd never before heard of. The recruiter explained that, when the options vested, I'd reap the profit from any rise in the company's share price since my starting date. The stock had been on a tear for nearly a decade. If history was any guide, she said jokingly, the options would make me a lot of money. Little did I know that all my options would expire worthless and that the stock wouldn't recover for 15 years, thanks to the bursting of the dotcom bubble. So much for getting rich quick.

Because I was naïve enough to extrapolate past performance of the company's stock into the future, the overall compensation package looked unbelievably attractive. Great work, beautiful place, generous pay. What more could I ask for? I accepted the job offer and moved to the U.S. in early 2000.

COMING TO AMERICA

The new chapter of my life started well. That summer, I visited a close friend of many years who was also now living in the U.S. It was refreshing to catch up with him and spend time with his family. His wife suggested that I buy a house. When I replied that I planned to go back to India in a few years, my friend laughed and made three predictions: I'd soon gain at least 20 pounds, I'd have no time to connect with friends, and I'd live in the U.S. permanently. I made a friendly bet that he was wrong.

Over the next few years, we lost touch—until tragedy struck. My friend suffered a cerebral stroke and was put on life support. I flew to see him as soon as I could but, alas, he never woke from the coma. I didn't get a chance to say goodbye, let alone treat him to something as payment for the three bets I'd lost.

My friend's premature death shook me. He wasn't even 40. I felt that my life also was ticking away. I started to picture my future self and the family who depended on me financially. What would happen to them if I died? Who would attend my funeral and what would they say about me? My midlife crisis set in early.

Meanwhile, I, too, had a few ups and downs. I went through a divorce in 2003. What followed was a period of ultra-frugality while I put my financial house back in order. I said goodbye to every hint of luxury—the almost-new car, the spacious rental apartment, vacation trips, cell phone, even going out with friends. To save on rent, I bought a poorly lit townhouse in a not-so-great location. I rarely bought anything beyond groceries and essentials. I cooked all my meals and limited my socializing to occasional get-togethers with close friends over home-cooked food. The local library became my only source of books and videos. With a four-figure cost of living and my six-figure income, it didn't take long before I was back on track financially and able to resume a less thrifty lifestyle.

A few years later, I remarried. I abandoned my plan to return to India and decided to settle permanently in the U.S. This last decision nixed my plan for financial freedom. I could no longer count on a lower cost of living later in life. I was 38 and effectively starting my financial journey from scratch.

My friend's demise was also a wake-up call. I needed to stop procrastinating and get serious about my financial responsibilities, especially now that I was not only remarried, but also had a stepdaughter. I bumped up the coverage amounts on my life- and disability-insurance policies. I named beneficiaries on my financial accounts. I figured that I needed to do more than just save aimlessly—I needed to plan. That was when I realized my biggest money blunder.

I was clueless about the stock market and its indispensable role in building wealth over the long term. I had wasted the first 15 years of my career taking shelter in bank certificates of deposit and savings accounts. I had, unfortunately, missed out on years of stock market compounding. No, I wasn't sitting on the sideline with cash, waiting for a better time to invest. Rather, I simply mistook the sideline for the playground.

Thankfully, I also possessed a valuable asset—my income-earning potential—and that offset my many financial mistakes, big and small. I was fortunate that software engineering turned out to be a dependable career for my generation, providing not only abundant job opportunities and high pay, but also enjoyment and satisfaction. The steady income, and the security it provided, was my greatest financial strength.

Fixing my money mistakes was easy once I took the time to learn about investments and personal finance. I maxed out my 401(k) contributions, putting the money in diversified stock funds. I got into the habit of investing my savings in inexpensive index funds. Because of the demands of work and family, and the pursuit of various hobbies, I was too busy to pay much attention to market noise. That was a blessing in disguise.

WRESTLING WITH READINESS

The 2000s went by swiftly. My wife went back to work, and the extra income bolstered our household balance sheet. My stepdaughter started elementary school and—seemingly before we knew it—was off to an in-state university. As empty nesters, our daily life slowed, and I had time to focus on something that had been bothering me.

A brief interaction with a stranger, whom I'll call Ted, left me anxious about our finances. Ted was a part-time driver for a shuttle service that my employer used for local commutes. One day, I was feeling unwell at work and needed a ride home. Ted showed up with a car.

Ted appeared to be in his late 60s or early 70s. He was eager to strike up a conversation and, from his remarks at stoplights and amid the rush-hour traffic, I figured he was disgruntled with his job. I was curious as to why he was still working at his age, especially if he disliked his job so much.

Ted didn't mind my inquisitiveness. He had retired several years ago after working for more than 35 years. The first few years of retirement went well—until the 2008 financial crisis. His nest egg had shrunk, and he was too afraid to dip into it. Instead, he needed ongoing income to supplement his investment earnings. He didn't think he could "re-retire" anytime soon.

I found his story hard to believe. How could a citizen of the world's wealthiest country be unable to afford retirement after a multi-decade career? Did he lose money flipping houses or in some other crazy get-rich-quick scheme? I didn't know what had happened, but I got a clue later when I learned about the effect of the financial crisis on new retirees. Ted was probably one of the many investors who had responded to the market plunge by panicking and cashing out their investments, vowing never to own stocks again.

Ted's story made me worried. Was I going to end up in the same boat when my paychecks stopped? How much money would I need for retirement, and how much longer would I have to work to get there? With my daughter in college, it was a good time to research my retirement readiness.

The exercise was overwhelming. As I navigated through the retirement planning maze, my spreadsheet got overly complicated, with dozens of parameters and macros. I didn't expect so many moving parts and so many unknowns. I was getting nowhere in figuring out a target size for my retirement nest egg. The number varied widely depending on my assumptions and inputs.

It then dawned on me that I was asking the wrong question. It wasn't about how much money I'd need to retire comfortably. Rather, the question was whether my personal time and independence were more valuable than financial comfort. It was about finding the courage to set a retirement date.

BUYING TIME

With this changed mindset, my spreadsheet appeared to tilt in my favor. Unless catastrophe struck, I wasn't too far from financial freedom. On my 47th birthday, I made a resolution to retire in three years, by the end of 2017. I wrote down the number 1,095—the number of days until my 50th birthday—and pinned it on our kitchen wall.

My daughter was amused. My wife was more surprised than anxious. Could I really afford to walk away from a golden-egg-laying career so soon, especially after a late start? Truth be told, I was a little puzzled too, until I analyzed our cash flow. The secret wasn't an oversized gain on smartly picked stocks, nor was it financial windfalls. Instead, it was that we lived far below our means.

Frugality was ingrained in me, thanks to my parents. They also imparted many other sound money habits that have paid off big time throughout my life. I had been able to handle money responsibly and keep expenses in check since my schooldays. Growing up in a middle-class family in India, I also learned to abhor debt. Paying off a loan always felt like an accomplishment.

Our low expenses helped in two ways. First, we didn't need a large nest egg to support our modest lifestyle. Second, our supercharged savings rate, which typically ran at least 60% of our household's after-tax income, quickly got us to our number—what we needed for financial security. The compound growth of our dollar-cost-averaged investments did its magic.

To be clear, our financial situation was far from rock solid, especially for an early retiree. The plan could've backfired. But I wanted to take my chances, knowing that I could reverse course if things didn't work out. My wife didn't intend to stop working in the near future. That, and the flexibility of my plan, made things easier.

As I approached my 50th birthday, I broached the subject of retirement with my supervisor. His brilliant suggestion turned out to be the best financial guidance I've ever received: He advised me to gradually reduce my work hours rather than stop abruptly. I took him up on his offer.

Switching to a part-time role at age 50 has worked out well, and I still love it. I get the extra time for my personal interests. Without the pressure of a high-powered career or the feeling that I'm dependent on a paycheck, I enjoy my work more. My modest spending habits may not appeal to others—but they've bought me one of life's greatest luxuries, which is financial freedom.

THREE LESSONS

* If you save more each year, your portfolio will grow faster—and you'll simultaneously shrink the nest egg you need to support your lifestyle.

* We all make investment mistakes. But if you earn a steady income starting early in your career and save diligently, those mistakes are usually easy to overcome.

* As you approach retirement, don't just think about how much you need saved to be financially secure. Also ponder what your time is worth—and whether it's worth more than the paycheck you're collecting.

EARLY AND OFTEN

BY
MIKE ZACCARDI

Mike Zaccardi is a freelance writer for financial advisors and
investment firms. He's a CFA® charterholder and Chartered
Market Technician®, and has passed the coursework for the
Certified Financial Planner program. Mike is also a finance
instructor at the University of North Florida.

M Y FIRST JOB was driving the golf-ball-picker cart on the driving
range at a local municipal course. That was 2003, when I was
a high school sophomore. My salary: $10 a day in cash plus free
golf privileges. Playing time was important to me. I was a mediocre
golfer trying to make my high-school team.

Eighteen years later, and now age 34, I have more than $1 million
socked away—the sort of sum my teenage self would have dreamed
about. But along the way, I've discovered that amassing seven figures
is far less meaningful than I once imagined.

Back in 2003, I saved all I could, stashing my $10 in a drawer after
each day on the job. While getting hit by golf balls in the picker cart,
I listened to FM radio. *The Clark Howard Show* ran during the late
afternoons. My parents sometimes also had that station on in the

car during errands around Jacksonville, Florida, where everything seems to be at least 20 minutes away. I had always been interested in money, so Howard's personal finance show resonated with me.

I learned about the wonders of the Roth IRA and the new target-date mutual funds from Vanguard Group. My first investment came in early 2004, although not at Vanguard. My mom accompanied me to a local bank, where I bought a certificate of deposit yielding a solid 2.1%. I thought, "I can make money without having to work for it? I'm in." In hindsight, I should have bought stock in Apple—which is up about 40,000% since then.

I left my money to grow at the bank while I continued picking up balls at the golf course. I got a pay raise in 2004—to $15 a day. The following June, I also began working at Publix, the main grocery store chain in the Southeast. My hourly wage was $7. I spent the summer of 2004 bagging groceries and sweating at the golf course. I went on to make the golf team that fall semester.

By late 2004, I had saved $3,000. Taking Clark Howard's advice, I opened a Roth IRA at Vanguard and bought shares of the 2040 target-date retirement fund. My $3,000 was the minimum investment needed at the time. When my certificate of deposit matured the following January, I used the proceeds to start on my 2005 IRA contribution. It took months, but I accomplished my goal, contributing the annual IRA maximum of $4,000.

My junior and senior years in high school were devoted to three things: golf, money and tracking hurricanes. I remember doing time-value-of-money exercises on my TI-83 scientific calculator in English class. I'd never heard the term 'TVM,' but that's what I was doing—forecasting what my net worth might be by the time I retired, some 45 years down the line. Hurricanes were also barreling toward Florida during those two active seasons. I enjoyed giving impromptu hurricane forecasts and weather reports in front of my classes, so much so that I chose meteorology as my first major in college.

WINDS OF CHANGE

In 2006–07, I spent my freshman year at Florida State University. I enrolled in a few 'met' classes and even launched a weather balloon from the roof of the Love Building in Tallahassee. I still thought of myself as a weather-nerd first and a money-nerd second. But I quickly realized that, while I loved presenting weather information to a crowd, I wasn't as excited about learning physics, chemistry and computer science. I made the switch from meteorology to finance in early 2007.

I still recall 2007's first quarter: I was earning a cool 6% in an online savings account and the stock market was doing well. I began dabbling more in international developed and emerging market stock funds since both kept beating the lousy S&P 500. I even took my speculative talents to the next level and opened an account at E*Trade right before the spring semester ended. Apple was my first individual company stock purchase. The shares went up 10% in a matter of a few weeks. I banked my profits and felt like a genius. In reality, it was the worst sell of my life.

While at college, I kept working at Publix so I could bolster my savings and pay some bills. One significant market trend wasn't in my favor—gas prices. A gallon of regular gasoline surged from under $2 in 2005 to above $4 by mid-2008. My 1998 Toyota Camry, while great on gas, was no fun to fill up as prices rose. It took nearly a full day's work, after taxes, to cover the cost of a fill-up. Still, I was able to keep hitting my goal of maxing out my Roth IRA each year.

Having switched majors from meteorology to finance, I decided to move back to Jacksonville and attend the University of North Florida (UNF). Meteorology was a specialty at Florida State. But since I was no longer going to be a weatherman, there was no point staying in Tallahassee. I also increased my savings rate by living at home and commuting to classes. My net worth swelled to $30,000 as of October 2007's stock market peak.

UNF was great because classes were in the evenings. I could work at Publix during the day and be in class at night. Unfortunately, I had extra time on weekdays, when the stock market was open. I began day-trading. Naturally, I lost a few grand during a year of trading individual stocks and options. But I learned a valuable lesson: I didn't have the talent or temperament to beat the market over such a short time frame. I realized I was on the wrong track and wouldn't become the next hedge-fund billionaire. I focused once again on my long-term strategies for building wealth, including continuing to max out my Roth IRA and maintaining a high savings rate.

One of the many benefits of pursuing a finance degree at UNF was the ability to work enough hours at Publix so the company paid part of my tuition. I took advantage of Publix's tuition reimbursement program from 2007 through my graduation in 2011. My grandmother was also kind enough to contribute to a college savings account that grew to $2,200. She endearingly dubbed it my "Legg Mason money", after the firm where she invested.

At the University of North Florida, I took part in several supplemental programs, helping with the student-managed investment fund, presiding over the finance society and even writing an investment column for the school's newspaper. Yes, for a young finance nerd, this was what constituted fun.

My final two years at college were a whirlwind. I worked for an independent insurance salesperson and then took a part-time job as a wealth management intern at a local registered investment advisor. River Capital Advisors was just across the road from college. I learned the ropes of the advisory business during the afternoons and then shot over to campus for evening classes. I was paid by the hour, allowing me to invest a tidy sum around the stock market lows of 2009. While my net worth had declined to under $20,000 by then, I knew it was smart to be buying at cheaper prices.

TRADING PLACES

Another internship opportunity came my way in 2010 at The Energy Authority, a nonprofit in downtown Jacksonville that assists utility companies in navigating the energy market. I woke up in the dark to be on the trading floor in front of four glaring computer monitors by 6:30 a.m., so I could help schedule trades. I didn't return home until 10 p.m.

With each job, I stashed away as much money as possible. I kept my living expenses low—like 'below poverty level' low. I maxed out my retirement accounts every chance I got. When I graduated from UNF in April 2011, my net worth was $80,000, with no debt.

I began working full time as a stock research analyst at a local mutual fund company, but found that I was too hyperactive to spend my days reading company 10-Ks and tweaking Excel models. I struggled to find my way. A bear market struck in 2011's third quarter. From its peak near $90,000, my net worth dipped below $70,000.

I took a job at a major brokerage firm in late 2011. I worked overtime and saved as much as possible, but burned out after a year. Still, my net worth hit a big milestone while I was a licensed representative, eclipsing $100,000 in July 2012. I celebrated by purchasing a 100 Grand chocolate bar—no joke. That early financial success got me featured in *Living Large for the Long Haul*, a book written by my childhood hero Clark Howard.

My new goal was to max out my 401(k) each year. I was even savvy enough to do an in-plan Roth conversion at the end of 2012, so my 401(k) would grow tax-free thereafter. I moved on from the brokerage firm and began work as an operations associate at a major investment bank with a large office on Jacksonville's Southside, just across the street from River Capital Advisors.

I settled in with a decent salary for someone my age. I continued investing as much as I could in my Roth IRA and 401(k). I drove a 2004 Honda Civic, which was better on gas than the Camry, and was dirt cheap. I paid just $4,200 in cash for it. It lasted about five years with little maintenance. Meanwhile, at the investment bank, I nabbed a few raises.

In late 2014, Pat, my old manager at The Energy Authority, contacted me about a job on the trading floor. We dined at a nearby Applebee's—which he and I look back on with nostalgia—to discuss what he had up his sleeve. A month later, I was back in front of four computer monitors, but this time I was the trader doing the deals. It was a steep learning curve. My salary also grew, including a 53% pay raise in 2015.

That's when my net worth started taking off. I ended 2014 just shy of $200,000. I moved closer to my new office, saving money in the process. After college, I rented from my parents at a rate of $1,000 per month, partly because I felt guilty about living at home rent-free during college. The 2014 move lowered my monthly rent to $469, including utilities and internet. Conveniently, I was within walking distance of Target, Walmart, Publix and church. It was a great situation—and thrifty, too.

I finished my MBA at the University of North Florida. Once again, the tuition was covered by my employer. I was on the hunt for my next challenge. I found it: the Chartered Financial Analyst (CFA) designation. Back in 2011, I had attempted to pass Level 1— and failed. Undeterred, I sought to round out my CV with the most respected and challenging finance designation around. I believed that, if I earned the CFA, I would boost my future earnings potential.

In late 2016, my net worth was rising fast. I was up to $350,000. I put my nose to the grindstone and passed each level of the CFA program, one after another. To this day, my greatest feeling of accomplishment was receiving that email confirming I had completed the program and earned the right to put those three letters—CFA—after my name. My net worth climbed above $600,000 by mid-2018.

When I was a wide-eyed undergraduate at UNF, Prof. Reinhold Lamb had overseen the student-managed investment fund. During my MBA studies, I had also enrolled in three of his courses. But it turned out I wasn't done with UNF. Lamb offered me the chance to teach his portfolio management class. I had been a regular guest lecturer for his students, but this was a whole new ball game. I had to ensure my finance knowledge and communication skills were on point.

I began teaching in the fall of 2017 and continued through spring 2021. Teaching taught me lessons, including patience, how to listen and how to present. A university adjunct is not big money, though. Whatever I earned, I plopped in the university's 403(b) plan, which complemented my employer's 457(b) plan. I also kept socking money away in my Roth IRA.

Following the CFA program, I felt the obligation to monetize my CFA to the fullest. I offered my analytical and writing services on an online financial advisor forum. I got a couple of bites. I began doing portfolio due diligence and writing blog posts at an hourly rate. I wrote early in the morning before my day job started, while also teaching at UNF at night.

Meanwhile, I was advancing at The Energy Authority. I went from trader to assistant portfolio manager to portfolio manager. My total income peaked in 2019 and 2020, thanks to my work as a portfolio manager, investment writer and instructor. My net worth swelled to more than $800,000 as the ball dropped in Times Square and the fateful year of 2020 began.

SEVEN FIGURES

A key lesson I learned over the past five-plus years: You can only drive down your expenses so low. I spent under $10,000 per year but couldn't get that figure down any further, short of being homeless. Still, that was low enough, especially with my income growing rapidly. Indeed, that was the key to my financial freedom—minimal expenses and a rising income. I switched roles at The Energy Authority to the risk group in early 2020. My writing business was flourishing, and I still taught at UNF. Everything was on track.

Then came the pandemic.

My net worth notched a short-term peak near $860,000 in January 2020. That's when I began writing for *HumbleDollar*. The following month, the stock market crashed. The numbers looked ugly on the personal finance spreadsheet I had kept since 2007. My portfolio bottomed at $640,000—the same level that I'd reached in September 2018. I didn't care. I was confident the markets would recover.

They did indeed snap back, plus I still had my various jobs. I approached a huge psychological number that so many savers strive to hit: $1 million. I'm not going to lie. I checked my net worth frequently in October 2020 as I neared seven figures. Then the day finally came. Guess what? It felt like any other day. I didn't have a profound sense of accomplishment, as I did when I earned the CFA designation. Eclipsing $1 million just seemed so empty. "Is this it?" I pondered the question on my daily walks. I'd achieved financial independence by saving early and often. But there were downsides to delaying gratification in such an extreme way.

I was also stressed about life at The Energy Authority. My work turned from something I looked forward to on Sunday afternoons to a job that no longer felt like a good fit. My former manager was helpful and encouraging, but I had no passion for the work, aside from the daily updates I published each morning on the energy market and weather. We agreed to a breakup in early 2021. I embarked down an uncertain road. I was writing and teaching, but doing so without a steady paycheck or comforting employee benefits.

Then the spring semester ended. After that, my only income came from the five to ten hours a week of hourly contract work for advisors and financial firms. It was rewarding to work with others by phone, email and Zoom. I was living the good life—on paper— writing a couple of hours at most in the morning, then reading and charting before lunch. In the afternoons, I got some of that awesome Florida sunshine while listening to financial podcasts during my regular walks. Unfortunately, it was also a rather lonely life, especially now that I no longer had a trading floor full of friends and happy acquaintances with whom to socialize.

You could call me 'the reluctant FIREist.' As of 2021, I was financially independent (FI)—and I discovered I'd unintentionally retired early (RE). It was never my goal to retire at age 33.

Realizing that I wasn't one for the FIRE movement, I started applying for jobs, not so much for the money, but to find a little more purpose in my life. Oh, and my net worth? It hit $1.4 million by late 2021. But I don't pay as much attention these days.

As for my portfolio, I've not scored big in crypto or high-flying tech stocks. My tilts toward value stocks, small-caps and international shares—along with keeping more cash than I need to hold—have resulted in relatively modest annual returns compared to a portfolio heavier on U.S. stocks and technology shares. That tells me that, in my financial success, my savings rate has mattered more than my rate of return. Maybe I'll have better investment performance in the years ahead. Who knows?

At 34 years old, I have much more work to do and, God willing, many joyous moments in life left to savor. I hope my future work will be less focused on money and more centered on having a purpose.

Still, it's comforting to know that I'm financially independent, barring a confluence of financial disasters. It's my goal to keep working, while resisting the urge to constantly track my net worth on my old spreadsheet. I should heed the wise words of a neighbor who recently wished me a happy birthday, and then said, "Now, go spend some of that money."

My story may inspire others to save. But I hope it also makes them realize that they also need to enjoy life. I've had extreme savings habits from an early age because I've always been somewhat anxious. I've long wanted enough saved in case bad things happen. I struggle with just going with the flow. Like many people, I feel the need to be in control. But, as I've discovered, money is not an elixir. Sure, ample cash and high retirement account balances provide financial security. But they will not bring peace and joy. My advice: Try to strike a balance, preparing financially for the long run—but also living in the moment.

THREE LESSONS

* Time is the lever that turns regular savings into seven-figure portfolios, and the earlier you start, the sooner you'll get there.

* A healthy portfolio can buy a sense of financial security. But it won't necessarily buy you a joyful life—and, indeed, excessive delayed gratification may hurt happiness.

* Early retirement is an admirable goal. But spend some serious time thinking about how you'll fill all those empty days.

TAKING CONTROL

BY
JIAB WASSERMAN

Jiab Wasserman, MBA, RICP®, has lived in Thailand, the U.S. and Spain. She spent the bulk of her career with financial services companies, eventually becoming vice president of credit risk management at Bank of America, before retiring in 2018. Her husband Jim also has an essay in this volume.

WAS BORN INTO an upper-middle-class family in Thailand. My dad was a doctor and my mom was a nurse. Both had a profound effect on me—on how I tackled my career, financial issues and life more generally.

I was the oldest of four children and the only girl. My father made sure I was given the same opportunities as my brothers, whether it was education, sports or other extracurricular activities. For him, 'because you're a girl' was never a reason to do or not do something. My father was the first feminist I ever knew—before I even knew what the term meant.

Each of us has our own strategy for coping with life, usually developed early on. I now realize that my strategy was a response to my mother's behavior. She has ADHD, as well as a personality disorder, but she wasn't properly diagnosed until a few years ago. Amid my otherwise orderly and privileged upbringing, her behavior was erratic.

My mother frequently lost her temper with those around her, and especially with me when I was young. She was often disorganized and irresponsible. In response, I early on developed a strategy of always maintaining control. Growing up, I played junior competitive tennis. I learned never to let opponents, or anyone else, see my emotions, especially anger. That strategy worked well for me in school, my career and when managing money, even allowing me to retire at age 53. But it came at a cost.

Although my parents made good money, they lived modestly. My father was frugal, always dressing in simple clothes. I remember being turned away by upscale restaurants because my father was in his tennis shorts and sandals. I never saw it bother him. He often shrugged and used the opportunity to teach me never to judge others by how they dressed.

My parents never talked to me about money. Part of it was that they didn't know much about investing or personal finance. What they knew was to work hard, live frugally and save as much as they could. One investment my parents believed in, however, was education. They were willing to pay and do whatever it took to give me and my brothers the best education.

With my father's encouragement, I passed the entrance exam for the College of Engineering at Chulalongkorn University—often known simply as Chula—which is Thailand's best university. When I was admitted in 1983, my class of more than 400 engineering students included just 25 women.

Though females were few, we were treated the same as our male counterparts and judged on our achievements. Chula is where I learned that men and women can collaborate to their mutual benefit and with mutual respect. It would become the standard by which I would later judge my work environment—and I often found myself disappointed.

MOVING TO AMERICA

After I graduated from Chula, I went to work as an industrial engineer in a garment factory and later for the government, where I reviewed machinery, equipment and raw materials imported into Thailand. I quickly realized that I didn't particularly like the actual job of engineering. My father and I discussed my career. With his support and encouragement, I moved to the U.S. in 1988 to pursue an MBA. That was when I met my first husband, Jeff.

I married Jeff in 1990, six months before graduating from business school. Jeff and I made very little money when we started out. I was employed full time at a small mortgage broker, while he was finishing his bachelor's degree while also working part time. We split rent and shared a mobile home with my then sister-in-law. We saved as much as we could. After a few years, we had enough for a small down payment and bought a home.

After we purchased the house, I accepted a job as a financial analyst at Associates Financial Services, which later became part of Citigroup. I quickly moved up to senior financial analyst and began managing a team of analysts, all of which brought more income. I maxed out my 401(k) plan and started a college fund as soon as my son was born in 1996. We traded our old car for a new, expensive SUV. The monthly payment was $450, quite high back then.

While my career prospered, my personal life didn't. Jeff and I separated, and I found myself a single mom. I didn't get a good lawyer and was intimidated by the divorce process. I just wanted to get it over quickly. I made two crucial mistakes: I waived child support payments and gave up the house, our only big asset. My ex later sold the place at a large profit.

Financially, I was starting over at age 33. I had about $5,000 in cash and $20,000 in my 401(k). I also had a big legal bill and was stuck with a large car payment. I moved into a small one-bedroom apartment with my toddler son. I got rid of the $450 car payment and bought a modest sedan that reduced my payment to $200 a month. I still managed to max out my 401(k) contributions and set aside college savings. Thanks to my father's example, I've always been frugal, so it wasn't a big deal to cut back on eating out and spending on clothes. I visited garage sales, looking for children's clothes, shoes and furniture. Almost all of my furnishings were used or passed down from friends or relatives.

After my divorce was finalized in 1998, I continued to excel in my career. In fact, I leaned on the office as a haven from the chaos in my personal life. My salary before bonus grew to $75,000. But I put in a lot of hours, sometimes 70 or 80 a week. During budget time, I often worked overnight, while the company paid for a babysitter. After a few years, I was burnt out. Once, when I asked for time off to take my son to a doctor, I was told I had to choose between being a mom and having a career. I took a few months' break in 2001, living off stock options that I cashed out. Later that year, I got a job as a financial analyst with Countrywide Financial, which was later bought by Bank of America. At $50,000 a year, the salary was lower but the work-life balance was better.

At Countrywide, I faced the harsh reality of gender discrimination. My first inkling: I found out that a male colleague received a year-end bonus, but I didn't. He had lesser qualifications and less experience, and there was no difference in our performance. I was angry. But as a single mom, I couldn't afford to cause a ruckus for fear of losing my job.

I was seen as a go-to analyst—but useful only in a supporting role, marginalized as the "smart Asian woman with an accent." My work contributions were ignored or claimed by my manager as his own. I often wasn't invited to important meetings with senior managers and executives, even when I did most or all the work. I was the only female analyst in the group and was often excluded from social and team-building events because my male manager was "uncomfortable." I was subjected to demeaning and sexually harassing comments.

Near the end of my career, things got better: I was fortunate to work for excellent managers who treated men and women equally. While I eventually thrived and was even promoted to vice president of credit risk management before retiring in 2018, no review of my money journey would be complete without mentioning the unfair and unequal treatment I received. It's a part of too many stories for women and minorities. That I was ultimately successful doesn't excuse a system that continues to discriminate.

MEETING JIM

After four years as a single mom, my girlfriends encouraged me to try online dating. Being frugal, I wasn't about to pay a year's subscription for something I wasn't sure I'd use. I skeptically signed up for a free 30-day trial. Just before the trial period ended, Jim and I connected online. I laughed so hard at his profile that I had to meet him. It was January 2002.

As it turned out, he was also funny in person, in part because of his take-nothing-too-seriously attitude. He was a divorced single dad with a son 11 months older than my son. After dating for more than a year, we bought a modest house in May 2003 and moved in together. We were married a few months later.

We didn't know how exactly to merge our two families, but we agreed on some basic principles. We set out to live within our means, save as much as possible, and focus on providing the boys with an excellent education. We began a period of minimizing expenses and maximizing savings. It was more difficult for Jim than for me. I was already used to a frugal lifestyle. I didn't mind packing my own and the boys' lunches, and cooking at home every evening. Jim had a harder time resisting the lure of restaurants. We ended up compromising. We would dine out if I could find a discount coupon or we'd go to cheaper, more authentic hole-in-the-wall restaurants.

Shortly after we got married, I took over the family finances. We opened a joint checking account and completely merged our financial lives. Jim had $17,000 in credit card debt, but his car was paid off. I still had car payments but no credit card debt. My first priority was to pay off Jim's card debt. Next would be my auto loan. After that was paid off, we made extra payments every month on the mortgage. I never liked being in debt. Owing money to others gives them control over you—something I abhor.

Being in the financial services industry, especially credit risk management, I knew the importance of credit scores. Having excellent scores gave us the power to negotiate and to choose the best financial products with the lowest costs. I managed to get Jim's and my credit scores up to 800-plus, out of a possible 850. They've remained there ever since. When we refinanced our mortgage, I was able to get a very low rate. We then used the extra savings to pay off our mortgage even faster.

Because I had taken a salary cut and Jim had a modest teacher's salary, our combined gross income was under six figures. To afford a home, our total mortgage payment had to be right at the maximum recommended 28% of income. I was concerned about committing to a house purchase. Having been a single mom for almost five years and having just recovered financially, I was wary of taking on more debt. I even suggested that we could all move into Jim's rented townhome, but Jim disagreed.

Being a teacher, he was more aware of the better schools in the area. We settled on a modest house in a great school district. It was less expensive than most nearby homes because the house had never been upgraded and, indeed, still had the original 30-year-old central air-conditioning system.

Jim and I have different spending habits. I comparison shop before committing to buy, while Jim is more impulsive. Still, we share similar outlooks when it comes to living simply. Neither of us insisted on spending a lot of money to renovate the house. We liked the old-fashioned wood cabinets, the original big-tiled Spanish floor, and the simple white-tiled bathroom. They were functional, good quality, and built to last.

We didn't spend a lot of money on home decor. All our furniture was secondhand, either passed on to us by relatives or found at garage sales, thrift stores and even on the sidewalk on bulk trash pickup days. We bought an entire living room sofa suite, including a couch and full chaise lounge, for $300 at a garage sale. The boys' bedroom furniture set was grabbed from the sidewalk when a neighbor put out his child's like-new furniture.

While we didn't devote much money to home decor, we did spend to make the house more energy efficient. We installed attic insulation ourselves. The house came with a pool and hot tub. It was already beaten up and needed a lot of year-round maintenance for just two or three months' use. We had the pool and hot tub filled in, installing a brick patio instead. Between the insulation and pool elimination, which cost $10,000 all told, we saved $200 to $250 in energy bills every month. We also made a few other updates to the house—and we did them as a family. We installed our own flooring. The boys built shelves for their rooms.

While our combined income wasn't huge, our savings rate was. The Great Recession of 2008–09 offered a wonderful investment opportunity, and we took full advantage by maxing out our retirement plans and choosing all-stock funds. While Jim didn't get paid much as a teacher, his employer match was generous. We also maxed out our contributions to Roth IRAs and invested in 529 plans for the boys' college costs. During this time, I bought a small rental property at a foreclosure auction with my youngest brother. That continues to provide us with a modest rental income.

When I got a raise or a bonus, or Jim earned extra from teaching summer school, we socked away the money, instead of splurging on, say, a new car or new TV. But we also didn't starve ourselves or skip family vacations. If Jim worked during the summer, we used some of the money to take a vacation. I knew it was inexpensive to travel in Thailand and the rest of Southeast Asia, especially if we didn't stay at tourist resorts. We would visit my parents in Thailand and then explore the region, visiting Vietnam, Cambodia, Singapore, Malaysia and elsewhere.

Even though we were raised half a world apart, Jim and I grew up with similar values. Both our families invested in education, something we also wanted to do for our boys. We were lucky that the boys got the message that school matters and that it would pay off later. My son got a full academic scholarship to university and even a small stipend. As a result, we only had to cover his living expenses, which were about $6,000 a year. That allowed us to help him in other ways on his path to becoming an actuary.

Meanwhile, when Jim went through his divorce, he opted to leave his investment accounts to his ex-wife to help pay for his son's future college tuition. That money grew over 18 years and was enough to cover most of the tuition at a private university. Jim's son is now a software engineer. When the boys graduated, we still had more than $60,000 in college savings accounts. We gave some to the boys as a gift, while keeping the rest in 529 accounts. We plan to use it for our own tuition, as we return to graduate school, and also hope one day to pass some of it on to our future grandchildren.

ARRIVING EARLY

In 2016, two years after our sons headed to college, we realized that it was a seller's housing market in our area. Our excellent school district now gave us a second benefit. Businesses and their executives were moving to Dallas in droves, and that growth pushed property prices to record levels. Our house, which we'd bought in 2003 for $200,000, sold for $340,000. After paying off the mortgage, we netted close to $240,000. We bought a smaller townhome for cash, leaving us mortgage-free just 13 years after we first bought a house together.

And with that, we were on the cusp of financial independence. After our sons graduated college, Jim and I retired at ages 57 and 53, respectively. Though it wasn't our goal to retire early, we got there in 2018, just 15 years after we married. We quit our jobs, rented out our townhome and moved to Spain for what turned out to be three years. We're now back in the States, happy to be closer to our sons. Because of our financial control in the past, we have power today— the power of choice.

My personal strategy of maximizing control has served me well, at least financially, but it came at a cost. My constant focus on money caused a lot of self-induced stress. For instance, when we were on vacation, I worried about staying within our budget. I didn't want to do certain activities if they cost too much. I sometimes carried a small notebook, recording every expense. Along the way, I robbed myself of some of the vacation's enjoyment.

I tend to see things in black and white, looking for what I can control. Jim likes to point out the gray areas—the absurdity of life and the illusion that we can control it. He makes me look up from my tallying notebook to take in the beautiful view or to laugh at it all. With Jim, I've learned to let things go when they don't go my way.

It didn't happen overnight. Instead, it's taken getting older and having more experience, combined with more than 20 years with Jim. I have slowly learned to embrace ambiguity—the grayness of life. Jim and I have an inside joke. In tennis, you shouldn't hold the racquet too tightly, especially between points, or you may get hand cramps. We often tell each other to "loosen the grip" when either of us is wound up by a situation. As I've discovered, loosening the grip means less stress—and greater freedom to just be.

THREE LESSONS

* When you're in debt, your financial life is not entirely your own. Don't want to be constrained by financial obligations? Never carry a credit card balance, minimize car and student loans, and pay down your mortgage faster than required.

* By tightly controlling how much you save and spend, you can rapidly achieve financial independence. But be careful not to overdo it: If you keep too tight a grip on the purse strings, you may miss the joy that life can offer.

* Money gives you power—the power to choose. But to gain that power, you need to make tough choices, deciding what spending is worthwhile and which expenditures you can happily skip. This is especially important for women, who suffer systematic disadvantages, as evidenced by the gender wage gap. By controlling expenses, we gain more power over our lives.

NOW AND THEN

BY
JONATHAN CLEMENTS

Jonathan Clements is the founder and editor of the personal finance website *HumbleDollar*. He also sits on the advisory board of Creative Planning, one of the country's largest independent financial advisors, and is the author of eight earlier personal-finance books. Jonathan spent almost 20 years at *The Wall Street Journal*, where he was the newspaper's personal-finance columnist, and six years at Citigroup, where he was director of financial education for the bank's U.S. wealth management arm. Born in England and educated at Cambridge University, Jonathan now lives in Philadelphia, just a few blocks from his daughter, son-in-law and grandson.

IT WAS YEAR-END 2007. I was about to turn 45. I was in the middle of an unhappy relationship that I didn't have the courage to end and that would drag on for three-and-a-half more years. I was coming up on my 1,000th *Wall Street Journal* column, but it had become a grind. I wondered how much longer I could keep it up before my articles descended into repetitive blather. My amateur running career—a huge part of my identity for the prior decade and a belated source of athletic pride for a once-wimpy English schoolboy—was spluttering, my Achilles tendon aggravated by the bone spur growing out of the back of my right heel. My two children were my only great joy. Hannah was then in college, Henry in high school.

As of 31 December 2007, I owned a house that was mortgage-free and a portfolio worth $976,000.

I mention this not to argue that money often fails to buy happiness, though I firmly believe that's true. And I certainly don't intend to boast. As a child, I might have imagined that self-worth and net worth were somehow correlated, but I sure don't think that today.

Rather, I mention year-end 2007 to draw a line across my life's calendar. The years that followed brought events—good and bad—that upset the somewhat predictable rhythm of my early financial life. I'll talk about those events later in this essay. But it was the humdrum early years that put me on the path to financial independence.

GROWING UP FAST

At university, I was the kid who swore he'd never get married and never have children. Two years after my 1985 graduation from Cambridge, I was married. A year after that, I became a father at age 25.

I can't claim to be naturally thrifty. I spent my college years and my first year in the workforce accumulating credit card debt, while also occasionally overdrawing my checking account. The card debt doesn't seem especially large today—it reached £1,000, the maximum allowed by my card. Still, at the time, it felt like a huge burden.

In August 1986, after working in London for a year, I moved to the New York area and settled down with my PhD-student fiancée. She had a modest stipend, so I was cast as the main breadwinner, initially earning a pitiful $20,000 a year at *Forbes* magazine. I had to grow up financially, and I needed to do it fast. There was no other choice.

We called these the "lean years," and they were. Takeout pizza on Friday night was a questionable extravagance. A car repair was a crisis. The apartments we occupied in Brooklyn left me with a dread of cockroaches and mice that I still can't shake. The occasional restaurant meal had me totting up the bill as the food was ordered— not exactly conducive to digestion.

Slowly, however, things improved. My salary rose, and my wife got an academic job. In 1992, we moved from Brooklyn to the house we bought in the New Jersey suburbs. The house cost $165,000, had three bedrooms and a single bathroom, and felt barely affordable. I lived there for the next two decades.

Financially, the only big hit during those two decades was our 1998 separation and subsequent divorce. But in truth, it wasn't that much of a hit because, at that juncture, we simply didn't have many assets to divide. I kept the house, and my soon-to-be ex-wife bought a place around the corner, so the kids could easily walk from one house to the other. A financial silver lining that I only later came to appreciate: Post-divorce, I got to call the shots on every dollar I earned.

Journalism wasn't exactly a high-paying profession then, and it's even worse now. Still, I had a knack for taking the somewhat tedious topic of personal finance and making it both interesting and understandable. By 1994, at the absurdly young age of 31, I was the *Journal's* personal-finance columnist, at the time one of just three columnists in the paper's news department. Within a few years, I was earning more than $100,000, the maximum allowed for a *Journal* staff writer.

I hustled to supplement my base salary. I signed up to write a second column each week for *The Wall Street Journal Sunday*, for which I was paid extra. I wrote three books over the course of a decade, each of which garnered me a low six-figure advance. I never took a book leave to write any of them, so the money earned was financial gravy—but it came at a price. I'd devote weekends and early weekday mornings to book writing, a schedule that left me ragged and desperate for a few days away from the computer screen.

I shoveled the extra money I earned into stock index funds while also adding large sums to each monthly mortgage payment. Among colleagues and readers, I became known—or perhaps notorious—for favoring stock-heavy portfolios built using broad market index funds. I've been wrong many times over the years, but that was one thing I got right, and I take pride in having been an early and outspoken advocate of indexing, even if my advocacy grew a tad repetitive.

While I viewed my stock index funds as my growth money, I saw my extra mortgage payments as a bond substitute. Why buy actual bonds at 4% or 5% when I could effectively earn more than 7%—my mortgage rate—by paying off my home loan? In late 1992, I remember spotting the line for extra-principal on my first mortgage-payment coupon and tentatively adding $10. The extra payments grew far larger over the years, and, by 2005, I was mortgage-free. It was the best bond investment I ever made.

While I feel I did an okay job of investing, the key to success was ensuring that I had plenty to invest—a simple enough feat: Even as my income ballooned, I kept my living costs low. A big reason was my modest home. Added to that was a general reluctance to spend on almost anything. I didn't eat out much. I drove the same used car for years. I took the kids on fun vacations, but always kept a close eye on the cost.

This was a great strategy for amassing wealth. I'm not sure it's a great strategy for enjoying life. I was working long hours. I wasn't counting pennies—I've never been one to budget—but I kept myself on a short financial leash. Despite making some substantial home improvements, I never much liked the house I lived in for those

20 years. An occasional indulgence, coupled with less self-inflicted work stress, would have taken some of the grind out of my march toward seven figures.

SECOND CHILDHOOD

While the two decades through 2007 were a long slog filled with predictable days, the years since my 45th birthday have seen all kinds of upheaval. I left *The Wall Street Journal* in 2008, spent six years at Citigroup, briefly returned to the *Journal* as a freelance columnist, and then tried my hand at a slew of different jobs. I taught personal finance at a small college for two semesters. I wrote a column for *Financial Planning* magazine. I took on two major writing projects for a Wall Street firm. I gave some paid speeches. I worked with three others to develop a financial app that never saw the light of day. Eventually, I focused my efforts on *HumbleDollar*, the website I launched at year-end 2016, while also doing work for Creative Planning, a sizable registered investment advisor based in Overland Park, Kansas.

Meanwhile, I largely gave up running and instead turned to bicycling, racking up six memorable accidents, three of which landed me in the emergency room. Over the past 15 years, I've written seven books, moved house four times, got married again and—alas—divorced again. Midlife crisis? No doubt that played a role. I didn't set out to try so much that was new. But after spending the first two decades of my adult life hewing to the straight-and-narrow path, and after saving my way to financial freedom, I was ready to explore.

In many ways, the past 15 years have seen the sort of experimentation and turmoil you'd expect from someone in his 20s—a life phase I never had because I was thrust so quickly into the role of family breadwinner. Indeed, I've taken to referring to the past decade or so as my second childhood. But while those in their 20s might do all this on a shoestring, I've been able to do it, in part, because money wasn't an issue.

How have I fared financially through this period? It's been a mixed bag.

When I joined Citigroup in 2008 and became director of financial education for the bank's U.S. wealth management group, my financial house was already well in order. But with the move to Citi, my income doubled even as I continued to live like a lowly newspaper reporter. Working for a Wall Street firm for six years was an education: I got to see the advice business from the inside, I learned about financial topics I'd rarely written about, and I was forced to overcome my fear of public speaking. Indeed, I found myself delivering 30-plus speeches a year to clients. But toward the end of my Citi career, I realized that—for the only time in my life—I was working solely for a paycheck. My dollar income might have been impressive, but the psychic income wasn't. I hung on long enough to collect a final year-end bonus, and then, in early 2014, I quit.

Meanwhile, I've sold three homes over the past decade. One was a rip-roaring success—the apartment I bought in New York City in 2011 during the depth of the housing crisis and sold three years later. But one was an unmitigated disaster that, when I factor everything in, probably left me more than $100,000 poorer. What went wrong? I made one crucial error, buying an apartment that had much higher ongoing fees than nearby properties, and that made it difficult to sell. But I was also blindsided—by a divorce, by a pandemic that nixed interest in owning apartments, by two buyers who made bids but then dropped out, and by the need to get a certificate of occupancy for work that had been done on the apartment more than 50 years earlier. The long-running drama—selling the place took 31 months—stole my peace of mind and cost me countless nights' sleep. Almost all of us suffer one or two big financial hits during our life. I count myself lucky: This particular storm was bruising, but it didn't threaten my financial future.

What about my portfolio? Like everybody else who owned stocks, my investments were crushed by the 2007–09 and 2020 stock market drubbings. But despite relentlessly arguing that the financial markets are efficient and can't be beaten, I saw both market declines for what they were—moments of overwhelming investor fear that caused share prices to become unhinged from intrinsic value—and I bought like crazy. I went into late 2008 with some 70% of my portfolio in stocks. By the time the market bottomed in March, I was at 95%. Obviously, this turned out well, but I mention it sheepishly, out of concern I'll be branded a market-timer. Fair criticism? I'd argue market-timing involves acting on a market forecast, whereas I was simply responding to market movements—and taking advantage of what I saw as temporary investor insanity.

Through the 2010s, my portfolio was entirely in index funds and mostly in stocks. But I had hefty holdings of index funds focused on value stocks, small-company shares, developed foreign markets and emerging markets, all of which badly lagged during the roaring 2009–20 U.S. bull market. I don't harbor any regrets—by its nature, broad diversification means you'll always own some of the market's stinkers—though I also recognize that I could have fared far better if I'd owned a lopsided portfolio that focused solely on the big blue-chip U.S. stocks in the S&P 500. Still, I'm not about to change strategy. I have no clue which parts of the global financial market will shine in the decade ahead, so I'll continue to own a little of everything.

Amid the financial triumphs and disasters of the past 15 years, perhaps the biggest change is this: Even as I continue to spend my days writing and thinking about money, I spend very little time thinking about my own finances. In a world where so many folks worry about how to cover day-to-day expenses, I've come to see not thinking about money as perhaps the greatest luxury that money can buy.

I have also become a little more carefree in my spending. I enjoy going out to dinner once or twice a week—and, unlike in my 20s, I never worry about the size of the bill. I'm quicker to book trips, both weekends away and longer vacations. Every year or so, I buy a piece of art, usually an oil painting. I enjoy helping my two kids financially and funding my grandson's 529, and I've belatedly become more focused on charitable giving. There is, I've found, greater happiness in spending on others than spending on myself.

Not all is right in my financial world. My big regret: I continue to work far too hard. As a teenager, I would happily take to the couch and surrender an entire day to a novel. Today, there always seems to be something that needs to get done, and that something is usually work. Like a force in motion that stays in motion, I've found that decades of working hard have created a momentum of their own, one I struggle to resist. In part, I chalk this up to the delusion that what I do is important, which perhaps it is, but not nearly as important as I imagine. I love what I do each day—the sense that, with my writing and editing, I'm helping folks to lead better financial lives. But in the end, managing time is more important than managing money, because time is the ultimate limited resource. I should lead a more balanced life. I know that intellectually. But I'm still trying to convince myself.

THREE LESSONS

* Low fixed living costs, coupled with a rising income, can allow you to save great gobs of money. Just make sure that you aren't sacrificing too much today for your future financial security.

* Instead of buying bonds, consider paying down debt, including mortgage debt. The interest you avoid paying will likely be far higher than the interest you could earn by buying bonds.

* A globally diversified portfolio of index funds means you'll always own some of the market's duds. But you're also guaranteed to collect whatever gains the global markets deliver—and those gains, coupled with good savings habits, should be more than enough for a comfortable retirement.

FAMILY FIRST

Family can be our most enduring source of happiness and worry, our motivation to make and amass money, and our greatest asset and greatest liability. You'll see those themes in the five essays in this section of the book. Why do we do what we do each day? More often than not, it's not for ourselves, but for those we care about most.

LEARNING BY HELPING by Richard Connor

MARGIN FOR ERROR by Anika Hedstrom

MY FAVORITE DETOURS by John Goodell

MAKING IT by Matt Christopher White

INVESTING TOGETHER by Sonja Haggert

LEARNING BY HELPING

BY
RICHARD CONNOR

Rick Connor is a semi-retired aerospace engineer with a keen interest in finance. He enjoys a wide variety of other interests, including chasing grandkids, space, sports, travel, winemaking and reading.

W HEN I THINK about my financial journey, I'm reminded of a line from a famous Grateful Dead song: "What a long, strange trip it's been." My journey has indeed been long and, on occasion, somewhat strange.

I was born in 1957, the second of three sons. My parents provided us with a loving home and an excellent education. At college, I studied to become an engineer and spent my career in aerospace engineering. No surprise, I've always been highly analytical, and that's been the way I've approached money questions.

Forty years ago, I married the love of my life. We had two sons, and now two wonderful daughters-in-law and three grandsons. I'm surrounded by a large, caring family. I consider myself extremely lucky: The chance to have a successful life—financially and otherwise—was placed before me.

As I've sought to make the most of that opportunity, four experiences have had a major impact on my financial thinking. Those experiences transformed my interest in matters of money from a modest hobby to a passion and, along the way, taught me the power of sound financial planning.

JOINING THE CLUB

The first experience was helping to found an investment club. My older brother and some of his in-laws wanted to start one, and asked me if I was interested. I'd never considered joining an investment club before. But they were good guys and I thought I could learn something, so I agreed. It was one of the best decisions I've ever made.

We started the club in 1993, at the beginning of the bull market in technology stocks. Legendary fund manager Peter Lynch's first two books were popular bestsellers. They filled the heads of novice investors like me with the idea that we could find undervalued stocks with strong growth potential if we just kept our eyes open.

Another contribution to our can-do investment philosophy was *Wall Street Week with Louis Rukeyser*. The long-running weekly show on PBS was entertaining and educational. It made us feel like we could invest using our own ideas and research.

We agreed that the club needed to be a legal entity—a general partnership. We created a partnership agreement, registered for a federal tax identification number, and set up a checking account, a brokerage account and an accounting structure. I volunteered to be treasurer. I was also the accountant, keeping the books on preprinted ledger sheets.

Initially, we all invested the same amount each month, so we each owned the same share of the club. It quickly became obvious that this would impede the club's growth. Any new member would have to invest the total amount of a founding member to keep things even.

What to do? Being the engineer that I am, I built a spreadsheet that became the backbone of the club's accounting structure. To allow unequal ownership, we needed to run the club on a per-share basis. The value of each share was initially set at a nominal value. Each member invested their desired amount and received shares. At the end of each month, we would value all of our stock holdings and calculate the new net asset value per share.

In effect, our investment club ran like a small mutual fund. Members contributed money, which was pooled to purchase stocks. Each member owned a pro-rated amount of the fund based on his contributions plus earnings. The club was a pass-through entity: All profits and losses passed through to the members.

Members could buy or sell as many shares as they chose at the share price calculated for that month. At the end of the year, we totaled up the dividends and capital gains. These were passed through to members by way of a Schedule K-1, an IRS partnership form. It took some time, but I was able to automate the process. Club membership doubled, and I ran the books and the treasurer's office for almost five years.

The club members decided to invest half our money in blue-chip companies. We used discounted cash flow analysis to find value stocks, those which seemed cheap relative to expected future earnings. We purchased household names like Merck, Exxon Mobil, GE, Motorola and Ford. We religiously bought more shares when their prices dipped and reinvested all dividends. I thought of these five stocks as our mini-Dow Jones index. All five were among the 30 giants in the Dow Jones Industrial Average.

The other half of our fund was devoted to speculative growth stocks. At this time in the 1990s, there were dozens of small, high-tech startups that held out the promise of becoming a big winner—the next Microsoft or America Online. Two companies, in particular, haunt me.

TRO Learning was a company that was early in electronic learning, the now-routine practice of teaching students at a distance. We bought in at around $5 a share, and the stock rose to about $20. All the company's reports said it wasn't making money, and didn't expect to for several years. To me, that was a sign we should sell. I brought it up at a club meeting but was voted down. The other members liked the company's sales momentum. We didn't sell, and the stock dropped. We eventually sold our shares at a modest profit.

The other company I recall was a small manufacturer called Plasma-Tech. It made the equipment that created screens for flat panel displays. Industry experts said the company made the best equipment of its type in the world. The future of flat screens was limitless, and this company was essential to America's plan to dominate that market. It was a great story and we bought it—along with a bunch of its stock.

Despite the great story, Plasma-Tech went nowhere. The company was having huge problems delivering its products. It had significant supply chain issues, as well as challenges in ramping up production. In 1999, the company was purchased by a Swiss conglomerate and is no longer listed on any exchange. I learned a valuable lesson from Plasma-Tech. A company can have great technology and a great story. But if it can't manage its business or turn a profit, you won't succeed by investing in its shares.

My five years in the investment club made me a much more knowledgeable—and humble—investor. We had our ups and downs, but overall our returns pretty much mirrored the broad market. Our blue-chip stocks, in aggregate, followed the Dow 30, and our growth portfolio averaged out to a similar result. The greatest return may have been the learning involved. By the end, the club had piqued my interest in all things financial.

HELPING MY PARENTS

The second key experience occurred about the same time as the investment club, but it was far more serious. I realized in my mid-30s that my parents, then in their early 60s, were falling into financial difficulty. My father hadn't worked in a while, and they were living off my mother's salary, plus some money she had inherited. We confronted my parents, and they reluctantly acknowledged that they needed help.

My brothers, my wife Vicky and I agreed to provide enough support to stabilize their situation. After a few years of helping them meet their bills, however, it became obvious that the small steps we were taking weren't enough to secure their long-term future. My wife suggested that we sell our home, purchase my parents' house, move in and let them live with us. When we presented our plan to them, we could see the relief on their faces.

My parents lived with us for the rest of their lives. My father's health was deteriorating. He soon needed a walker and oxygen. He died in 1999 at 71 years old. My mom lived with us for another six years. In summer 2004, she suffered a seizure. Over the next two months, she gradually lost control of the left side of her body. It took a few months to diagnose, but doctors discovered a tumor in her brain. It was a B-cell lymphoma, fairly advanced.

She had brain surgery and follow-up chemotherapy. Although she showed some improvement after chemotherapy, her symptoms returned within a few months. At that point, there were no good options left. She passed away a few weeks after Christmas, in early 2005, with her family and friends around her.

The experience of caring for my parents' health and finances taught me so much. I think it marked my final transition into adulthood. I dealt with resolving debts, fighting with Medicare, retrofitting our house to accommodate my parents' mounting disabilities and—finally—settling two estates.

All this made me determined that my wife and I wouldn't be a financial burden to our children. Though it was a lot of work and challenging at times, I never considered it a hardship to care for my parents. It was a profound experience that I would do all over again if required. And soon I was.

ASSISTING MY IN-LAWS

The third experience began about five years later, when I took over the finances of my wife's widowed aunt. Aunt Pat was childless. She started showing signs of cognitive decline in her late 70s. She gradually lost the ability to manage her affairs, and even lost track of some assets, as I was to discover.

Aunt Pat moved in with my in-laws in 2007. My wife was granted power of attorney over her medical and financial affairs. I assumed the responsibility for understanding, organizing and managing her finances.

She was fortunate to have ample fixed income from several pensions and Social Security. My biggest job was organizing and simplifying her finances. It took several years, but I consolidated everything in a Vanguard Group account and a checking account. I automated her income and expenses payments. I found evidence that Aunt Pat had lost track of assets. After an extensive search, I recovered more than $75,000.

My financial plan for Aunt Pat ensured she would have the money needed to pay for a decade or more of high-quality care, if required. That didn't come to pass. Sadly, she died suddenly in May 2011 at age 81. From helping Aunt Pat, I learned the benefit of simplifying your finances as you age, and making sure that all your estate documents are in place.

Meanwhile, my in-laws provided a fine example of how a middle-class couple can build a successful retirement. They had spent their lives working hard, living well within their means and saving diligently. After their five children had grown, they began to invest in earnest in their retirement accounts. Between their traditional pensions, Social Security benefits and their savings, they were able to enjoy a comfortable retirement starting at 65.

My father-in-law passed away in 2009 at 82. Following her husband's death, my mother-in-law seemed to lose interest in managing her finances. Again, I took over. As well as they planned and executed their retirement, there was one crucial mistake I discovered when my father-in-law died. When he'd taken his Teamsters' pension, he'd chosen a single-life-only payout. That meant the checks stopped cold when he died. This greatly reduced my mother-in-law's income.

My initial task was to organize her assets by simplifying the number of accounts and assets that she owned. Once again, I consolidated them at Vanguard. Her portfolio consisted of a 403(b), some Vanguard funds, a few individual stocks and some certificates of deposit. She kept a large amount of her assets in cash.

A year after her husband died, she decided that she was ready to sell her home and move together with her sister—Aunt Pat—into an independent living facility. She chose a two-bedroom apartment. This community didn't require a big entry fee. But the monthly charge was about $6,000. Fortunately, the combined fixed incomes of my mother-in-law and her sister could cover it.

We sold my mother-in-law's home and invested the proceeds in her Vanguard account. I felt comfortable that her finances were now in good shape. But then Aunt Pat suddenly passed away. Now, my mother-in-law had to pay $6,000 a month for the apartment on her own.

Not long after that, she developed some medical issues. During a routine procedure, there was a complication that led to emergency surgery. Further complications from that surgery caused a significant reduction in her cognitive abilities. At age 84, she was no longer capable of living alone without assistance.

We were forced to quickly investigate several senior living facilities. Each had its own financial structure. I had to evaluate each one to see if it fit her financial situation. We chose a quality facility near us with a small initial deposit but larger monthly charges. Her monthly cost went up to $7,000. I calculated that she had enough assets and income to cover her care until she was 95.

Because of her dementia diagnosis, the majority of her living expenses qualified as tax-deductible medical expenses. I used this tax deduction to her advantage from 2011 through 2014 to offset her IRA withdrawals, greatly reducing her income taxes. After we emptied her IRA, I used her medical deductions to offset long-term capital gains taxes. Her reported income was so low that she qualified for the 0% capital gains tax rate.

I set up a three-bucket approach for her short-, medium- and long-term expenses. We kept three years of cash in the first bucket to cover current needs. The second bucket was invested in short-term bonds, and the third in an S&P 500-index fund. Because she was already in her mid-80s, we planned on drawing down her assets over ten years. But she only lived for another three-and-a-half years.

TAKING CARE OF OURSELVES

While looking after my in-laws, my wife and I were also preparing for our own retirement. In 2007, on my 50th birthday, we had a local financial planner do a detailed retirement assessment. He performed a portfolio analysis, retirement income projections and a so-called Monte Carlo analysis, which looked at how our investment mix might fare in a host of market scenarios. His detailed report showed that we were on a solid path to retire at age 62.

We all know what happened next. In 2008 and 2009, our assumption of 8% average annual stock returns suddenly looked foolish. But it didn't change our retirement plans. Our two sons had just finished college, so we focused on maxing out our 401(k) contributions. As share prices plunged toward their March 2009 low, we kept buying stock index funds at ever lower prices.

In 2010, my employer—a division of aerospace company Lockheed Martin—was sold to a private equity firm. Employees were very concerned that this meant the end of our traditional pension. I was a senior manager at the time, and many of the employees looked to me for guidance on the complicated pension rules. I realized that, as a leader, I needed to become much more knowledgeable about the pension. This was my fourth key experience—taking my financial education to a new level.

I spent a week studying the plan and building some spreadsheets that helped explain our options. Over the next seven years, I became an expert on our pension plan, providing consultations and lunchtime briefings to many employees. In 2014, the new company froze our pension plan, meaning we could accrue no more benefits. At the same time, they added the option of a lump-sum payout but provided few details. Luckily, one of my sons had a friend who was an actuary in the pension industry. He was able to educate me on the new option.

Many employees came to me to understand their choices and figure out what they should do at retirement. I enjoyed counseling them. I decided to continue my education, so I enrolled in the Certified Financial Planner program at the American College of Financial Services. I completed the program in about nine months, and then passed the comprehensive exam. A few years later, I completed the Retirement Income Certified Professional program as well.

I stopped working full time in April 2017—two years ahead of the schedule we'd drawn up before the Great Recession. I started taking my pension several months later. I briefly considered switching careers and becoming a financial planner. But the thought of starting a new career at age 60 was daunting. Several months after I stopped working, my former employer asked if I'd be interested in some consulting work. I agreed, and I've done a meaningful amount over the past four years.

I'd always intended to give back during retirement. I volunteered for AARP's Tax-Aide program. We provide tax return preparation, free of charge, with a focus on older clients with low incomes. This proved to be a great choice. It melded my passion for finance with my desire to help the wider community, and it connected me with a great group of smart, caring people.

I also discovered the *HumbleDollar* website. I thought I might be able to write articles and become part of the web's ongoing financial conversation. More than 100 articles and blog posts later, I'm happy I took the chance. It's enriched my life and, I hope, entertained a few readers.

In 2021, Vicky and I sold our home in the Philadelphia suburbs and moved full time to our house on the Jersey Shore. Will this be our final stop? It might be. We love the area, and our children and grandchildren are within a few hours' drive. But after helping my parents, Aunt Pat and my in-laws, I've learned to be prepared—but also stay flexible. I'm not so sure how the rest of our lives will go, but I'm optimistic that our years of saving will provide the wealth we need to live comfortably.

THREE LESSONS

* Retirement might seem like a time to slow down, but—in reality—the financial changes often come thick and fast. Be prepared to help your parents and other elderly relatives, and be prepared for large changes in your own financial life when you get into your 70s and beyond.

* Never stop learning. Whether it's asking others for advice, scouring the web for information or taking educational courses, there's a wealth of financial information and insights on offer.

* Remember, the journey is the thing, not the destination. Along the way, cherish the family and friends in your life. When you get to the point where you can help others, do it freely and often.

MARGIN FOR ERROR

BY
ANIKA HEDSTROM

After completing her MᴅA, Anika Hedstrom joined a major corporation, working on investment trading floors in the U.S. and as an expatriate in Southeast Asia. Working alongside exceptionally bright and accomplished professionals, she was surprised how few had a vision for their own financial lives. She became a Certified Financial Planner and cofounded Uplevel Wealth to help families design and lead intentional lives, while eliminating as many unexpected financial surprises as possible along the way.

B ESTSELLING AUTHOR RYAN HOLIDAY believes that, if you want to be a great writer, you must first lead an interesting life. To understand the world, you need to cultivate experiences and gravitate toward things that challenge you. Holiday remarks, "What will the person who never risks hope to ever gain?"

Everything that happens to us, including our embarrassments and misfortunes, is material we can apply toward better handling the future. David Epstein, author of *Range: Why Generalists Triumph in a Specialized World*, believes such events are also the key to finding meaning and fulfillment. He notes that, "Our insight into ourselves is constrained by our roster of previous experiences. We actually have to do stuff, and then reflect on it."

It's through our adversities that we are given the opportunity to lead an interesting life. The old Irish blessing says, "May you be poor in misfortune, rich in blessings." Perhaps it should be recast as, "May you be rich in blessings *and* misfortunes." Which brings me to my money journey.

TWIN CHALLENGES

I was age 36, and working for a financial services firm in Portland, Oregon, when I was lucky enough to get pregnant. I have endometriosis—a condition that affects one out of every ten women, can take up to ten years to diagnose and can cause infertility. One of the best investments I've ever made: pursuing answers about my condition—and then getting help.

For $10,000, my husband and I were blessed with two 'positive' pink lines, something many with my condition can only dream of. On the spectrum of infertility treatments, $10,000 is quite inexpensive. We didn't have to endure in vitro fertilization or other, more involved, courses of action.

Shortly into my pregnancy, however, my luck turned. What started as routine nausea and fatigue escalated into countless doctor appointments, visits with various specialists, and extended hospital stays. At just 27 weeks and six days, I gave birth to our twin daughters in an emergency delivery.

There's nothing that can prepare you for this type of storm. Overnight, we went from a September due date to a June delivery. Instead of dealing with months, we were thinking in minutes. At every step, we had to make decisions where there were more questions than answers.

It's difficult to articulate what it feels like to see your babies failing to breathe—for their hearts to stop while alarms go off and lights flash in the neonatal intensive care unit (NICU). The babies simply weren't yet at the gestational stage where they had developed the capability to consistently remember to breathe. Every ounce of you wants to react, to pop open their isolette incubators, and start digging through wires and tubes to help.

But as counterintuitive as it sounds, the right antidote was to do nothing. The babies needed a chance to recover on their own. If they didn't, the nurses would flick their feet or lightly stroke their skin to stimulate a response. Through this process, they were simultaneously training the babies' brains and setting the pace for our marathon. Watching these nurses care for our babies offered an important lesson: The novice reacts while the professional responds.

The best nurses did something else differently: They spent considerably more time bedside than they did chart-side. They got to know their newborn patients at a level that enabled them to make calls that the numbers or protocol didn't always support. I didn't walk away from the NICU experience remembering every blood oxygen saturation level or the breakdown of nutritional intake from the dietitian. I walked away feeling incredibly grateful and confident in the team that cared for our babies.

I came to appreciate their empathy and EQ—emotional quotient—just as much as, if not more, than their IQ. All too often in finance and other endeavors, we focus on the prescription and not enough on the diagnosis. We don't spend enough time wrestling with and analyzing the inputs. We flip the 80–20 rule, spending too much time with the 80% and not nearly enough with the 20% that matters most.

A LIFETIME'S PREPARATION

There's less than a 1% chance of having a pregnancy like mine. The cost involved was staggering. Yet my husband and I weren't entirely unprepared. Before we ever set foot in the delivery room, we'd spent many years laying the groundwork, financially and otherwise.

For me, that preparation began early, learning money habits by watching my parents, especially my father Ole. He was both a sports enthusiast and a total nerd. As a tenured veterinary pathology professor, Ole's work attire would mainly consist of Clarks dress shoes, Wrangler pants with a belt that often missed at least one loop, a collared shirt and coke-bottle glasses. He was the king of brown-bag lunches and DIY. His fashion sense reflected his unassuming nature and humility. From him, I learned that wealth accumulates thanks to the money you don't spend.

Layered on top of that was my education and career as a financial advisor. I've learned that much of financial success is related to behavior, that managing money is less a hard science and more of a soft skill. Taking action, for the sake of doing something, doesn't build wealth. Adhering to a sound strategy—and focusing on what we can control—ultimately enriches us the most, while also allowing more time for the important things in life.

Ever since my husband and I were married in 2014, there were two things in our lives that we've been maniacally consistent about: saving money and investing in ourselves. Don't get me wrong: We love indulging in good food, beer, wine and friends—the prerequisites for the good life in Portland. We do our best to align our money and our time with what's important to us: adventure, knowledge, financial independence, experiences. But we also minimize or cut out the rest. Our financial approach is simple. We devote our money to things we care about, make sure we spend less than we earn, and invest the difference.

That's not to say we haven't had missteps. One of the biggest: We overpaid for our first home, which wasn't uncommon in Portland in 2015. Three months into homeownership, we discovered how many shortcuts were taken by the home's previous owners and how much we needed to fix.

It was December 2015 and one of the wettest winters on record in Portland. Our new neighbors invited us to their annual holiday party, where we met another neighbor who asked my husband a few things about her house and the weather. This led him to look in her home's crawlspace, where he found a few feet of standing water. We incorrectly assumed ours was dry.

Our house had a sump pump, and it had clearly failed. The one-year insurance that came with the house purchase would replace it, but only after the three feet of standing water was gone. We MacGyvered a makeshift sump pump by placing a bucket full of holes and a pump from Home Depot in the deep end of the water. An attached garden hose then carried the water to the street through the exterior crawlspace vent. After the water was mostly gone, it became evident that the flexible insulated conduit from the heating and air conditioning ducts was damaged. This, in turn, led us to discover multiple other problems, which required a complete renovation of every single heating and air conditioning duct throughout the house. It was close to $8,000 for all the work.

Other projects followed. Our largest started as a fence replacement and turned into a 360-degree structural landscaping renovation, involving retaining walls, fencing, drainage, sewer and gas lines, irrigation, plants and lighting. The final push was creating a covered and heated patio that my husband tackled. That unknowingly set us up for social distancing when the pandemic hit six months later.

Two days after we'd finished that project, we finally brought home our twins. It was September 2019—the month they were meant to be born. The twins had spent 87 days in the hospital's neonatal intensive care unit. The hospital bill for each baby was well north of $1 million. We were profoundly grateful for good insurance and for 2010's Affordable Care Act, which prohibits insurers from setting a lifetime dollar limit on coverage. Our policy's annual out-of-pocket cost was capped at $14,000. That was a hefty sum but one that pales next to the total medical cost that our twins incurred.

Our ability to make it out of this storm with our finances intact wasn't just the result of health insurance. It also hinged less on the savings we had added over the years and more on what we had subtracted—the expenses we chose not to take on. We may have overpaid for our 1962 fixer-upper, and yet its value to us has proven far greater. When we bought the house, we made sure we could qualify for the mortgage with just one of our incomes.

Those low housing costs, coupled with our resistance to lifestyle creep even as our incomes increased, left us with ample financial breathing room. That allowed us to save a healthy sum in the years running up to the twins' birth—and it gave us the financial flexibility to deal with the upheaval that followed.

BIRTHING A BUSINESS

With the arrival of the twins, I went from working full time to taking six months off. I then tried for some normalcy in my life by returning to work four days a week. But I quickly found myself caught between the needs of our young daughters and the demands of work. I was trying to keep up when life took yet another unexpected turn. In March 2020, COVID-19 hit.

Like countless others, 2020 gave me an opportunity to reflect on my life's path. I realized that what I needed and wanted for myself and my family didn't exist. Later that year, I had a routine lunch with a colleague. We were two working professional women with young children. Research suggests this is a problem: Working mothers are less likely to be hired, taken seriously and perceived as competent. They're also typically paid less than male colleagues with the same qualifications.

We decided to take matters into our own hands—by launching a fee-only financial planning firm, Uplevel Wealth.

The financial services business is a fairly tough industry with a decent failure rate. The intangible nature of what we do means it can take a long time to acquire clients. There are also high barriers to entry. For instance, one large custodian—the firm you use to hold clients' investments—requires that a financial-advisory firm manage at least $50 million to use its platform. That $50 million is on the lower end of the industry's asset minimums. Other custodians require your previous—and often much larger—employer to sign off before they'll allow you to use their platform. Financial advice is also a business where women and minorities hold few leadership positions. A 2019 study by Bella Research Group and the Knight Foundation found that 99% of all asset management firms were owned by white men.

Despite these barriers, COVID brought some key opportunities. The pandemic forced the industry to operate virtually. This allowed my partner and me to get a better understanding of our clients' lives. Instead of meeting them in an office, we were—aided by the internet—able to open the door to their living room, join them at the kitchen table and meet their family. It added a much-needed human element at a strange and uncertain time.

Want a richer life? Someone once said kids are the hardest, best thing you will ever do. I agree. Want financial freedom? I believe entrepreneurship is the hardest, best thing you will ever do. I was able to make that leap because of the breathing room that my husband and I built into our financial lives. To launch my new business, we used money we had saved for years in an account labeled 'opportunities.'

In the short term, I believe financial freedom is the ability to thrive and experience life while you're in it. It's the confidence to take a sabbatical, to change direction or to cope with the unexpected with ease. It's the ability to take a calculated risk while staying in the game. In the long term, it's the ability to determine your definition of enough, and have the humility and discipline to be satisfied once you reach it. I haven't yet reached my *enough*. But I've been captivated by the journey—both the blessings and the misfortunes.

THREE LESSONS

* Never go without health insurance. The out-of-pocket maximum may seem large—but it's possible to incur medical costs that are far, far higher and which would bankrupt those without insurance.

* Be intentional in how you use your money. Spend on those things you care about, while eschewing expenses that bring little satisfaction.

* Challenges will drop unbidden into your life. Make sure you have the financial breathing room to deal with them.

MY FAVORITE DETOURS

BY
JOHN GOODELL

John Goodell is deputy director of policy and general
counsel at the Texas Pension Review Board. He has spent
much of his career advocating for military and veterans
on tax, estate planning and retirement issues. His biggest
passion is spending time with his wife and kids.

THIS ISN'T THE story of how my wife and I reached financial
independence. Technically, we haven't—but we will. Instead, it's
a story about the power of stories.

I was raised listening to tales of my grandfather's life during the
Great Depression and Second World War. A few themes always
stood out: family, service, and the constant need to squirrel away
as much money as possible for a rainy day. I was fascinated to hear
about a world that seemed so distant from the comfortable existence
I grew up in—one that my grandfather helped make possible.

My grandfather never told me these stories. Instead, my
grandmother or mom shared them. They would talk about how
my grandfather had to graduate from Stanford University a year
early, in 1930, despite having been offered the starting quarterback

position for his final year by the famous football coach Pop Warner.

When the fallout from the 1929 stock market crash finally reached Main Street, my great-grandfather was unable to keep the family's California milk-crate business afloat without his son's help. My grandfather never complained about missing the glorious culmination of his many years of hard work on the football field. Instead, like so many of the Greatest Generation, he dutifully rolled up his sleeves and struggled to ensure his family's survival. A decade later, my grandfather volunteered for the Army, using his mechanical engineering degree to build and maintain aircraft while serving in the Pacific. After the war, he returned to run the family business, and did so successfully for many decades.

Through his actions, my grandfather taught me many things. But two lessons stand out: When it comes to money, you can never save too much. And when it comes to family, you make whatever sacrifices are necessary to give them the best life possible.

That brings me to the final years of my education. I resolved that I would do everything in my power to ensure I never found myself in need of money. I went to college on an Army ROTC (Reserve Officers' Training Corps) scholarship. Deciding that I wanted to be a military lawyer, I applied to law schools. I had paid for college with the promise of my future Army service, but law school required money I didn't have. Rather than allow me to go into debt, my grandfather offered to pay the whole bill for law school shortly before his death. His lifelong aversion to debt stemmed from seeing so much financial and personal carnage created by Wall Street speculation. He had struggled and given up much to achieve financial freedom, and he hated the idea of his grandson going into debt.

These are stories that I now tell to my children. But to my grandfather's story, I have added three of my own. In each case, however, they aren't about amassing money, but rather about the virtue of occasionally letting it slip away.

MONEY WELL SAVED

After graduating from law school, I reentered the Army. By then, I had married my high school sweetheart. We learned to live on my military income while she went through medical school and residency. We lived frugally and saved roughly a third of my salary, which ranged from $60,000 to $75,000 during those seven years.

In 2012, just as my wife was about to finish her residency, I deployed for a year to Afghanistan. That was one of my life's bleakest periods. How did I get through it? I continued to save voraciously—but I spent the year saving for what most personal finance experts would consider one of the worst uses of money: buying a new car. Four months into my time in Afghanistan, I committed to buying the car through a program offered to deployed service members. I paid a big chunk of my salary each month until the vehicle was paid off at the end of my deployment. In return, I received a small discount on a car that I was allowed to customize.

And it wasn't just any new car. I bought a 2013 black Ford Mustang GT Premium California Special Edition. I spent months choosing the color of the car, the color and location of the racing stripes, and the sleek custom touches like window louvers. I longed for that car, and thinking about it offered an escape from the war's daily reality. When I was back stateside, and eventually got to feel the full power of the 442-horsepower V-8 engine on a back road somewhere between Tennessee and Texas, the feeling was indescribable.

I paid roughly $36,000 for that depreciating asset. Had I invested that sum in an index fund, today it would easily be worth three times as much. But looking back on my year in Afghanistan, having something to take my mind off all that was happening around me was, without a doubt, the best investment I could have made.

FROM ZERO TO THREE

I still recall the shock of seeing our bank balance jump when my wife finished residency and got her first doctor paycheck. I know some men, especially those who are older, prefer to be the family's main breadwinner. Not me. I've always felt a deep sense of gratitude that my wife makes roughly double what I bring in.

Many physicians spend their first major paychecks on expensive cars and large houses, items they'd been deprived of during their long years of training. But we remained frugal after my wife's residency. Our annual expenses were still a little less than $32,000, thanks in large part to the military allowance for housing. Occasionally, we would even live on base, where housing is free.

Because my wife earned scholarships and attended the cheapest medical school she could find, all our education expenses were paid off by age 32. That's when we really began to save and to see our wealth compound. If you were to use the standard 4% withdrawal rate, my wife and I could have come close to covering all our expenses from savings by the time we reached 35. Four more years of saving at that clip would have easily clinched our financial independence.

But instead, we hit the pause button. Why? We began asking ourselves a key question: "What good is money if there's no one to share its many uses with?"

Over Thanksgiving dinner, I had a conversation with my brother and his wife about the child they'd adopted. I was struck by his offhand comment that so many kids are awaiting adoption. As my wife and I mulled over the issue, it became clearer to us that we might be wired differently from most people. While we reasoned that the important part of having a family is raising and loving kids, neither of us really wanted a baby. We realized it didn't matter to us if the children we raised shared our genes.

We decided that adoption would be our next journey, even though that decision set us back many years on our path to financial independence. Partly, that's because kids are expensive. But partly, it's because we chose the most expensive path to adoption. For those unfamiliar with the process, international adoption is far more costly than domestic adoption. But we were wary of U.S. judges, who might reopen an adoption at the request of a biological parent, so we decided to adopt internationally.

We traveled to Medellin, Colombia, embarking on the greatest—and perhaps most expensive—adventure of our lives. The U.S. offers phenomenal tax credits for adoption costs, covering up to $14,890 of expenses per child in 2022. That credit phases out entirely at higher incomes. Believing that we would have our adoption expenses effectively reimbursed by tax credits, the decision to adopt internationally became a no-brainer. We expected to travel to Colombia in early 2018, so we planned our taxes and work schedules to take full advantage of the tax credit.

Then the adoption agency called—in October 2017. We'd been approved by the Colombian government much faster than usual. Three kids were waiting for us if we were still interested. When you work with a foreign government, these types of offers are take-it-or-leave-it, not something you can negotiate. Our agency emailed us the children's files. As we looked at the photos of the three beautiful siblings and read their histories, we saw—in the eyes of these adolescent kids—God's beauty staring back at us. My wife and I knew then that we were not going to let this opportunity pass us by. The lodging for five weeks in Colombia, plus travel costs, totaled roughly $15,000. The fees to adopt—paid to a Colombian attorney, agency caseworkers, and the U.S. and Colombian governments—added some $40,000 more.

In the midst of all this, it dawned on me: We wouldn't qualify for the adoption tax credits.

Our joint income in 2017 was above the top of the tax credit's income phaseout range by less than $1,000. We missed out on all three tax credits by the narrowest of margins. To lower our taxable income and collect as much as $44,000 in tax credits, I tried to recharacterize that year's Roth retirement savings as traditional, tax-deductible contributions. But this proved impossible with both of our employer plans.

Clearly, it was a financial setback. Still, the adoptions have proved to be the best investment of our lives. Part of the return on investment comes from love, but much of it comes from the parts that haven't been easy. As a parent, I have learned so many lessons. Fatherhood has helped me improve from the woefully unprepared, overconfident person that I was—a version of myself that I look back on now with a grimace.

SACRIFICING MY PENSION

Two years after we welcomed our three kids, I decided to cut short my active-duty Army career. I notified the Army that 2020 would be my final year as a full-time soldier. When I left at age 39, the military had been the only professional life I'd ever known.

It would be hard to argue that this was a smart financial decision. On the civilian side, defined-benefit pension plans have mostly been replaced by 401(k) and similar plans, where the onus to save and invest rests on the employee's shoulders. But the military still offers a traditional pension. In fact, it might be the gold standard of pensions, one that's indexed to inflation and backed by Uncle Sam.

If you remain in military service for 20 years, your pension will amount to 50% of your highest 36 months of base pay. For each additional year of service past 20, the pension increases by 2.5 percentage points. How much you receive varies substantially depending on rank and years of service. Given my active-duty career path, I estimate that a 50% pension would have equaled about $60,500 a year in today's dollars. I could have drawn that amount—for life—starting at age 45.

I'm still pursuing those 20 years of service, but I'm now doing so in the Army Reserve, which will earn me a reduced pension that won't kick in for 20 years. Pensions for Reserve and National Guard members are far less generous, and hinge on the amount of time spent in uniform—working on weekends, mobilizing to assist during natural disasters, fighting in combat zones and so on.

My pension will depend on how actively I participate in the Reserve, but I estimate I'll draw roughly 39% of my Army salary. That means I'll receive about $46,000 a year once I turn 60. That's roughly $15,000 less than I would have received if I'd stayed on active duty for six more years, plus my payout will start 15 years after the larger pension I could have received by simply remaining in the Army.

The obvious question: Why forgo the comfort, security and immediacy of that pension money? Among the many reasons, the chief one was that my family had lived in four places over the prior two years. Moving and military life are, alas, synonymous. With older kids, those moves get harder, as they repeatedly have to say goodbye to friends.

Although some people might disagree, I believe such moves are enormously disruptive to kids' well-being, and never more so than when your children are learning a new language and cultural norms. Our kids are resilient, but it seemed selfish to pursue opportunities and promotions at the cost of the children finding their footing as new Americans. On top of that, my wife has constantly had to interrupt her career to support my military service. Few outside the military are aware of how much spouses and kids sacrifice to support their family member's military career.

MEASURING WEALTH

In our winding path toward financial independence, I find that the best parts have been defined by those times when I left money on the table. That's because building true wealth requires balance. I think back on my grandfather's journey, and the role the Great Depression played in his life. He saved, invested and built a successful family business. But I also think about the many sacrifices he made for those he loved. His wealth was measured not only in dollars, but also by his family, friends and legacy.

I expect to reach financial independence long before age 60. But if I'm unsuccessful, I'll have my Reserve pension and Social Security to fall back on once I get into my 60s. As that paranoid kid who was affected deeply by the stories of the Great Depression, I've ensured that we have financial backup, should we fall short for any reason.

For now, my wife and I save most of our income. The bulk of those savings go to ensure that we don't saddle our kids with college debt, passing on the gift that my grandfather gave to me. Our kids are older, so the college timeline is tighter and the urgency to save is greater.

Some say that you should secure your own financial future before saving for your children's college. If we were closer to retirement, and if I didn't have a pension in my future, I'd say these folks might have a case. Still, I'm not sure about the me-first mentality and, frankly, I don't care—because I'd rather follow the path laid down by my grandfather.

THREE LESSONS

* Financial independence is important—but so, too, is family, and sometimes supporting loved ones means a slower road to wealth.

* For couples, a shared willingness to hold down living costs can open up all kinds of possibilities, including career changes and a growing family.

* Pick your role models carefully. A financially savvy parent or grandparent may provide invaluable lessons that carry you through a lifetime.

MAKING IT

BY
MATT CHRISTOPHER WHITE

Matt Christopher White is a CPA and CFP® who writes about money and apprenticeship to Jesus. He's the author of *How to Love Money: Four Paradoxes That Breathe Life into Your Finances*. Matt is equally comfortable talking about Luke 6:43, Section 643 of the Internal Revenue Code and the 6-4-3 double play. There's no place he'd rather be than with Sarah and their two girls, Lydia and Eliza, at their home in the foothills of the Smoky Mountains.

FLETCHER WHITE, MY great-grandfather, was one of the young American doughboys drafted to fight in the First World War. He also helped set the financial direction for our family for generations to come.

Fletcher may have lacked military acumen, but he compensated with ingenuity and resilience learned growing up in rural Appalachia. In fall 1918, he and a million fellow American soldiers pulled off in a few months what the French had been unable to accomplish in four years. At a cost of more than 26,000 U.S. lives, the Meuse-Argonne offensive dislodged the German soldiers from their trenches, helping to bring an end to a terrible war.

I'll let Fletcher tell you about it in his own words. They're preserved in a book, *Around Home in Unicoi County* by William W. Helton, that chronicles the history of our Tennessee town:

"On the morning of November 11, 1918, a bunch of us soldiers had taken a load of ammunition to the front, and when we got there it was just before 11:00, and in a few minutes, it suddenly got quiet, and the word spread fast that it was all over. What a change—the thunder of war one minute, then quiet as a tomb the next. It was like that until that night, when you could hear firing here and there in celebration. We slept on the ground that night, and although everything was quiet for the first time in four years, they set a guard. But we slept well that night, and were thankful—even the ground felt good."

A decade after making it back to Erwin, in the Appalachian Mountains of northeast Tennessee, Fletcher and his wife Lottie found themselves raising their three kids during the Great Depression. My dad smiles as he recalls listening to his Gramps spin yarns on the front porch: "Whenever he talked about the Depression, he would always say, 'We got along just fine. We always had a roof over our heads and food on the table.'"

In 1924, Congress passed a bill to compensate First World War veterans for the income they lost while serving. The only problem was, the first payment wasn't slated to happen until 1945—21 years later. In 1932, thousands of frustrated veterans and their families converged on Washington, D.C., in peaceful protest, urging lawmakers to deliver the aid right away. Eventually, in 1936, they succeeded in getting the stipends paid in full, and the momentum they created led to legislation that would become known as the G.I. Bill.

My great-grandfather received $800, which he used to buy several acres. The land meant opportunities to improve his family's life. He grew fruits and vegetables, raised livestock, built a barn and cellar, and rented his cane mill for neighbors to make their sorghum molasses. Years later, my grandparents built their house on the land, which is where my dad and his sister grew up. Later, my parents built their house there, too. That's where my brother and I grew up. My grandparents and parents still live in those same homes today.

Fletcher didn't just set a path for our family with his land purchase. He also had a 38-year career as a carman with the Clinchfield Railroad, which had brought its headquarters to Erwin at the start of the 20th century. His son—my grandfather—studied accounting at Steed College in nearby Johnson City and then made it his career, also working for the Clinchfield Railroad. In fact, all of my great-grandfathers and grandfathers worked for the Clinchfield. Only my maternal grandfather—Pap—didn't retire from there. Instead, he left the railroad to serve with the Air Force in Korea. Upon his return, he attended college thanks to the G.I. Bill, and then went on to a career as a teacher, principal and superintendent with Unicoi County Schools. My mom and dad followed in his footsteps, my mom primarily as an eighth-grade science teacher and my dad as an elementary school principal.

My parents worked their entire careers for the same employer, one that had a strong defined benefit retirement plan. They had watched their parents show similar loyalty and be rewarded with a financially comfortable retirement. When your pension is overseen by the U.S. Railroad Retirement Board or the Tennessee Consolidated Retirement System, you don't have to worry much about retirement. That's probably why my family didn't talk much about investing or the financial markets.

TENNESSEE ORANGE

As a kid, I didn't think about money much, either. All I wanted to do was play sports—basketball and baseball, to be specific. I was a child of the 1990s, so I wanted to be like Michael Jordan or Ken Griffey Jr. I believed with everything in me that I could do something great in sports.

I performed well enough in high-school basketball and baseball to earn some local recognition, but I received zero college offers. My pride was wounded. Watching my dream die, I felt acute pain. Had I failed? In 2004, going into my senior year, I accepted that this would be it—my last year playing sports. Resolutely putting that dream behind me was like dousing my face with ice-cold water. It was the first time I ever gave much serious thought to what I wanted to do with my life after high school. Until then, I had only entertained thoughts of continuing my athletic career for as long as possible.

I needed a new vision for my life. A few years earlier, I had decided to follow Jesus, and I remember thinking hard then about what that really meant. I intended to pay attention to what Jesus said. I read in the Bible where he said, "Life is not defined by what you have, even when you have a lot." I also read, "For where your treasure is, there your heart will be also." I filed these ideas away.

I visited a few colleges that would've gladly charged me a fortune, but I decided they weren't for me. Instead, I opted to attend the University of Tennessee (UT) in Knoxville—a place where I felt at home, could cheer on my beloved Vols and would have no shortage of opportunities to explore.

The summer before college, I read a biography of Howard Schultz, the founder of Starbucks. That sparked my interest in business and finance. Then I picked up business book No. 2 of my life, *Personal Finance for Dummies* by Eric Tyson. I figured there was no better place for a complete novice to start. I skimmed through several chapters, was intrigued and decided I wanted to learn more. At college orientation, I found out that I could start school as a business major with an undecided concentration. I thought that would be perfect.

Preparing to move to campus, I thought about how I could meet new people at UT. I wanted to find others who also sought to follow Jesus, so I looked into various campus Christian groups. I noticed that the Baptist Collegiate Ministry had some fun welcome week activities, so I decided to participate. My future wife Sarah did, too. Neither one of us even went to a Baptist church at the time. By December, we knew we wanted to marry.

As Sarah and I became close, she told me how her life had been shaped by losing her dad suddenly when she was age 12. He'd had a brain aneurysm while on a business trip. I got to know Sarah's mom—a first-grade teacher. She easily connected with my parents, and it felt like we had always known each other. I also got to know her older brother, and I began to see how admirably he stepped into managing the family's financial responsibilities. I was only 18 years old, but I had already found the woman I would spend my life with. We had dreams of raising a family together. As clearly as I could see that vivid shade of orange all over the UT campus, I could see that my actions every day—even at age 18—would directly impact the future of my family.

In my sophomore year, I decided to study accounting and finance. I was excited about the opportunity to increase my personal finance knowledge. I was no doubt influenced by the legacy of my accountant grandfather, as well as stories of Sarah's dad, who had been the director of audit for the University of Tennessee.

I remember sitting in one of the old brick buildings up on the Hill at UT for my first day of finance 101. I couldn't tell the teacher from the students. He was a young guy, casually dressed. He began the first lecture by telling his story. In the late 1990s, he had been part of a fast-rising Silicon Valley technology startup. Many of his friends had cashed out their stock options at the right time and were now multi-millionaires. He held on too long. The company went bust—along with his stock options—and that led him to return to school to pursue a doctorate in finance.

As I processed his story, I thought to myself, 'How could he have seen that coming? I doubt that his tech friends were that much more financially savvy than him. It seems like there was a lot of luck involved. There has to be a better way.'

Later that semester, I studied how a mutual fund provides diversification, and I was introduced to the concepts of asset allocation and correlation. In my next finance class, I gawked at the professor's illustrations of compounding returns. I began to realize that I could build financial success on a foundation of discipline—a firmer foundation than either luck or purported skill.

FALLING INTO PLACE

On June 20, 2009, Sarah and I were married in the church sanctuary that her dad had been instrumental in building as a leader in the church. We both began master's degree programs at UT—Sarah in nutrition science and me in accounting with a tax concentration. During the recruiting season that fall, I secured a job with a boutique Knoxville CPA firm called Burkhart & Co. that provided tax compliance, financial planning and consulting services. I would start the fall after I graduated.

In one of my tax courses, we delved into the mechanics of IRA taxation, including the difference between traditional and Roth accounts. Our professor illustrated how compounding returns look even better when they're tax-free. I took notice. I opened a Roth IRA at the Edward Jones office of a family friend. The active funds he suggested were the first investments I'd ever bought. Sarah already had a Roth IRA there, and she added to hers. We began investing regularly at clearance prices—this was right after the stock market bottomed in 2009.

Sarah and I both left school with a master's degree and no debt. Over school breaks, I had already knocked out two sections of the CPA exam. Before I started my job, I passed the third and fourth parts.

Not long after the real estate bubble burst, we bought our first house in Knoxville, using some funds that Sarah had received from her dad's estate as our down payment. Our realtor told us it was the best deal he had ever seen. With our two incomes, the payment was manageable. A few years later, we jumped at the chance to refinance to a 15-year mortgage at 3% interest. We realized that we were benefiting from good circumstances and timing, but we didn't chalk it up to luck. Instead, we were thankful to God. We believed what David said in the 23rd Psalm: "The Lord is my shepherd; I have all that I need." We knew we were reaping what had been sown by several generations of our families—working hard, fighting to keep their marriages strong, and investing in a better life for their kids.

Not everybody had the kind of opportunities we had and we wanted to do something about it, so we chose to sponsor a seven-year-old boy in Tanzania through Compassion International, a charity that connects donors with children in poverty. We started giving $38 every month to help finance his local Compassion program, which functioned through a church that was already serving the community. We wanted to help Stanley have the same things we cherished in our own upbringing—a close-knit support system focused on his spiritual formation, character development and education.

Meanwhile, at church, we took counseling classes for a year and then started serving in the peer counseling ministry, which allowed us to help others in the local community. The director of counseling became a trusted friend. Before switching careers, he had also been a CPA. He and his wife had two boys—one with special needs. He implored us to save as much as possible during our two-income-no-kids years. We listened.

At work, Burkhart & Co.'s founder and president, Renda Burkhart, quickly became a mentor to me. I remember sitting in her office as she explained how index funds work. She enthusiastically recommended Jack Bogle's *The Little Book of Common Sense Investing*. I devoured it. Sarah and I built a sturdy financial foundation with a Roth IRA for each of us, a qualified retirement savings plan through each of our employers, a health savings account and a taxable brokerage account. We consolidated our accounts at Vanguard Group, where we favored index funds and put an emphasis on low fees for the active portion of our portfolio.

NOT LIKE WE PLANNED

When the time came to have kids, we assumed there would be no issues. It wasn't long before we discovered how naive we were. We tried to conceive for more than a year but couldn't, so we were overjoyed when we found out early in 2013 that Sarah was pregnant. A few weeks later—when I was buried with work during the spring tax season—I got a call from Sarah in the middle of the workday. I ducked into the library to take it. I can still recall the wall of books I stared at, while she told me through tears that we'd lost our baby. Only our parents had known that we were pregnant—or even trying—so we told very few people about our loss. For the next three months, I was consumed by the demands of tax season. That, in part, meant Sarah and I didn't really have the chance to grieve together.

Around that same time, I started leading client relationships at the firm. I wanted a more thorough and confident knowledge of estate planning and investing, so I enrolled in the University of Georgia's executive education program to prepare for the Certified Financial Planner (CFP) exam.

After the miscarriage, we were unable to conceive for another year. Then, in spring 2014, we found out that we had another baby on the way. Learning of this pregnancy was again a joy, but it was far from a relief. Instead, it was the start of a long season of agonizing anxiety for Sarah. At work, my responsibilities continued to grow. The fall tax season arrived and again brought long hours for months on end. On top of that, I had a November CFP exam date looming.

It all became too much for me. I suffered from my own intense anxiety and fear. I felt like I was letting everyone down. I didn't have enough to give to satisfy the demands of work. I was falling behind in my CFP exam preparation. But more than anything, I was fiercely determined to support Sarah with more of my time and presence. I was angry and bitter that work had prevented me from being more supportive after Sarah's miscarriage. I stumbled along but ended up passing the CFP exam in November. Our daughter Lydia arrived five days later.

It took some time, but I eventually swallowed my pride and asked for help. I learned to accept that I didn't have what it takes to carry all these burdens on my own. I stopped doing peer counseling for a season and, instead, learned how to be on the receiving end. A lot of people showed me a lot of grace in those days.

HUNTING FOR TREASURE

At Burkhart & Co., we all benefited from Renda's stellar reputation in the Knoxville community, which attracted an impressive clientele. I developed a specialty working with high-net-worth families, including helping with their trusts and estates. Working with these families was a fascinating opportunity to study people who—by all objective measures—had made it. It didn't take me long to understand that 'making it' didn't stop people from having to wrestle with money and other issues. Several of my clients were living my childhood dream as professional athletes or as Division I college coaches. Those with first-generation wealth struggled to discern who their real friends were, when to share their newfound financial surplus and when to put up healthy boundaries. As the generational wealth passed further down the family tree, kids had trouble with entitlement and finding value in work. With possessions came worries and burdens. Relationship strife usually followed close behind.

At the dawn of another spring tax season, Sarah and I got the good news that we were expecting for the third time. Soon after, we suffered our second miscarriage. We were heartbroken, but I had learned from my past mistakes. Even though it was the busiest time of the year, I canceled all my client meetings and worked from home for a week, so I could grieve with Sarah and Lydia. We received an outpouring of love and support from friends and family. We were both weary, but we still longed to add to our family. This time, we didn't have to wait another year. Within a few months, we celebrated the news of our fourth child. Eliza arrived the next February.

Each time we lost a baby or celebrated a birth, we sponsored another child through Compassion International in honor of the miracle of their life. We now have eight children, from all over the world, in our extended family. We've exchanged hundreds of letters where we share our lives and learn about each other's cultures. We send birthday and Christmas gifts every year. We pray for them and they pray for us. We love involving our two girls in all of this. Our Compassion friends have money concerns of their own. The kids' parents often can't find consistent work, and their families do without much of what we consider to be basic necessities. The kids usually spend their birthday money on shoes for themselves or on rice and beans for their family. Rarely, if ever, do they get to buy a toy.

As I've gotten to know both many high-net-worth families and those who are used to doing without, I have observed something that surprised me: We are all more alike than I ever would've thought. We all have to make the same fundamental decision. Sure, we come at it from different perspectives and different parts of the wealth spectrum. But we all have to decide: What do we ultimately treasure? What we treasure will, in time, determine who we become.

THE VIEW FROM HERE

This morning, as I write this, I sit on the front porch of my parents' house, taking in the view of the mountains and the fields below, where my grandparents' house sits. I worry about my 93-year-old Paw's failing health and mind. I worry about Grandmaw and Dad as they take care of him. I am thankful for the visit we had this weekend—four generations enjoying this moment together.

As I reflect on my money journey thus far, I notice that two contrasting mindsets have regularly guided my decisions. Sometimes, a long-term view has led me to make current sacrifices for a future payoff. Other times, I have chosen slower progress toward a long-term goal in favor of the moment. The hard part has been knowing when to take which approach. There's usually no fanfare alerting me that it's time to perk up and focus on this important choice.

I constantly have to remind myself that it's the mundane days that really are the substance of my life. And it's for those days that I'm especially in need of some wise and practical advice. I find it in the words of longtime University of Southern California philosophy professor, Dallas Willard. He wrote in *Renovation of the Heart in Daily Practice: Experiments in Spiritual Transformation* that, "At the beginning of my day, I commit my day to the Lord's care. ... Then I meet everything that happens as sent, or at least permitted, by God. I meet it resting in the hand of his care. I no longer have to manage the weather, airplanes, and people." To that list, I might add the financial markets and the status of my retirement nest egg.

When I start my day with Willard's exercise, I find I'm more likely to live that day as though I treasure what I say I do. I treasure Jesus. My apprenticeship to him leads me to value people—my family, my neighbors—over possessions and accomplishments. Sarah and I have been in agreement for some time about what we treasure, but that hasn't confined our money journey to a predictable path—far from it. For a season, we pursued our financial goals at a rapid pace. As circumstances changed, we chose to let go of some promising financial opportunities to free up space for other priorities.

That led to a career change for us both. I left the public accounting profession to put better boundaries on my career's demands. Now I get to put my expertise to good use at one of Knoxville's largest employers—and have the freedom to do freelance writing, too. Meanwhile, Sarah took a part-time teacher's assistant position that gives her the ideal schedule and invaluable connectedness at Lydia's school. We prefer a lifestyle of measured frugality. It affords us the ability to continue progressing toward tomorrow's financial goals—albeit at a slower pace—while still enjoying today's profound gift of unhurried presence.

This year, Lydia played in a basketball league for the first time, and I got to coach the team. Being in the gym again had me reminiscing about my glory days. I have to admit: I'm a little embarrassed about how one-track minded I used to be about playing sports, without ever thinking seriously about whether it was worth it. I wonder, where did I think 'doing something great in sports' was going to get me? Back then, I failed to recognize that no matter how far I went, eventually it would end—and life would go on.

'Making it' is an illusion. I have already accomplished some meaningful financial goals and some are within reach, but I still have a long way to go to reach many others. When I achieve them, life will go on. I'll make new goals then. But whether it's then or now, I want my life to emanate the same qualities: thankfulness, contentment, discipline, diligence and charity.

THREE LESSONS

* Reflecting on your family's history is the start to understanding your money journey. Before you figure where you want to go, you need to think about where you came from.

* One day, our progeny will look at our lives to help them understand their own money journeys. What do we want them to see? Your legacy isn't just dollars and cents, but also the example you set and the values you live by.

* We may think achieving a vaunted financial goal will give us access to the life we treasure. But in reality, a one-track-minded pursuit of that goal can be a distraction—one that causes us to miss those parts of life we truly treasure.

INVESTING TOGETHER

BY
SONJA HAGGERT

Sonja Haggert is the author of *Invest, Reinvest, Rest: Investment Advice for All Generations*. The book is based on what she's learned as an individual investor. A second edition is in the works, which will reflect changes that have taken place in the financial world. Sonja spent the bulk of her career at a local manufacturing company, eventually becoming vice president and general manager of one of the company's divisions. She was born in Germany, moved to Alberta, Canada, with her parents and eventually settled in the U.S. Sonja is a graduate of Villanova University, which is where she met her husband. Today, they live in suburban Philadelphia.

M Y 1975 GRADUATION from college was a momentous occasion for my parents. We had emigrated from Germany, first to Canada and then to New Jersey. They didn't have college degrees, but they had worked hard and epitomized the American dream. Proud that they'd been able to pay for my education but also relieved that college costs were over, they were looking forward to the start of my career.

Wait, what about marriage and a house in the suburbs? They

wished those things for me, just not right away. My mother, in particular, wanted me to have a career. She'd had hers at Flemington Furs in Flemington, New Jersey, as the firm's seamstress extraordinaire. I'll be forever grateful for her inspiration and direction at a time when women weren't encouraged to pursue a career. She earned more than my father and retired with a healthy pension.

My mother was also the ultimate 'what if' person. What if you never marry or you get divorced? Would you be able to support yourself? What if you lose your job? How will you live? What if you get sick? Could you pay your medical bills? What if you don't save and something happens?

Being immigrants and anxious about financial security, my parents were savers. I was not.

OFF TO WORK

When I graduated college, jobs were scarce. I was lucky. A professor I worked for secured an internship for me at a Philadelphia department store during my junior year. After graduation, the store hired me. I spent every penny I earned.

I met my husband at college. He had plans for graduate school and none for marriage. He took a teaching assistantship and subsisted on almost nothing. Growing up, he had learned how to save by doing jobs around the house for his parents, earning dimes and quarters along the way. Being frugal came naturally.

All that changed when we married in 1980. It was the start of our ongoing partnership—financial and otherwise—that's seen us make countless joint decisions, often for the better. But sometimes not. Being among the lucky ones without college debt and with good jobs, we thought nothing of becoming big spenders. We bought a house with a 16% mortgage, a timeshare for our vacations and, not long afterwards, a piece of property in Maine. The house we bought was a duplex, a relatively intelligent purchase because our renters helped pay the mortgage. It was the only way we could afford that 16% mortgage. But we also discovered that we didn't like being landlords.

Writing those mortgage checks and having little left over for fun made us realize that we needed to make some changes. Fortunately, I had moved on from retailing, where I bought everything in sight, to a manufacturing company where the products were decidedly less glamorous and the potential for career advancement greater.

Meanwhile, my husband took a position with a large pharmaceutical company. He initially hoped to spend his career in the chemistry lab but changed course and went into sales. Making that sort of a career change could have been a significant undertaking, but he was able to do it within the confines of his current employer. The relative security that provided, along with the greater career opportunities, made it easier to take the plunge. We were now looking at two pensions. We thought we were set and acted as such, continuing our high-spending ways.

Then my husband went back to school to get an MBA—and that would eventually change everything. How so? His favorite course was finance. The final project was to outline a path to retirement. He got an A. We decided we'd follow the plan he drew up, one that would allow us to retire at age 55. The only problem: It took us a decade to implement the plan.

Instead, in the late 1980s and early 1990s, we purchased not one property but two, invested in a startup, and decided we needed another timeshare to enjoy our vacations. When I think back on the debt we accumulated, I marvel that we could juggle it all.

The properties turned out okay. We sold one for a substantial gain during a real estate boom. We used that money to remodel our existing home. We held onto the other property for a long time and, in the end, managed to do reasonably well.

The startup, however, was a complete disaster. What in the world did we know about startups? The company was called Flea Fare, which provided franchise services to flea markets. Yes, really. Today that sounds like a laughable concept. At the time, we were enamored, in large part because we spent many a weekend with my in-laws visiting flea markets.

What about the timeshares? They provided some beautiful vacations for us and family members. Eventually, we gifted the timeshares to our nieces, who still enjoy them, so we don't regret the purchases, except the steep financing charges that were involved.

GETTING SERIOUS

In our 40s, we were doing reasonably well financially. We had a few promotions under our belts but started to tire of the constant travel our jobs required. It was time to get serious about following that retirement plan my husband drew up in his MBA course. Our age 55 goal wasn't that far away. We saw our parents, who were already retired, enjoying their lives. They were traveling, and spending more and more time with family and friends. We wanted those things for ourselves.

Up until then, our investments consisted of certificates of deposit and some randomly selected mutual funds. We decided we needed a financial advisor. In 1996, we picked one based on an American Express promotion—not the greatest reason. At the time, Ameriprise was under the American Express umbrella, and signing on with Ameriprise earned us Amex credit card points.

But we lucked out. Our advisor got us through the 2008 crisis with our sanity intact, provided solid investment advice when we wanted to pursue a foolish investment, and gave us more and more leeway as we became comfortable making our own investment decisions. We still use him today.

By 2003, we had managed to pay off our debts, including our mortgage. My mother's voice echoed in my ears. "Pay off your house as soon as you can because you always want a roof over your head." In addition to our pensions, we now had two 401(k) accounts, to which we contributed the maximum each year. In 2003, we also reached the magic seven-figure savings number. Still, it was clear to us that we would need more to enjoy the retirement lifestyle we wanted.

How would we swell our retirement nest egg? My husband and I had tried golf together, taking numerous lessons before deciding it was all too time-consuming. Instead, we decided to take up a new hobby—investing. We told ourselves, "We can do this." But how were we going to do this? It might seem like the world is divided between investment do-it-yourselfers and those who rely on the advice of others. But we ended up doing a mix of both.

My immigrant parents were all about security. The majority of their investments were in certificates of deposit. Their one foray into the stock market ended badly. They had purchased Sun Microsystems when it was a hot stock and held on too long, seeing their gain shrivel from $50,000 to zero.

My in-laws were a different story. For years, they had successfully invested in the stock market. Like us, they had a financial advisor, but they also liked to do their own independent research using the Value Line Investment Survey and a financial newsletter. They started passing along those newsletters to us.

I wasn't convinced my in-law's financial newsletter was the best option, so I researched others. When I had narrowed our choice down to three, I set up an Excel spreadsheet and tracked the newsletters' recommendations for six months. During that time, we didn't buy any of the suggested investments.

After the six months, we opted for *The Oxford Communique*, the newsletter my in-laws subscribed to. It's published by the Oxford

Club in Baltimore. It would become our key source of investment recommendations.

Every month, the newsletter sends out an in-depth writeup on a stock. This research has provided us with direction on which stocks to buy. Best of all, the newsletter also sends out alerts when it thinks we should sell. That takes away the fear that history will repeat itself and we'll end up, like my parents, with a stock like Sun Microsystems.

The Oxford Club also provides seminars, where we learned about topics like investment taxes, evaluating dividend payout ratios, how to invest in options (not for us) and using trailing stop-loss orders. At those seminars, we also got to know the people who were providing us with investment recommendations. Putting faces to their names gave us peace of mind.

Our investing hobby has made us money over the years, though I can't tell you how we've done relative to the market averages. Like our attempt at golf, my husband and I enjoyed investing together—but, once again, it started becoming too time-consuming. In addition, we became frustrated with the tax bills from our mutual funds, so we've been moving into exchange-traded index funds (ETFs) instead. To guide our index fund investing, we turned to a book, *The Gone Fishin' Portfolio*, written by Alexander Green. Green is the editor of the Oxford Club's *Communique*.

Our 'gone fishin' portfolio' is made up of ten different asset classes, each represented by a Vanguard Group ETF. The portfolio only needs to be rebalanced once a year. The premise: The rest of the time, you can go fishing—or whatever it is you enjoy. Today, these index funds account for a quarter of our total portfolio.

TIME TO RETIRE

In 2004, after ten years at the helm of one of the company's manufacturing divisions and working with three different CEOs, I was burned out. My current boss was thinking short term and I kept stressing long-term goals. He also wanted to bring in his own people to head the various divisions. I was floundering. My life had become defined by my job and my happiness with it. My boss and I agreed to part ways. I found myself in my mother's 'what if' mode. What if I had been more conciliatory—and less insistent that the company focus on long-term goals?

The good news: Being debt-free gave me the option to retire. But first, I had to prove to myself that I was still up for a challenge. I threw myself into a startup with a friend. The premise was to provide courses for women on everything from finances to decorating. The company never took off, but I enjoyed working with a dear friend. When we decided to disband, I once again started questioning myself.

Fortunately, at the time, another friend asked me to join the board of Laurel House, a nonprofit in Norristown, Pennsylvania, that helps women dealing with domestic violence. I threw myself into the work, both as co-president of the board and as a member of various committees. It seems I had found my new purpose and was finally ready to retire. I'm still active in the organization and a huge admirer of the work it does.

Writing has been a lifelong dream—one I've been able to pursue in retirement. In addition to contributing to *HumbleDollar*'s website and putting together a book on investing, I write a newsletter, *Simplified Investing for Smart People*, about how the financial news affects us personally.

In 2008, my husband joined me in retirement, which meant we both met our age 55 goal. A few years later, we decided to do away with the responsibilities of homeownership and move to an over-55 community. We found our ideal home, but it would be four more years before we moved in—because tragedy got in the way. We started losing our parents in rapid succession. There were four lives whose affairs we had to untangle, which meant there was no time to move. The builder of our new home agreed to lease the model we had purchased, and the resulting rent payments helped cover the mortgage on the new place.

In retirement, we continue to invest in individual stocks and bonds, but our focus has shifted. Thanks to a book about dividend stocks, *Get Rich with Dividends* by Marc Lichtenfeld, we decided that this was our niche. Why not get paid to invest? We had gotten to know Lichtenfeld, another Oxford Club employee. His newsletter is now our go-to source for stock picks. We've seen some doubles and triples in stocks like Broadcom, Franklin Resources, Texas Instruments, Eaton and AbbVie. Have we had losers? Of course. Have we made a killing in tech stocks? No. But we're okay with that.

Being retired means owning more bonds. When Lichtenfeld started a trading service for corporate bond investors, we signed up. Lichtenfeld's recommendations have allowed us to invest in bonds that provide the comfort of regular income and a known payout at maturity, with the added advantage of the occasional capital gain.

What fun would investing be if there wasn't a bit of a thrill in it? We've gotten involved in startups again—this time through MicroVentures, a crowdfunding website that lets us diversify across numerous venture capital investments. We did well with Spotify, not so much with the others.

We've also dipped our toes into cryptocurrency. We started with bitcoin and went on to add others as well. As I write this, we're up sixfold on our initial investment, but that could quickly change. Knowing the volatility involved, we cashed out a sum equal to our initial investment, so now we're playing with 'house money.'

My husband and I have many heated discussions about which investments to buy—but that's part of the fun. You'll rarely find us silent at the dinner table. Investing is one of the things that keeps us close, along with travel, theater, concerts, museums and fine dining.

In his recent book, *The Psychology of Money*, Morgan Housel defined happiness as having enough. We enjoy a retirement lifestyle that lets us do what we want when we want and with whom we want. For us, that is indeed enough.

THREE LESSONS

* Many investors opt to either do it themselves or rely on a financial advisor. But there's no reason you can't do both.

* Make sure you talk regularly with your spouse or partner about the household finances. If you're agreed on long-term goals, it can provide the motivation to save—and your financial journey can help bring you closer together.

* Many of us make financial mistakes when we start out. But don't despair: You'll likely have time to make up for those early missteps.

SLOW AND STEADY

The prospect of a big investment win may be tantalizing, but its pursuit often leaves us worse off financially. Instead, for everyday investors, wealth typically lies in collecting a regular paycheck for many decades, diligently saving one dollar after another, and then leaving those dollars to compound in the financial markets. Sounds dull? Perhaps it is—but the results can be thrilling.

LESSONS UNLEARNED by Howard Rohleder

DRIVEN TO SUCCEED by Richard Quinn

PROJECT MICKEY by Phil Kernen

FILLING PIGGYBANKS by Kyle McIntosh

MONEY VIGILANT by Greg Spears

LESSONS UNLEARNED

BY
HOWARD ROHLEDER

Howard Rohleder, a former chief executive of a community hospital, retired early after more than 30 years in hospital administration. In retirement, he enjoys serving on several nonprofit boards, exploring walking paths with his wife Susan, and visiting their six grandchildren. A little-known fact: In May 1994, Howard was featured—along with five others—on the cover of *Kiplinger's Personal Finance* for an article titled 'Secrets of My Investment Success.'

M Y PARENTS WERE profoundly influenced by the Great Depression and—as their only child—I was, too. My father had seen my grandfather, who was a successful small grocer, lose everything when banks failed in the 1930s. My father never trusted banks or the stock market again. He fully expected another depression somewhere just over the horizon.

My mother grew up in Appalachia without electricity or indoor plumbing. She had a tremendous work ethic, making it clear to me that work always came before fun. She readily deferred spending in favor of saving. Her greatest fear was to experience once again the cold she felt in winters during her childhood.

My father imparted wisdom through a series of pithy phrases. These included exhortations such as "initiative is doing the right thing at the right time without being told" and "what's worth doing is worth doing well." He promoted and practiced the Golden Rule: "Do unto others as you would have them do unto you." These positive influences shaped my character.

But when it came to business and personal finance, I was taught "it's not what you know, but who you know," implying a rigged game. "You need to have money to make money" suggested the little guy wasn't welcome in the financial world. He preached that, when it came to money, "you can't trust anyone, not even your grandmother." And he'd say—in a derogatory tone—that an acquaintance "has more money than he knows what to do with." Money to him was ephemeral and not worth devoting time to. These negative images colored my early thoughts about money.

Neither parent was extravagant. Neither spent to maintain social status. My mother scrimped. My father spent somewhat more freely.

My father was a self-employed general practice physician with no pension, little savings, and no ownership of stocks or bonds. He had a wide variety of interests and readily contributed time to community projects and boards. But he was unwilling to put effort into understanding the business or financial world. This lack of interest led him to make 'investments' without doing basic due diligence, leaving him at risk of being scammed.

FROM THREE TO TWO

My father's retirement was forced by a cancer diagnosis. He came home ill from work one day and never returned to the office. His retirement lasted nine months, most of it consumed by the illness. When he died, I was aged 17. He had life insurance that provided my mother with a small nest egg. The house was paid for, and she had a job with solid benefits, so our immediate needs were met. I qualified for both Social Security and veteran's dependent benefits, which went a long way toward covering future college expenses.

My mother was left with 15 years to prepare for retirement. She and I had zero investment experience, and our family had no investment advisor to turn to. My father's words about trusting no one rang in our ears, making us fearful about whom we could approach.

It was the late 1970s, and interest rates were much higher than today. Our initial investment of the insurance proceeds consisted of certificates of deposit (CDs) at a savings and loan, which offered a fixed rate of interest until the CD matured perhaps 12 or 18 months later. In the regulated environment of the time, the Federal Reserve's Regulation Q allowed S&Ls to pay a quarter-percentage point more than banks, and they often handed out a household appliance as an inducement to open new accounts. This could be considered our first strategic investment: a quarter point and a toaster.

With the spike in interest rates in the early 1980s, there was a lot of press about a relatively new concept: money market mutual funds, which sought to maintain a steady $1 share price while paying a healthy amount of interest. They were discussed in my college finance classes. We took the plunge and moved some maturing CD money into Fidelity Investments' money market fund, which was paying double-digit rates.

I came to realize that we needed to prepare for my mother's retirement. She had the beginnings of a retirement fund. If we managed it well, it could support her. If not, I would be supporting her. From my reading, it was clear that we needed to think about investing in the stock market. My mother had a small amount of stock in her name from her employer and had, at some point, put money into a stock fund from Investors Diversified Services

(IDS), a forerunner of Ameriprise. We contacted IDS to identify a representative, who came to the house to talk with us. I remember jotting down his profound statement "buy low, sell high" on my notepad. To invest with him, my mother wrote a check for $20,000 from a maturing CD.

As I continued to learn, I started to understand the amount of commission and fees built into our IDS investments. I couldn't get comfortable with the representative profiting off our transactions. We eventually liquidated those investments and moved the money to Fidelity, where we had previously opened the money market fund. During the severe recession of 1981–82, as a result of research plus a bit of luck, we put money into Fidelity Magellan Fund, run at that time by legendary mutual fund manager Peter Lynch. Later, we invested in Fidelity Equity-Income Fund. When individual retirement accounts first became available to all workers, we immediately opened a Fidelity IRA for my mother and bought stock funds.

With this foundation, my mother had the makings of a sound retirement. Her work would provide a modest pension and excellent health insurance to supplement Medicare. Ultimately, her company offered a buyout, and she was able to retire early with sufficient assets for the rest of her life.

MY TURN TO INVEST

Learning to manage money for my mother at an early age had the benefit of setting the stage for my own investing. After college, I married into a family where stock ownership was the norm. This was a novelty to me: a middle-class family that had faith in the markets and invested for their future. My father-in-law was a conservative investor, and he was preparing thoughtfully for retirement. I learned from his example. He was also frugal, a trait he passed on to my wife.

He had given my wife five shares of AT&T and five shares of General Electric as a college graduation present. For many years, these were our only individual stock holdings, but we added to them with reinvested dividends and zero commission purchases through each company's dividend reinvestment plan. GE, in particular, soared during this period, with the stock splitting multiple times.

While my mother had a nest egg from the life insurance proceeds, my wife and I had to come up with capital to start investing. From my mother, I learned frugality. Over the decades, I've enjoyed some investment success. But what I do better than most is save. My wife and I lived below our means and spent only what we could afford.

In my mid-20s, I realized that—with even a modest salary—30 to 40 years of earnings would represent $1 million to $2 million flowing through my checking account. Siphoning off some of those earnings along the way, and then investing them, would allow me to build our savings for retirement and other goals. Early on, my wife and I scraped together $1,100 and opened an account at Twentieth Century Investors, now American Century, a mutual fund family that sold its funds without a commission, or 'load' in Wall Street lingo. James Stowers ran the company then and had an impressive track record from investing in growth stocks.

Through the 1980s, our investments worked out well for my mother and for us. Still, I had a big fear of losing money and no perspective on market gyrations. At various times, I was scared into selling some of our winning positions by what turned out to be normal market fluctuations. I'm certain that, in every case, I would have done better to hold or even buy more. Over time, I learned that dollar-cost averaging and rebalancing help take the emotion out of investing.

Looking back, I see that this was all part of the normal learning curve. As a new investor, you can gain perspective by talking to mentors, listening to experts and reading up on market history.

But there's no substitute for living through multiple up and down markets, and learning from your successes and failures.

I also recognized that, when it came to my mother's account, I was not investing for myself but for her retirement. We were at different life stages. I had a much longer time horizon. Losing money for her would be much more painful. I drew a distinction between how I invested for myself and how I invested for her, taking more risk in my account. I saw investments go to zero, but I never saw anything close to that in her account.

REPLAYING THE MESSAGES

Like many children, I got mixed messages about money from my parents. Those early lessons have proven hard to shake. When it came time to invest for my mother and me, I had to examine my father's lessons about money and decide what to keep and what to discard. This took time.

The one lesson from my father that I took to heart—and still struggle with today—is not trusting money advice from others. On the positive side, this drove me to educate myself. I prepared tax returns for my mother and myself, which required that I understand the tax implications of financial decisions. If my investing decisions turned out poorly, I had no one to blame but myself. We had to trust Fidelity, but no individual broker was profiting from our buys and sells.

Through my college and graduate school years, I found opportunities to learn more about investing. Andrew Tobias's *The Only Investment Guide You'll Ever Need* was the first comprehensive book I read about financial planning. I took a tax accounting class as an undergraduate and an evening adult education class in personal financial planning while in graduate school. And I continued to read everything I could about saving, investing and financial planning.

As a result of this do-it-yourself approach, I saved on professional fees and commissions. I'm sure there were times when, from lack of expertise, I made decisions that were less than optimal. Whether these offset the savings in fees, I'll never know.

My father didn't just distrust the financial advice of others. He also didn't trust the entire financial system and felt the little guy wasn't welcome. But while my father thought the game was rigged, I decided that there were rules to the game, and it was incumbent on me to learn those rules in order to win. I accepted that the markets were far better regulated in the late 20th century than during the boom that led up to the 1929 market crash and which shook my father and grandfather.

When I started working, I immediately opened an IRA. With babies and a mortgage, it was six years before I could max out my annual contributions, at which point I also opened a 403(b) account at work. I increased those contributions each year until I reached the maximum allowed. Dollar-cost averaging, with money flowing into investments every payday, required a faith in the system that my father never had. I had to accept that, even when I was 'buying high,' the market's long-term upward trend would overcome the inevitable dips.

What about my father's notion that you could "have more money than you know what to do with"? I catalogued my responsibilities: assuring my mother's retirement, supporting my family, educating my children, and planning for my retirement. It struck me as irresponsible to myself, my family and society if I didn't prepare to meet these financial obligations.

The flipside lesson of "having more money than you know what to do with" is the notion that, at some point, enough is enough. Continuing to aggressively accumulate after you have 'enough' risks making money the end goal, not the tool to achieve financial security. With financial security, to paraphrase the recent book *The*

Psychology of Money by Morgan Housel, you can do what you want, where you want, when you want, with whom you want, for as long as you want. In short, you have choices. If you fail to properly manage money, your choices will be limited or made for you.

In the end, my mother lived out her life with financial security, and my wife and I are set to do the same. Goals achieved—and perhaps that's all that matters.

THREE LESSONS

* We're all heavily influenced by the money messages we heard growing up. Strive to identify those messages, and figure out which make sense for you.

* To be successful investors, we need faith in the financial markets' ability to deliver long-run gains. If we're sensible in our investing, that faith should be handsomely rewarded.

* We need to save diligently and invest prudently to amass wealth. But prudence also requires that we recognize when we've amassed enough—and no longer need to take so much risk.

DRIVEN TO SUCCEED

BY
RICHARD QUINN

Before retiring in 2010, Richard Quinn was a compensation and benefits executive. He writes regularly for *HumbleDollar*, and also blogs for his own site, QuinnsCommentary.net. Dick and his wife Connie have four children and 13 grandchildren, and they've been married for more than 50 years. Since retiring, they have been to 44 countries and driven across the U.S. twice. Dick takes pride in having kissed the Blarney Stone, drunk from the Fountain of Youth, and placed a prayer in the Western Wall.

THIS IS ABOUT a journey, about what can happen and what you can make happen. It's about starting at the bottom and, over more than 50 years, achieving financial independence.

My financial views were heavily influenced by my parents, especially my father, but not in the way you might imagine. My father was a car salesman. For many years, he worked seven days a week, from 8 a.m. to 8 p.m. He was let go from his job at age 67. Thereafter, my parents lived solely on Social Security. But I never heard my father complain. I never heard him express envy of others.

In his final working years, my father sold Mercedes. He could never afford one himself, but he was allowed to use one of the demo cars. When I was 17, I got to drive a 300SL in a parade. Owning a Mercedes became a lifelong dream. That's all it was until 2004, when I opened a bank account solely to save for that car. It took me a decade, but eventually I paid cash for a Mercedes E350 in 2014. Three days later, my wife and I started off on a trip across the U.S. I was age 71.

I had seen my parents struggle financially for their entire lives, and I wanted to avoid that at all costs. I wrote in my 1961 high school yearbook that, "I will be a millionaire someday." Adjusting for 60 years of inflation, I didn't make it, but I did okay.

I was born in 1943, and I have a very different perspective from many younger Americans. I recall periodically crawling under my schoolroom desk, practicing for a nuclear attack. I remember when a woman's place was in the home and discrimination was the norm. I recall when the mandatory retirement age was younger for women than for men.

I'm aware of how lucky I've been. My current financial state was achieved with a lot of help from others and thanks to a life largely devoid of significant uncontrollable misfortune. For all that, I am grateful. Still, I do take a modicum of credit for perseverance and fiscal prudence—greatly assisted by my wife.

CLAMBERING UPWARD

When I graduated high school in 1961, two things were on my mind. First, find a job—any job—and, second, when would I be drafted. At age 18, I started my career as a mail boy, the lowest-paid person in a company of 15,000 workers, earning $1.49 an hour.

Four months later, I attempted to sign up to buy U.S. savings bonds through payroll contributions. "Don't bother," my manager said, "you won't be here that long." I had only just started working and I was about to be laid off.

Fortunately, the union stepped in and convinced the company to give me a job as a clerk in the employee benefits department, provided I went to night school to learn to type. There was a side benefit to that newly acquired skill: When I entered active duty in the Army in 1968, I quickly went from truck driver to personnel sergeant. That meant I got to work in an office.

My initial foray into investing involved penny stocks. It lasted several years—and it didn't go well. When I was on active duty, my wife and I were engaged, and I came home one weekend so we could buy her a ring. In anticipation of paying, I sold one of my stocks at a loss. But when it came time to pay for the ring, the jeweler told us we could wait until the fall, when I next came home on leave. That stock I'd sold at a loss? If I had waited to sell, the profit would have paid for the ring.

Meanwhile, it took me several years to get the message about college, in part because it was a subject never mentioned when I was growing up. My father and mother only graduated high school, my grandfather 8th grade, my great-grandfather was illiterate. While two of my high school friends were off to Princeton and Harvard, I was off to find a job.

Still, I knew that, if I wanted to get ahead, I needed a degree. But I was never a motivated student. Finally, 17 years after graduating high school and after nine years of school at nights and weekends, I obtained a degree. I barely saw my four children during those years. But there were no student loans involved. Veteran's benefits—the result of my time in the Army—paid for most of it.

Several years later, I was in a department staff meeting. One of the participants—she had a PhD—suggested we go around the room and tell where we'd received our degrees. I immediately felt embarrassed. I knew some of the schools that the others had attended: Stanford, Carnegie Mellon, Princeton, Vassar. When they got to me, I named a community college and a mediocre state university. But by then, time and experience had done their job: I was the highest-paid person in the room.

By 1982, I was a manager in the company's employee benefits department. That was the year we introduced a 401(k) plan—and the year I became serious about investing. I always contributed at least enough to obtain the company's matching contribution. My wife and I adjusted our spending to make sure that happened, even during the years when we were paying college costs for our four kids.

But my best investment was the pension I earned based on 50 years of service. That pension, coupled with my 401(k) savings and other investments, mean my wife and I today are financially secure. Indeed, my pension—along with Social Security—covers our basic retirement expenses and much more.

If you spend 50 years at one company, you become pretty loyal— maybe too much so. After my time in the Army was up and I was back at my employer, I signed up for the company stock purchase plan at $5 per week. I continued contributing my entire career. More than 50 years of regular investing and reinvesting dividends really adds up.

On top of that, in 2000, I started receiving stock options as part of my compensation. The size of the grants was quite modest by most standards, but I was pleased. Unlike most recipients, when the options vested, I converted most into company stock. Today, shares of my old employer are 34% of my taxable investment account and my accumulated shares generate significant dividends. But I won't pretend that sort of big investment in a single stock is prudent.

FULFILLING DREAMS

Yes, I've been fortunate. But my wife and I also never caused bad things to happen. We lived on one income, never carried credit card debt, and saved every month, no matter what expenses we faced.

Our first house was built in 1918. When we bought it—with a mortgage costing 9½%—we agonized over our ability to afford it. I tallied the total payment, including the mortgage and property taxes. Try as we might, it didn't look feasible, but we did it anyway.

We lived in that first house for five years. Our second house was a few blocks away. It had been built in 1929, with none of the amenities expected of homes today. It had three bedrooms, one the size of a large walk-in closet, two bathrooms—one a converted closet—and a tiny kitchen. We lived there 43 years.

Until I purchased a Mercedes in retirement, we only ever owned basic vehicles. No power anything, no air-conditioning. We kept them until—in three cases—the engines blew up. Once we had an older Chevy stolen. The police called to say they found it abandoned. I went and "stole" it back, cleaned up the food and other garbage in the backseat, had it repaired and kept it for five more years—until the engine blew.

For ten years starting 1988, we had one, two or three children in college at once. Frankly, I'm not sure how we paid for all that, but I do recall a 401(k) loan, a home equity loan and remortgaging our house. I also started what folks now call a 'side hustle.' I published a newsletter about employee benefits and put on conferences. In the process, I'd often put the entire family to work, including paying the children to stuff envelopes.

The financial stress of putting our kids through college would have been less, but we were determined to pay the entire cost of their education—plus I made a large, emotionally driven financial decision just before the oldest went off to college.

For many years, my father worked totally on commission, with no paid vacation. But in 1953, when I was ten years old, we went to Cape Cod for a week. It's the only family vacation I can recall. A friend gave my father a tip on a great place to stay. In his enthusiasm, my father booked for a week and paid in advance.

The motel turned out to be worse than an Army barracks. My mother refused to stay. To get his money back, we all agreed that I would have a sudden asthma attack, necessitating our immediate departure. That worked, my parents got their money back, and we then stayed in several places on the Cape, ending up in Chatham, Massachusetts. Even at age ten, I was hooked.

Fast forward 23 years. In 1976, in a moment of enthusiasm, I said to the family, "Let's go to Cape Cod." Amazingly, most of the places I remembered from 1953 were still there. From that summer on, we spent vacations on the Cape in a motel or a rented house. On every trip, I expressed my desire to buy a vacation home in Chatham, as unrealistic as that was. I even subscribed to a local newspaper. Every week, I longingly checked the homes that were listed for sale. After several years, my family didn't want to hear about my daydreaming anymore. But I kept looking.

In February 1987, I found a house that was old but appeared financially feasible. I was warned that if I didn't buy a place this time, the family was never going house-hunting again. By mistake, we went to the wrong real estate office and they showed us a new house that, at $159,000, was in our price range. It had three bedrooms and two bathrooms—just right.

After some wrangling with the bank, we put down 10% and got a 30-year mortgage at 9¾%. I was delighted, as was my family, partly because they wouldn't have to listen to me each time the Cape Cod newspaper got delivered. In the initial years, we could afford the house only by renting it for most of the summer.

Over the past 35 years, we've spent more than $300,000 on

additions, remodeling and maintenance on the Chatham house. On top of that, there's been property taxes, utilities and insurance. Today, the house is valued at more than twice what we paid, including the cost of improvements. But no matter—I never saw the house as an investment. It was fulfilling a dream and buying years of family memories. My only regret is that my father never got to see the house—or, for that matter, the Mercedes.

THREE LESSONS

* If you want to achieve great things financially, it starts with setting goals. If you don't know where you want to go with your financial life, you'll likely end up somewhere you don't like.

* Job-hopping may get you a pay raise and a loftier title. But finding a company you enjoy working for, and putting in many years, can be a surer road to financial freedom.

* We can't control what others do and we can't stop misfortune from striking. But we can control our own actions. Those who are financially prudent will most likely enjoy success, even if events don't always go their way.

PROJECT MICKEY

BY
PHIL KERNEN

Phil Kernen, CFA®, is a portfolio manager and partner with Mitchell Capital, a financial planning and investment management firm in Leawood, Kansas. When he's not working, Phil enjoys spending time with his family and friends, reading, hiking and riding his bike.

I DON'T MAKE NEW Year's resolutions. I exercise to feel good, not to lose a certain number of pounds or notch some personal athletic record. I save because my future self will appreciate the sacrifice I make today, not because I'm targeting some specific level of wealth. I've never had a defined life plan. My career has been opportunistic. Yet, despite all that, my wife and I settled on and pursued two goals early in our marriage that had a lasting impact on our family's finances—and on the stories we share with our kids as they, too, become adults.

In 2000, our daughter was born. In early 2002, we were expecting again. After a prenatal visit early in the pregnancy, my wife called me during a hectic day at work.

"We're having twins," she said.

I told her to be serious. She was. I took the afternoon off to come home and process the news with her. We knew how much it cost for one kid. We were two working parents, but it was a financial struggle. Now, the cost would be multiplied by three.

As 2003 ended, our oldest was three and our two youngest were one-year-olds, and the expenses felt huge. Daycare and preschool cost $24,000 a year. It represented a hefty line item in our family's budget. We also paid $24,000 every year on our mortgage, though that included regular extra-principal payments. Fortunately, we had no student debt and no credit card debt, and we owned our two cars. Despite the financial commitments of a growing family, we made it a priority to save for the future.

Every year-end, we talked about our personal and financial objectives for the following year—how much to save in your retirement plan, how much in mine, how much for this home improvement project, how much for that trip. As 2003 turned into 2004, our discussion took an unusual turn. We both felt the pull to try something different. After more discussion, my wife proposed a new idea: pay off the mortgage early.

HOME AND AWAY

We had bought our home when we moved to Overland Park, Kansas, in 1997. We were only six years into a 30-year mortgage. We'd paid $175,000 for the house, borrowing $167,100 for 30 years at 7.875%. Less than 12 months later, we refinanced to 7.25%. In 2002, we modified the loan, lowering our rate still further, so we now paid 5.625% on the remaining $143,168 balance. Our required monthly payments were $1,200, but we continued sending $2,000 each month, the same payment we'd made when our mortgage rate was higher.

We compared the 5.625% to what we thought the stock market might deliver. After the 2000–02 bear market, share prices had moved steadily upward. Perhaps stocks were indeed the better bet. But in the end, we had an emotional reason for continuing with the extra-large mortgage payments.

To us, financial freedom didn't mean retiring early. We were two 30-somethings with three kids age three and under. The idea of not working was impractical and silly. Instead, at the time, achieving some level of financial freedom meant owning our house and never having to worry about where we would put our heads. If I lost my job, losing our home wouldn't be a risk. If we wanted to pursue different careers, we could afford to earn less. It was easy and fun to think about what we could do with an additional $20,000-plus that wouldn't be going toward house payments anymore.

In addition, we felt confident this would be our home for the long haul. We loved our city. We had put down roots in a new place we called our own, and we both wanted our kids to grow up in one house. It was big enough to meet our needs for a long time. We had already moved multiple times and we had no desire to do it again. More important, we wanted to be in control of our money rather than letting it control us. Paying off the mortgage was a crucial step in that direction, plus it felt like something different from what everyone around us was doing. It was a long-term financial goal— daunting yet achievable—that we could both get behind. Maybe we could even turn it into something fun.

By 2004, when we began in earnest, $130,000 remained on the mortgage. We worked down the balance to $125,000 with several payments, and then the excitement waned. The numbers were still too big and the undefined end date seemed too far off. We needed something to help us refocus, something long term to keep us moving forward and excited.

We had always been a traveling family. Earlier, in 2001, we had driven with our one-year-old daughter to Arlington, Virginia, to spend time with family. When I reviewed the route, I noted it would be our daughter's first time passing through eight states. Wouldn't it be fun, I now mused, to visit all 50 states with our kids by the time they finished high school? It would be a good excuse to see new places, show our kids the country, open them up to new perspectives and create a love of travel. The likelihood that they wouldn't remember anything at such a young age was of no consequence. We were after shared experiences and stories we could tell later.

By 2004, the kids had visited 16 states, every one of them by car. Our budget didn't allow for flights for five people. Could we somehow weave together our mortgage and travel goals? My wife proposed that we fly to Disney World to celebrate once we paid off our home loan. Celebrating the achievement with a once-in-a-childhood trip to Disney seemed like an idea that we could all get behind. As a bonus, we would also experience Florida—another state to add to the kids' list. Suddenly, our two goals became one.

MATTERS OF PRINCIPAL

Later that week, my wife came home with a 1,000-piece puzzle of Mickey Mouse and explained her idea. We would assemble the puzzle, then take it apart, placing contiguous pieces in separate baggies. One thousand pieces, divided by 125 reductions in the loan balance of $1,000 each, meant eight pieces per bag. Every time we reduced the mortgage principal by $1,000, we would put eight more puzzle pieces together. We would glue the pieces to a poster board and then put the partially completed puzzle away, while we awaited the next time we could add pieces.

About the same time that we started this project, I changed jobs, moving to a corporate credit union. My pay didn't change much and our progress continued. We would go overboard from time to time, postponing some small, immaterial purchases to make larger payments on the mortgage. If expenses became too large, we instituted a checkbook lockdown until they moderated. My new job was located near a branch of the bank that held our loan. I would drive to the bank branch over my lunch hour to deposit the check and receive the receipt. By the end of 2004, the mortgage had declined to $97,000. We could see Mickey's ears and part of his face.

In 2005, my twins joined their big sister at her school, and I changed jobs again, joining an investment advisory firm. It meant a pay cut, but my wife and I agreed that was an okay price to pay because it was the type of role I had envisioned when pursuing my Chartered Financial Analyst designation several years earlier. Still, that didn't make it any easier to reach our goal of being mortgage-free, but that was a tradeoff we were willing to make. By the end of the following year, the mortgage had declined to $52,000. We could see Mickey's gloves and pants.

The years passed, the principal declined, the puzzle filled in and the goal grew nearer. Every month, we brought out the poster board, tallied up how much we had paid off and added more pieces to the puzzle. The kids didn't grasp the 'why,' but they liked puzzles and always clamored to add more pieces. As the end approached, they came to understand the celebration that was to come.

We continued traveling, and we did it inexpensively. We drove to see our extended families, and slept on guest beds and floors. We met friends in state parks for long weekends. We camped, something both our families had done growing up. Neither had a lot of money to spare when we were young, and camping offered a way to have a vacation and get away. We drove everywhere, all five of us in a little Subaru Forester, getting creative with three car seats and boosters in the tight space. We did have one indulgence. Every January, my mother-in-law would stay with our kids for a few days, while my wife and I flew somewhere warm.

Paying off the mortgage wasn't done at the expense of other savings priorities. We made sure to contribute to our workplace retirement plans. We funded 529 college savings accounts for each of the kids. We set aside money for home repairs, both expected and otherwise. We were willing to do without extra 'wants' that others often see as needs.

By the end of 2007, the loan balance was down to $27,000. We thought the final payoff might happen in 2008, so we began researching Disney World. We decided to build savings to the point where we could pay off the entire balance with one final check. In 2008, we booked the trip for October.

Our plan was to spend a week and visit the four Disney parks: Magic Kingdom, Hollywood Studios, Animal Kingdom and Epcot. Normally, we would have chosen to stay somewhere nearby to save money. But instead, we stayed on the Disney property and saved time by avoiding the commute to and from the parks.

We also decided to buy Disney's meal plan. Paying individually for each meal would have left us feeling figuratively spent and in a sour mood. By buying the plan, even if it was likely overpriced, we knew each meal was covered, leaving us in a much better frame of mind to remember the trip's purpose—a fun family celebration. If the kids wanted an expensive menu item for dinner, or ice cream in the middle of the day, no problem. The approach worked beautifully: happy kids, happy parents.

FREE AT LAST

In truth, the trip's timing was far from ideal. In September, the long-simmering housing crisis erupted, markets crashed and a global financial crisis was upon us. I had been with my employer for three years. Suddenly, everything looked uncertain. We were investment managers and markets were collapsing, with no end in sight. Was my job safe? At least no one was going to take our house. In November, we wrote a check to the bank for $9,400. The next day, my wife walked into the lobby to present our final payment, 11 years after we first took out a loan to purchase the house. We let the kids put in place the last pieces of Mickey's golden shoes.

Being mortgage-free didn't lead to any immediate changes. We couldn't openly celebrate. Amid the financial hardship caused by the Great Recession, it seemed insensitive. We didn't know who might be worried about their job or home. We did, however, call our insurance guy to share the news—because we'd now have to pay the premium on our homeowner's policy directly, rather than as part of our monthly mortgage payment. The financial freedom we sought came in subtle ways. We redirected the extra cash flow into a new and bigger car for our growing family, trading in an older car for a Honda Odyssey. We increased college savings for our kids, whose tight age difference meant we'd be paying college costs for three students simultaneously for at least two years.

We continued traveling. After covering all the states in the middle of the map by car, flying became necessary to visit the states we'd yet to experience. Having a few extra dollars set aside made those trips possible. In 2011, we visited Delaware, Pennsylvania and New Jersey. In 2013, Washington and Oregon. In 2014, California. In 2015, we toured New England. Waiting in line for a ride at a fun park in Killington, Vermont, we fell into conversation with the family in front of us. When we explained our 50-state goal, the parents expressed surprise and shared that they had only ever been to five nearby states, while we were in the process of clicking off six states over ten days. It was then that our kids began realizing the magnitude of their travels.

Three years ago, my wife left a job that had turned toxic. It was late spring, our oldest was graduating high school and our younger kids were entering their junior years. She took the summer off to spend as much time as she could with them. We also had the money saved to visit Hawaii, state No. 49. When our oldest entered college that fall, we were ready to shoulder university tuition.

The following year, my wife again took the summer off before finding a better position in the nonprofit world. That was when we traveled to Alaska, reaching our goal. A paid-off house made us comfortable with the short-term drop in income, even as we visited our 50th state.

Admittedly, paying off our mortgage early probably wasn't the best financial decision. My wife and I didn't—and don't—care. Today, the completed puzzle sits in a closet. Our kids will likely decide what to do with it after we're gone. It stands as a lesson for them—and for us—that you can set big goals and reach them little by little by little. What about the celebratory trip to Disney? Along with our travels to 49 other states, it continues to provide memories and stories, which we share around the dining-room table when the kids are home.

THREE LESSONS

* Paying off debt—especially your mortgage—buys you the financial freedom to pursue a less-lucrative career and makes it easier to weather financial storms.

* If the entire family is focused on a financial objective, and you bring a sense of fun to its pursuit, you're much more likely not only to reach your goal, but also to enjoy the journey.

* It can take years and sometimes decades to achieve our financial goals. Be sure to celebrate.

FILLING PIGGYBANKS

BY
KYLE MCINTOSH

Kyle McIntosh, CPA, MBA, is a full-time lecturer at the California Lutheran University School of Management. He turned his career focus to teaching after 23 years of working in accounting and finance roles for large corporations. Kyle lives in Southern California with his wife, two children and their overly friendly goldendoodle.

CHRISTMAS 1981. THE location was Huntington Beach, California, and I was visiting my grandparents' retirement community. It was sunny and 70 degrees, with a mild ocean breeze. Despite the temperate weather, I had poured my six-year-old self into an itchy sweater for the annual holiday party. We sang carols, ate store-bought cookies and drank Kool-Aid. The climax was Santa passing out gifts toward the end of the celebration.

It was no secret that grandparents would plant the gifts with Santa. The familiar wrapping paper and handwriting were easy to spot. I was hopeful that I'd see a *Star Wars* action figure or anything G.I. Joe. When I ripped open the wrapping paper and saw a piggybank, my heart sank. Having given a few dud gifts to my own kids in recent years, I can only imagine how clearly the disappointment showed on my face.

My gloomy look that day didn't stop my dad's parents from focusing on the savings theme. I'd go on to receive two more piggybanks from them during childhood. My maternal grandparents jumped on this gift idea, too. By the time I was 12, I had a fleet of piggybanks. While I didn't appreciate the gifts at the time, the message sank in: Saving was important.

Beyond the piggybanks, my grandparents helped make me an effective saver in other ways. My paternal grandfather opened an account for me at a local savings and loan. We would visit the teller window from time to time to get an updated imprint on my passbook. I loved listening to the clatter of the S&L printer as it updated my balance. The account was modest, but each imprint—especially given the interest rates of the 1980s—delivered a meaningful increase to me. I could see the compounding effect right on that passbook page, with my current interest earned on balances that included the interest I'd earlier received.

My maternal grandfather was a stock-picker. When we visited his house, he would often be in his home office researching stocks. I would sometimes pull up next to him to see what he was doing on his Apple 2e computer. I remember seeing the green-and-black screen filled with graphs and charts.

I distinctly recall him telling me about Bollinger Bands, which chart a stock's price and volatility. I had no idea what he was talking about, but it sounded important. I would have benefited from starting with a less technical topic, but these visits did get me interested in stock investing.

A final grandparent influencer was my stepmom's father, Tony. My parents divorced when I was young, and I had many holidays with my stepmom's family. During these gatherings, I spent most of the time battling my cousins on the latest Nintendo console. One holiday, our video game marathon was interrupted by Tony, who gave us a brief speech about building wealth. My expression must have looked similar to the time I received that first piggybank.

While I can't remember all he said, one sentence stuck with me. "If you want to be rich," he started, "you need to use dollar-cost-average investing." While I didn't appreciate the concept, I stored the phrase in my memory. Years later, when I started reading about investing in *The Wall Street Journal* in the mid-1990s, every time I saw the phrase "dollar-cost averaging," I linked it to getting rich. Eventually, this Nintendo intermission speech led to the 'set-it-and-forget-it' investing approach I'd follow starting in my early 20s.

EARLY HUSTLE

With my savings habit established, it was time to hit the play button on earning income. Like most young kids, I dabbled in lemonade stands, washing cars and doing other odd jobs to make a few dollars. During my middle school years, however, I got serious about making money.

From age 11 to 13, I was a paperboy for the *Daily Breeze* in Torrance, California. This required delivering 60 newspapers, seven days a week. Without a doubt, this experience was more consequential than any other job I had on my financial journey. For the first time, I made enough money to build a meaningful savings account. More important, it instilled a work ethic and a business acumen that I've carried throughout my career.

At 3:30 p.m. every weekday, I'd arrive at the neighborhood route station, along with a dozen other paperboys. Our route leader—the only adult in the room—would let us know the number of advertising inserts for that day, and we'd set off folding papers. After 30 minutes of folding and exchanging banter, we'd load our bikes. Weekday papers had to be delivered by 5:30 p.m. and there was no time to spare. Each route had at least one customer who would lodge a complaint if the paper was a minute late. In my case, Mr. Pirtle watched the clock and had the *Daily Breeze* on speed dial.

On weekends, the job was a harder slog. The papers and inserts were slammed down on our driveways around 5:30 a.m. and had to be delivered by 7:30 a.m. The highlight of the weekend delivery was my mom bringing me hot cocoa while I was folding papers on cold mornings. The bagel shop owner on my route tossed a warm cinnamon raisin bagel my way every Saturday and Sunday. Let it be noted: I didn't drop a bagel once in three years.

As paperboys, we were running our own business with full profit-and-loss responsibility. Each month, I got a bill from the *Daily Breeze*. The newspaper charged me for the papers I delivered, as well as for the canvas carrier bags on my bike and even for rubber bands. Looking back, it seems unbelievable that 12-year-olds were getting charged for rubber bands.

My monthly bill for papers and supplies was around $200, minus a credit for all the advertising inserts we folded into the papers. It would then be up to me to collect $5.50 per month from each of my customers. If I collected from 100% of my customers and received a few tips, I would make about $150.

At the beginning of the month, I'd return to my customers after delivering the paper to collect what was owed. I used my route book to keep track of my receivables. Most customers would pay promptly and include a modest tip. In the case of Mr. Pirtle, the tip was very modest.

Sometimes, I had to follow up with customers multiple times to collect. These follow-up visits were make or break for my monthly profitability. I needed to collect from two-thirds of my customers to break even. Whatever I collected from the last third was my profit. While the collection process might have been awkward for some, I was never rattled by asking adults for the money they owed me. I rarely carried a receivable for more than a week.

In addition to being a paperboy, I found a few side hustles in middle school. They included cleaning the bagel shop's boiler and working at Honeybaked Ham—a seller of precooked glazed ham—over spring break. My favorite side hustle was the one that nearly got me sent to the principal's office.

For about six weeks in seventh grade, I was really ticking up the savings account by selling Coke—the beverage—from my school locker. I started small, selling six-packs and then 12-packs, but quickly built my empire to selling 24 cans each day. A case of Coke cost me about $6 in those days, so my cost per unit was 25 cents. Throughout the day, I'd meet people at my locker and sell them cans for 50 cents.

I sold out every day. While I hadn't yet seen the movie *Wall Street*, I somehow channeled Gordon Gekko in my selling practices. Greed was good and I raised my price to $1 on hot days. There were no giveaways and I never drank one can myself.

Unfortunately, Ziggy, our physical education teacher, didn't appreciate my business. He caught me selling twice, and threatened to turn me in to Mr. Colby, the principal, upon a third bust. I still unloaded my inventory after that second infraction, but I knew I needed to stop. After earning more than $100 in profit, this side hustle came to an end.

Eventually, the savings from these different jobs grew to be a few thousand dollars. When I went to college, I deposited the money to open a checking account on campus. I spent carefully—sometimes taking out just $5 at a time—knowing how hard I worked to earn that money.

CORPORATE YEARS

Fast forward to 1997. After graduating from college, I continued to hustle as I started my corporate career. I landed my first job with Arthur Andersen as an auditor. I raised my hand for extra projects and I pushed to work on the San Francisco office's top clients. By the time I left in 2002, I had received an early promotion to manager and my salary had doubled.

My starting salary was $34,100, which was modest considering I was living in San Francisco. Even so, I maxed out my 401(k) in 1998, my first full year of work. This kicked off a streak of maxing out my 401(k) contributions for more than 20 years. In keeping with Tony's dollar-cost-averaging advice, I plowed the money into stock index funds without regard to the market's ups and downs.

During these first years of working, I also set up a brokerage account with Charles Schwab. I started by investing $1,000 in Schwab 1000 Index Fund. Whenever I had an extra $100, I was sure to transfer it to my Schwab account and put it to work. I made a few horrific investments early on, including $500 on Webvan, a dotcom grocery delivery stock that flamed out in 2001. From lessons like that, I learned to stick mainly to index funds. I also opened a Roth IRA with Schwab during these early years.

After Arthur Andersen's accounting business folded in 2002, during the Enron crisis, I became the corporate controller for Digital Insight, a small publicly traded company that was later acquired by Intuit. The CFO had seen my hustle—I was an auditor for her prior company—and she took a chance on having me, at age 27, lead her accounting team. My learning curve was steep, but I worked long hours to make up for my inexperience.

My compensation increased substantially, and I was eligible for a bonus and stock compensation. My wife and I were then DINKs— double income, no kids—so we increased our savings and paid off our student loans. I set up a regular transfer of funds from our checking account to Schwab, with that money automatically invested in an S&P 500 index fund every two weeks. I don't have many financial milestones etched in my mind, but I do know that our brokerage account reached $100,000 during these years. That was a big deal to us.

The pace at Digital Insight was fast from day one. I arrived at my office every weekday at 6 a.m. with a venti Starbucks coffee, and I rarely left before 6 p.m. Most weekends, I spent several hours—if not full days—catching up or getting ready for the week ahead. While I was well-compensated, it wasn't a healthy work environment for me. After pushing hard for three years, I realized that making money didn't matter if you were miserable. I decided to shift to a lower-paying and less demanding role that allowed me to decaffeinate and enjoy life more.

Near the end of my tenure at Digital Insight, I received one of the best phone calls of my life. Adam Kaufman, a recruiter who I'd gotten to know over the years, got right to the point: "Patagonia is looking for someone like you. Are you interested?" Over the next four years, I worked as corporate controller for the privately held apparel firm.

While I took a pay cut, I loved going to work, and I had my nights and weekends back. I exercised more and was able to travel without work looming over me. In addition, the regular work schedule allowed me to complete a part-time MBA program at the University of California at Los Angeles's Anderson School of Management.

Even with less pay at Patagonia, plus the cost of an MBA, our DINK status let us continue to sock money away. Around this time, we purchased the house that we still live in today. We initially considered homes that were smaller and less expensive, but we knew they wouldn't work once our family expanded.

We're glad that we stretched for the bigger home. We saved the considerable commission costs that come with moving up the home ladder. And we gained deep relationships with many of our neighbors who have known our children—now ages 11 and 14—for their whole lives. Such ties are invaluable.

When we bought our home in November 2004, we started with

a 15-year fixed-rate mortgage. The payments were a stretch, but with annual pay increases, the monthly note became manageable. We refinanced a few times as interest rates fell, always sticking with a 15-year fixed-rate loan.

With each refinancing, we continued to make the same lofty monthly payment required on our original 2004 mortgage. Our aggressive extra-principal payments left us mortgage-free after just a dozen years. In theory, we'd have been better off paying down the loan at a slower pace and investing the difference in stock index funds. Having a paid-off home, however, has been mentally freeing, and provided us more flexibility as we navigated our careers.

After four years at Patagonia, and having completed my MBA, I was ready for a new challenge. I spent the next 11½ years working for Amgen, a biotechnology firm that's a member of the Dow Jones Industrial Average. I started in corporate accounting. After two years, I put my hand up for an international assignment and we soon found ourselves living in Switzerland. After 16 months leading an international project from Amgen's Swiss office, we moved to the U.K., where I was the finance director for Amgen's U.K. and Ireland commercial operations.

Two years later, I was offered a temporary role. The U.K. general manager asked if I'd be interested in leading a commercial business unit for the final seven months of my overseas assignment. This was an unconventional role, given my accounting background, but the general manager said he trusted my business instincts and acumen. Little did he know that I'd honed those skills delivering papers and hocking carbonated beverages as a kid.

For the next seven months, I stretched myself to lead a team of 35 professionals selling bone health and nephrology drugs. Dealing with Mr. Pirtle set me up well for negotiating pharmaceutical contracts with the U.K.'s National Health Service.

Five years earlier, when I was at Digital Insight, a colleague who saw me working extraordinarily long hours urged me to view my career as a marathon, not a sprint. I didn't follow his advice then, and—as he no doubt expected—I burned out. But during my time at Amgen, I finally heeded his words.

My slow-and-steady approach paid off when I was promoted in 2017 to lead the finance team for Amgen's operations function. I oversaw 50 employees, based in six global locations, and a budget of more than $3 billion. Because of the global nature of the role, my days started early with calls to Europe or Puerto Rico, and they often ended with evening calls with Singapore. I traveled to each global location at least once a year. The travel and hours were grueling, but I was always home on weekends to referee soccer games or watch swim meets.

Amgen offered not just professional challenges, but also the financial benefits that come with staying put with a single employer. My compensation rose, I built a substantial retirement account and I received restricted stock grants each year. All this allowed me to shift to a second career at age 45.

SWITCHING GEARS

After 23 years in corporate roles, I flipped the cassette in 2020 and pivoted to a second career as a teacher. I'm now in my second year as a full-time lecturer at California Lutheran University in Thousand Oaks, California. While I mostly enjoyed my corporate roles, I had long had a passion for teaching and wanted to make it my full-time work.

While some coworkers and friends assumed this change was an impulsive decision driven by an epiphany during the pandemic, it actually was years in the making. From a financial standpoint, it took decades of hustle and savings to prepare for the change. More important than money, however, was my wife's support. In 2016, we decided it was time for me to start taking steps toward teaching.

I carefully test-drove my new career. In 2017, I taught two evening classes at Moorpark College, located not far from our home in Southern California. Next, I taught evening classes at California Lutheran University, in the summer of 2018 and 2019, while continuing to work for Amgen.

The rewards I felt from coaching and mentoring students fed my long-held desire to teach. The parts of the job I'd imagined as possible downsides—the time spent grading and prepping for classes—weren't bad at all.

There's no perfect time to make a major career shift, especially one that involves a pay cut. Once I knew I was headed toward teaching, I contributed as much as possible to Amgen's nonqualified deferred compensation plan. That money, which I withdrew in 2021, helped smooth the pay difference between my corporate and teaching careers.

Still, I could have come up with countless reasons to remain in a well-compensated corporate job. Ultimately, however, I knew we had a good plan—plus a reasonable amount of money saved. I had to go with my gut.

I love my new job and the lifestyle it brings. While we save less now, we'll be fine thanks to the savings—and the hustle—of the past several decades. I'm not sure that dollar-cost averaging made us rich, as I'm not precisely sure how to define that term. But that slow-and-steady investing approach, along with the many early lessons in saving, set me up for a second career that I can see doing for the rest of my life.

THREE LESSONS

* Remember the wisdom of step-grandfather Tony: "If you want to be rich, you need to use dollar-cost-average investing."

* If there's one financial virtue that trumps all others, it's saving diligently. Strive to sock away money starting early in life, and then raise your savings rate as your income grows.

* "A career is a marathon and not a sprint." While promises of higher pay often prompt folks to change jobs, you will likely garner more value—both professionally and financially—by staying with an employer for longer.

MONEY VIGILANT

BY
GREG SPEARS

Greg Spears is *HumbleDollar*'s deputy editor. He also teaches behavioral economics at St. Joseph's University in Philadelphia as an adjunct professor. Earlier in his career, Greg worked as a reporter for the Knight-Ridder Washington Bureau and *Kiplinger's Personal Finance* magazine. After leaving journalism, he spent 23 years as a senior editor at Vanguard Group on the 401(k) side. Greg is a Certified Financial Planner certificate holder.

I BELIEVE THAT OUR earliest financial experiences set lifelong patterns. It's certainly been true for me, though I didn't recognize it until recently.

My father was an Episcopal priest. When I was born in 1956, our family lived in a big stone parish house located in a large graveyard in Harlem. It was the overflow burial ground for Wall Street's historic Trinity Church, whose churchyard was all filled up. Dad never voiced concerns about money and, as it turns out, enjoyed financial security his entire life. My mother took the opposite view. She was always worried the bottom might drop out, and for good reason.

She was born into a prosperous family that employed a chauffeur and a maid, as well as a nanny who was responsible for raising my mother. Her father, a lawyer, was a Gatsby-type figure who'd installed a putting green on the lawn and had his suits tailored in London. First, he lost a bundle in the 1926 Florida land bust. Later, he lost his job as the New York representative of Lloyd's of London. He was among those tragic men who committed suicide during the Great Depression. My mother was age 11.

After college, she joined the American Red Cross in 1943. At the English airbases where she was stationed, many U.S. flight crews—people she knew—never returned from the big bombing raids. After D-Day, she followed behind Patton's 3rd U.S. Army, which broke out of Normandy, fought across France and Belgium, and drove into Nazi Germany. In her 90s, she told a caretaker that she was taught how to drive a tank "just in case" the unit got surrounded and the women needed to break out. This possibility was codenamed Alamo.

My mother learned early that life—and even Western civilization—is shockingly fragile, and can be destroyed in an instant. One protective measure she took against this existential threat was to build a bulwark of savings, a lesson that she passed on to me. When I was two months old, she opened a passbook account in my name at the Harlem Bank for Savings. She took me there to make deposits, some as small as $5, to impress on me the importance of saving. The account grew to be worth $366.54 by 1968, according to my old bank book.

When I was around five, we moved from Harlem to Princeton, New Jersey, where Dad was rector of (another) Trinity Church. I was a scholarship student in local private schools, my tuition paid by a wealthy parishioner. My school friends had beach homes and every new G.I. Joe toy. My mother took me to a consignment store to buy clothes. It must be true, I realized—we're as poor as church mice.

Actually, that wasn't true at all. We were a solidly middle-class family surrounded by immense wealth. My friend Chip came from the family that had founded Bristol Myers. Another friend's father, J.

Richardson Dilworth, managed the Rockefeller family investments. My hazy impression of our poverty, combined with our friends' wealth, turned me 'money vigilant' for life.

Money vigilant describes people who are alert, watchful and concerned about their finances. We tend to work hard and save a lot because we feel our destiny—good or bad—is entirely in our hands. It's as if I took my father's religious faith but transferred it to finance. I always wanted to do the right thing, starting with saving. I wasn't going to count on good luck or a windfall.

I earned $6.25 a month singing soprano in the church choir. Comic books cost 12 cents, popguns a quarter. How could I spend it all? I saved coins and bills in a Band-Aid tin. Occasionally, I'd spill it all onto my bedspread to count it. It felt protective.

The pleasure I received from saving turned out to be permanent. I have always saved, even when I didn't earn much. For instance, I earned $130 a week in New York City one summer during college. To keep costs down, I squatted in the Bowery loft I was being paid to renovate. Later on, I rented a room in a single-room-occupancy hotel for $40 a week, where I cooked most of my meals on a hot plate.

Despite the film noir vibe, I didn't feel deprived. My life was rich with experiences. I had a bicycle and would pedal around lower Manhattan, then mostly deserted on weekends. There was no cover charge at CBGBs, the club where punk bands played. I haunted the many used bookstores then on lower Broadway. And I managed to save enough for a week's vacation in Jamaica before returning to college.

I'm not miserly but I am frugal. What's the difference? I get pleasure from spending on things I value, which includes travel, antique furniture, Mark Twain first editions and large old houses. To afford them, I can do without new cars, wine pairings and flight upgrades. I also avoid casual spending, like Starbucks coffees or cafeteria lunches.

When I do spend, I want to feel that I'm getting a good deal. My wife, two kids and I began taking European vacations in 2002 because so few people wanted to fly after 9/11. We took the children to Rome, Istanbul, Amsterdam and Paris on successive annual vacations. We'd pack our coats and go in the fall, which cost much less than high season.

I always mowed my own lawn and raked the leaves. I'd tell myself the money I was saving would pay for our next trip to Europe. During summer vacations, I'd scrape down and repaint a side of my parents' house in Maine, a house my wife and I continue to enjoy to this day. Our family always did the maintenance—that was how my parents were able to afford the place. I have a bias toward repairing old things rather than buying new ones. I've repaired Adirondack chairs for decades until they finally collapsed from rot. A sampler I saw once expressed my philosophy: "Make It, Make Do, or Do Without."

READ ALL OVER

Growing up, my parents made it clear that I was on my own once I graduated college. After a year working for a weekly newspaper in Upstate New York, I enrolled in Northwestern University's journalism school in 1980. I rented a room in a shared apartment for $100 a month and lived on pizza slices. I told my girlfriend I had turned down the last installment of my student loan because I didn't need the money. She told her business writing professor of my decision, and he said he had a better idea.

Following his advice, I went back to the bursar's office to sign for the loan. Then I rode the L downtown to Chicago's financial district and opened a money market fund with Kemper Securities. The money fund yielded something like 18%, and I'd borrowed at 5%. I was playing the float, although I wouldn't have known what that meant. It was my first investment outside an FDIC-insured account.

My introduction to stock investing was another happy accident.

I'd landed a job at *The St. Petersburg Times* in Florida. My editor assigned me to write about the restoration of a Spanish-revival building from the 1920s. Looking around the building, I asked my guide what all the mainframe computers were doing. He explained that this was the back office of the Templeton Funds, and it was his job to run it.

He picked up a laminated poster he called "the Alps chart," which showed the growth of $10,000 in Templeton Growth Fund since its inception. I could see that it had turned into a mountain of money. After my story ran, I returned to invest $2,000 in a Templeton IRA. I took home $243 a week then, so the investment represented about two months' pay.

The night editor would sometimes call me out of bed to cover house fires and fatal car wrecks. My day assignment was aviation, including plane crashes. I'd also written about bank robberies, murders and one fatal shark attack. After four years of tragedies, I was ready for something calmer. In 1985, I made the jump to the Washington, D.C., bureau of the Knight-Ridder newspaper chain. There, I covered Social Security, Medicare and Florida's colorful congressional delegation.

I also received a jump in pay to $576 a week and gained entry to Knight-Ridder's pension plan, 401(k) and employee stock purchase plan. The 401(k) was administered by Vanguard Group, which gave me entry to the often-closed Windsor Fund. Its manager, John Neff, was among the 20th century's great value investors. I bought Windsor shares through the 401(k) for the next decade.

A source on Capitol Hill recommended her stockbroker. I opened a small account and he bought stocks for me. Soon after, on October 19, 1987, the Dow Jones Industrial Average fell 22.6%, its largest one-day decline. I remember the Washington bureau coming to a standstill as we watched the wires. The only story that mattered was up in New York, and we hadn't a clue as to what was happening. Still, I felt certain that I knew what to do.

A few days later, I walked into my broker's office and sold all my stocks at a loss. I used the money to invest in a Van Eck gold fund. At the counter, there was a man beside me buying stocks. I remember thinking he was making a mistake. Of course, I was the fool. The stock market recovered nearly all its losses by year-end.

Luckily, I continued to stumble onto well-managed mutual funds, usually on the advice of someone else. I started saving for our son Michael's college in June 1989, the month he was born. At first, I put the money in the bank. Then I followed a friend's recommendation and met with a financial planner in Maryland to talk about how to invest the money.

Larry had a beautiful office on an upper floor of a glass office tower. He was friendly and persuasive, and recommended that we invest in First Eagle Global Fund. It was managed by Jean-Marie Eveillard, a canny Frenchman who had a broad mandate to buy stocks and bonds that he thought undervalued. He even stashed around 10% of the fund's assets in gold, a reserve against unforeseen catastrophe. Like my mother, he had seen the Second World War.

I was happy with the fund's excellent returns, but I didn't know how my advisor was paid. Larry never sent us a bill. Only later did I understand that we'd purchased shares with an 8.5% load. There was also a trailing 12b-1 fee of 0.25% a year. Fortunately, Eveillard's returns beat the market, despite his fund's high expenses. We held onto the fund until the year before Michael entered college.

At work, I bought shares of Knight-Ridder stock at a 15% discount. It was a breakeven investment. The most valuable benefit was getting my employer's annual report in the mail. I found it fascinating—and alarming. The charts showed a decline in newspaper circulation and advertising revenue. I got a sinking feeling as I realized my employer might not exist by the time I reached age 50. I needed to find a new job before the music stopped.

Worrying about my employer's health was another sign of my

money vigilance. I was surrounded by smart reporters, yet no one seemed to share my concerns. What iceberg? I felt that companies rose and fell in health, just as people do. Eventually, a competing newspaper company bought Knight-Ridder, which was like catching a falling anvil. It dragged the acquiring company into Chapter 11 bankruptcy. Thousands of reporters lost their jobs, and the pension plan—underfunded by $1 billion—was taken over by the federal government.

I sidestepped the whole catastrophe by leaving in late 1994. A good friend recommended that I join him a few blocks away in downtown Washington at *Kiplinger's Personal Finance* magazine. I wrote a tryout piece and was hired as an associate editor covering mutual funds. One day, I interviewed the CEO of Kemper Securities, who had dropped by our offices. I escorted him out and saw him climb into the back of a limousine that had been idling at the curb. I went back in and called Kemper to sell my money market fund shares. The CEO had seemed uninspiring, and I thought he was taking shareholders for a ride.

The hardest part of my job was finding investments worth recommending to readers. I had no financial training and had serious doubts about my abilities as a forecaster. Also, I noticed a disconcerting tendency: The fund managers who explained their investment approach most persuasively seemed to fall flat on their faces in the race for performance. I steered my stories toward safe bets, like the best electric utility stocks or U.S. savings bonds. One day, I had an epiphany while reading *Bogle on Mutual Funds*, which made the case for index funds. I drove up to interview Vanguard Group founder Jack Bogle at the company's headquarters in Malvern, Pennsylvania.

Bogle was a commanding presence. He had a deep voice and spoke with the confidence of an Old Testament prophet—but backed up by reams of data. He called his proofs "the relentless rules of humble arithmetic." I came away convinced that index funds could solve the big problem of investment selection. Bogle was also a passionate practitioner of thrift, which certainly got my endorsement. The article I wrote said investing in a low-cost S&P 500 index fund was like having a ten-yard head start in the 100-yard dash.

IN THE VANGUARD

Soon after, the telephone rang in my office and a recruiter asked me to interview for a job with Vanguard. The company needed an editor to support its 401(k) communications. Indexing was still something of a cultish investment then, yet I was convinced it was going to help a lot of people—and conquer the financial world. Print journalism, meanwhile, continued to circle the drain. I accepted Vanguard's offer of a big raise and reported for work in December 1996.

For the first three months, I rented an apartment while my wife and kids completed the school year in Maryland. I spent lonely nights idly paging through a huge book of listings looking for a new house in a good school district. I saw a picture of an old farmhouse near Valley Forge Park, but my real estate agent wouldn't take me because it was out of our price range.

My wife, kids and I drove over anyway, and the property looked enchanting. A light snowfall had dusted the overarching sycamores, and a brook ran through the large front yard. It felt as if we'd left the modern world. I saw there was a second house on the property, a small cottage attached to an old stone barn. I told my wife I thought that house could be rented and help us carry the mortgage. I hired a new real estate agent and made a low-ball offer to the owners. They countered and we eventually settled at $471,000. The rental income paid half the mortgage, so our monthly payment was about the same as that for our old house in Maryland.

I threw myself into my job at Vanguard. Within a year, we'd published an in-depth investor education series on subjects like investing, retirement, insurance, taxes and estate planning. My sources were primarily Certified Financial Planners. Eventually, I realized that I could vet the content myself if I earned the CFP designation. Vanguard agreed to pay $5,000 for my education. I studied before work, on weekends, even in the stands of Little League games. Being money vigilant, I wanted to know everything I could about finance. Still, it took years of self-study. I passed the comprehensive exam in 2005.

Vanguard pays less than most investment firms, but far more than I'd earned as a newspaper reporter. That allowed me to contribute the maximum to the 401(k), plus save $10,000 a year in 529 college funds. When college came around, we threw everything we had into making eight consecutive years of tuition payments for our son and daughter. By the end, college costs had ballooned to $65,000 a year, and we had emptied our 529s accounts and were paying $1,000 a month from income. My wife sold some jewelry to help pay the college bills.

After both kids graduated, we had more income to save. My wife opened a solo 401(k) funded from her work as a psychotherapist. I maxed out my retirement plan contributions and Vanguard kicked in another 14% of my pay through various retirement schemes. We were saving more than $50,000 a year. By 64, I had more than enough to retire. My job—managing ten writers—had become more administrative during the pandemic. Distance and technical hurdles made it harder to write and edit.

My goal in life was never to become wealthy or lead a life of luxury. I'd rather paddle a kayak than buy a speedboat. What I wanted first was to take care of my family. Then I wanted to reach a stage where my wife and I didn't have to worry about money. After all these years of vigilance, perhaps I could relax and forget all about it. Am I there yet? Sometimes, but old habits die hard.

Recently, my wife was hospitalized overnight. At her bedside, we fell into conversation about the various checking accounts we use to pay the bills, including the property taxes. What I wanted, I told her, was to have a large enough balance in each account that I could write a big check without worrying. Afterward, I realized I'd been bargaining with fate. If we had enough savings, maybe nothing bad could happen to my wife.

Perhaps my father had it right: God will provide. He made more from his church pension than he'd ever earned working. Besides, I think he knew from presiding over so many funerals back in Harlem that every day above ground is a treasure—no matter what the size of your bank balance.

THREE LESSONS

* Keep abreast of your employer's financial health because it affects your job security. Take advantage of employer-paid education and training to keep your skills marketable. Set high standards for your work.

* Unless you have an independent source of wealth, save at least 10% of your pay for retirement, and 15% would be better.

* A large pool of savings has cascading benefits. If you pay cash for a used car, you'll avoid years of financing charges. If you make a large down payment on a house, your monthly mortgage check will be smaller. These lower household expenses will enable you to save yet more.

WINDING PATHS

Sometimes, we choose to stray from the straight-and-narrow path—and sometimes we're forced from it. This disruption usually isn't good for our finances in the short term, and it may not be good for our happiness, either. Still, such change can help us better understand ourselves and what we truly care about, motivate us to fix our finances, and start us on a journey to a happier, more fulfilling life.

MAKING A COMEBACK by James Kerr

A ROCKY ROAD by Don Southworth

FINDING MY BALANCE by William Ehart

COURSE CORRECTION by Jim Wasserman

INVESTING IN MYSELF by Catherine Horiuchi

GETTING BY by Matt Trogdon

FOLLOWING MY MUSE by Rand Spero

MAKING A COMEBACK

BY
JAMES KERR

James Kerr led global communications, public relations and social media for a number of Fortune 500 technology firms before leaving the corporate world to pursue his passion for writing and storytelling. His book, *The Long Walk Home: How I Lost My Job as a Corporate Remora Fish and Rediscovered My Life's Purpose*, was published in early 2022 by Blydyn Square Books. Jim blogs at PeaceableMan.com.

IT WAS JANUARY 2009 and my world—like the world around me—was coming apart at the seams.

A year and a half after our divorce, my now ex-wife and I were finally getting around to divvying up our investment assets, and it couldn't have come at a worse time. The world's financial system was melting down, and the stock market along with it. Every day, the market was down another percent or two, and that was on a good day. There seemed no limit to how low it could go.

Compounding my distress, we'd agreed on the terms of our financial settlement back in the fall when the stock market was higher. Four months later, our accounts were worth 30% less and, because my ex-wife's split was based on absolute dollar amounts rather than percentages, the entirety of the market losses would be tallied on my side of the ledger.

For more than 20 years, I'd been following the playbook for financial security and independence: socking away money in my 401(k), taking advantage of the company match, contributing to my kids' 529 college savings plans, living below my means, and investing whatever extra money I had at the end of the month in broad-based index funds within a taxable account. I was doing everything I was supposed to be doing, and now—after all that diligent saving and investing—I was going to be left with barely a six-figure portfolio.

To make matters worse, the multi-billion-dollar tech company where I was working as director of public and investor relations was struggling financially. Its stock price had dipped precariously below $1 and there was talk the company might have to declare bankruptcy. I was worried about my position at a time when the job market was in the tank, and I was on the hook to pay thousands of dollars every month in alimony and child support.

I was 49 years old and nowhere close to where I needed to be financially at that point in my life. I was effectively starting over—and I was terrified.

BECKONING BETTER TIMES

Like most human beings, I'm a security-seeking creature. I don't like taking risks and I crave the feeling of having solid ground underneath me, which is one of the reasons I spent nearly my entire career working for large companies before leaving the corporate world in 2021. You'll never find me jumping out of an airplane or bungee-jumping off a bridge toward a rushing river below. It's just not me. I like certainty. I like knowing I have resources at hand should I need them. I have backup plans for my backup plans. It helps me sleep at night.

To be facing so much uncertainty—in my personal life, in my career, in my finances—was deeply unsettling. I remember one particularly cold, dark night that January when I was lying in bed unable to sleep, thinking about my financial situation, and thinking as well about how strange it felt to be single again after 14 years of marriage. Worries circled around my head like a cloud of buzzing flies. Would I be able to meet my financial responsibilities? Would I be able to recover from this and get back on track? Would I ever be able to retire?

One of my job duties at the time was to interact with Wall Street analysts and help them build their financial models for my employer. Given the concerns about the company's finances, I was spending a lot of time on the phone talking the analysts and investors through arcane balance sheet items, like accounts receivable and working capital.

For that reason, I suppose, I had balance sheets on the brain one sleepless January night. As I lay there staring at the ceiling, I found myself doing a frank assessment of my own liabilities and assets at this crossroads in my life.

On the liabilities side, I had a sizable mortgage on a house I'd bought the year before. But aside from the mortgage, along with child support and alimony obligations, I had no other substantial debt. I owned my car, and I always paid off any balance on my credit cards at the end of the month. Those were all positives.

On the assets side of the balance sheet, I had the equity in my house. Unfortunately, it wasn't much since I'd bought the place near the peak of the market, before the real estate bubble burst. I owned, along with my brother, a piece of property in northeastern Pennsylvania where I hoped to build a cabin one day.

I had whatever scraps would remain of my 401(k) and our taxable account after the financial settlement. I would be entitled, at retirement, to half of my pension, although the company had curtailed the defined benefit plan a number of years ago and my benefit wouldn't amount to much.

Overall, a rather skimpy accounting. No financial analyst would issue a 'buy' rating on my stock.

But I had other non-financial assets that could not be discounted. I was alive and in good health. I had a fantastic, loving family that supported me. I had a good relationship with my three sons. I had marketable skills should I need to get another job. For all of these things, I was deeply blessed.

I also had a deep well of resilience. I'd been through a lot of tough stuff in my life—periods of depression and anxiety, a long list of accidents and mishaps—and I'd somehow survived. Along the way, I'd done a lot of work on myself and had reached a point where I knew deep down that I could get through anything.

I'd always been a seeker and a big reader and, through my reading, I'd discovered meditation, mindfulness and other Eastern spiritual practices, all of which had helped me immensely.

Lately, I'd been reading about the so-called law of attraction. The basic idea is that human beings attract into our lives whatever we're focused on, both good and bad, and that we manifest states and experiences that match the energy of the thoughts we are putting out. If we're putting out positive, optimistic energies about a happy and prosperous future, that's what we will get. Conversely, if we are filling our minds with dark imaginings of a hopeless future and fears of what we don't want, we'll get that, too.

According to the principle of attraction, if we want to manifest something in our lives, we need only state our desires clearly and unambiguously to the 'universe' and it will be delivered to us on a platter. The more specific we are in our requests, the better the chances that we will get what we want.

Now, in addition to being a security-seeking creature, I am also a highly rational one—too rational at times, my girlfriend will sometimes tell me. For me to believe something, I need facts. I need to see some objective evidence that this thing I'm being asked to believe actually exists.

I was skeptical about this so-called law. Gravity was a law. Entropy was a law. The law of attraction? It sounded like new-age psychological claptrap.

Still, much of what I was reading made logical sense to me. I knew, from my time both on and off the therapist's couch, that our unconscious thoughts and belief patterns shape our realities in very real ways. I'd learned how to defuse anxiety and panic attacks by paying closer attention to the things I was saying to myself. I'd become undeniably a more peaceful, grounded and productive person through my daily practice of meditation and mindfulness.

All of this was clear evidence to me of the power of rightful thinking and intention in creating our outward circumstances. I thought, why not try this law of attraction? What could it hurt?

So that sleepless winter night, as I stared up at the dim-lit ceiling, I stated my intention in precise detail. In ten years, when I was 59, I would be happy, healthy and peaceful. I would have a wonderful, supportive partner in my life. She would have dark hair and be a yoga teacher. She would get along well with my kids. Financially, I would be secure and independent. My portfolio would be worth ten times what it was at the moment—enough for me to be able to step away early from the corporate world and pursue my passion for writing and storytelling.

A tenfold increase in ten years. Sure, why not? If I was wishing on a star, why not go big?

Item by item, I laid out my wish list, envisioning a new, more fulsome balance sheet for my life. It didn't seem possible at the time, as dark as the world was back then, that these things would come true. But from what I read about the law of attraction, whether my desires seemed possible or not didn't matter. All I had to do was set the intention and then give power over to the universe to deliver it to me.

MAKING IT HAPPEN

Having stated my intention, I went to work. The law of attraction is clear about that as well. It's not enough just to put your intention out there and roll back onto your pillow. You need to actively take steps toward it.

I didn't have a problem with that. I liked working hard. I liked setting goals and seeing myself making progress toward them. I had a decade to bring this plan to fruition. It was possible. I just needed to be persistent and have faith.

That was, as I said, January 2009. Two months later, the stock market finally bottomed and began a slow, tenuous climb out of the abyss.

I knew from my MBA and investor-relations training that, despite the terrible market sentiment at the time, things would turn around in the long run and this was a good time to be putting money to work in the market. I also knew of the power of dollar-cost averaging and was a firm believer in John Bogle's philosophy of investing in low-cost, broad-based index funds. In addition to my 401(k) contributions, I opened up a taxable account and started investing a set amount every month in low-cost Vanguard Group index funds.

At first, I favored bond funds, since they were doing well and seemed safer at the time. But within a few months, I went on the offensive and began investing all of my money in stock funds, weighted toward aggressive growth companies in the U.S.

My company was also on the upswing. A new CEO had come

onboard, promising shareholders a turnaround. I appreciated his no-nonsense, MBWA (management by walking around) leadership style, and he and I developed a strong working relationship. I was put in charge of global communications and given the job of telling our story to the media and the public in general.

It wasn't long before our financial results, and our stock price, started turning around. We were hitting our numbers and granting bonuses. In addition, as a member of the executive team, I was entitled to annual stock option grants. As the share price rose, those options were suddenly worth something. Whenever I got a bonus or cashed in any stock, I put the money in the market.

Looking back now, I was probably being too aggressive in allocating so much of my investments to the U.S. stock market. But I just felt the market was so low that the risk was also low. What's more, I had faith in American business innovation and felt that, over time, my faith would pay off.

With my investment strategy set, I sat back and watched the seeds grow. We all know what happened in the market since that dark winter of 2008–09. From its low of 676 on March 9, 2009, the S&P 500 quadrupled over the next ten years. It hasn't been a straight line up, of course, but through the ups and downs of the market, I have stayed disciplined and kept my investments on autopilot.

Along the way, life has tossed me plenty of surprises, as it is wont to do. In 2013, I found out I had stage three colon cancer and had to go through six months of chemotherapy. Fortunately, I caught it early and am now cancer-free.

In 2016, at age 56, I lost my job at the tech company after 28 years—a profoundly unsettling experience that I write about in my book *The Long Walk Home*, published by Blydyn Square Books. I was fortunate, however, to quickly find another job at a large and very successful financial technology company. That same year, I met my current girlfriend—and, yes, she has dark hair and is a yoga teacher. We've been together ever since.

As the market continued to do well and my investment accounts grew, I decided to move my investments at Vanguard into a managed account under an investment advisor. That advisor, who is terrific, has diversified my portfolio to a mix more appropriate for someone my age.

FAITH REWARDED

In 2019, ten years after I set my intention, I hit my target investment number. That year, I downsized, sold my house, paid off my mortgage and built my dream mountain house up north. I worked for another two years at the financial technology company as my investments continued to grow. Then, in September 2021, at age 61, I stepped away from the corporate world to pursue my long-held dream of being an author. I am now in the second act of my career, and loving every minute of it.

Some might say that it wasn't the law of attraction that enabled me to get to financial independence. It was just plain dumb luck that I was putting money to work during one of the greatest market booms in history—a circumstance that's unlikely to ever happen again.

To which I would reply: It may have been luck that got me here, but it certainly wasn't dumb. I set the intention, worked hard, scrimped and saved, and made investment decisions based on accepted market wisdom.

It also took faith—both in myself and in the markets. Anyone who was investing back in those dark days of 2008–09 was taking a leap of faith. The greatest investment opportunities are found in the greatest periods of uncertainty. The equation goes something like this: opportunity + intention + knowledge + hard work + faith = good luck.

One thing we know for sure: There will be more downturns in the market. Those are the times that create opportunity. When they do, I will be ready.

THREE LESSONS

* Don't lead an aimless financial life. Create a vision of where you want to be financially and otherwise—and then devote yourself to getting there.

* If you want to make rapid financial progress, supplement your workplace retirement savings with monthly investments in a regular taxable account.

* Make no mistake: Investing in stocks takes faith—faith that businesses will continue to grow and innovate, and that their success will be reflected in rising share prices. History suggests such faith will be richly rewarded.

A ROCKY ROAD

BY
DON SOUTHWORTH

Don Southworth is a semi-retired Unitarian Universalist minister, consultant and tax preparer living in Chapel Hill, North Carolina. He recently completed his Certified Financial Planner education. Don is passionate about the intersection between spirituality and money, and he encourages people to follow their callings wherever they lead.

M Y PATH TO financial freedom began when I was seven years old. Of course, I didn't know that at the time, but that was when money became something I started to worry and care about.

I was living with my mom and my sister in a one-bedroom apartment in San Francisco when my dad came over to bring us Valentine's candy. Mom and Dad had been separated for a few months and, within minutes of his arrival, they began screaming, yelling and throwing our candy at each other. The next day, when my sister and I came home from school, our grandmother was waiting for us at the front door. She told us that our mom was in the hospital after attempting suicide.

For the next three months, I lived with my grandmother, and my sister went to live with our aunt and uncle, while Mom healed in the hospital. When she came back to live with us again, she advised me that I was now the man of the house, and it was partly my responsibility to help take care of her and my sister. Money was tight. But thanks to my grandmother's generosity, we had an inexpensive apartment to live in. Most of the time, I didn't realize that we didn't have much.

My first job came at age nine. I would take my grandfather's shoeshine kit to the corner and offer to shine shoes for a quarter. We lived a few blocks from the Haight-Ashbury district, where hippies roamed, many without shoes. The shoe-shining business wasn't very profitable, but fortunately there was a bar on the corner. I had a gapped-tooth smile that some people found irresistible, especially after a few drinks. On most nights, I would go home with enough to buy a candy bar or two and have a few coins left over to give to my mom.

I got my first real job in sixth grade, when I began selling newspapers after school. The better the headlines, the better my take-home pay each night. I averaged $2 to $3 a day, and I gave my mom $8 a week toward rent. I was probably one of the few 12-year-olds who had to pay rent, but I was also one of the few who had a couple of dollars to spend each week.

Despite my mom's strong encouragement—and even demand—that I save something, I usually dropped just a quarter into my piggybank at the end of the week. I would spend my savings on a couple of packs of baseball cards or a ticket to see my beloved Giants or 49ers. Tickets for kids were only 50 cents in those days, and the games were much more exciting to me than having a rainy-day fund.

UNDER THE INFLUENCE

I don't think any of us can get to a place of financial freedom or peace until we've dealt with the money-related stories and experiences of our youth. Whenever I've had the opportunity to lead classes or coach people on handling money, I ask them to reflect on the lessons and values—many of them unexamined—that they have carried from childhood.

I've known wealthy people who are constantly anxious about money. Others think of money as evil or feel guilty about having too much. Still others decide that saving and budgeting are for fools. Usually, they were taught these perspectives when they were growing up. Some rebel at their childhood experiences, and choose to be as different financially from their parents as they can.

In my case, my mom was always worried about money. We rarely took vacations, and my parents were always fighting in court about alimony and child support payments. She thought that working was more important than education. Thus, when I turned 17, I focused on working full time as a fast-food manager instead of going to college.

Mom began receiving disability benefits when I was in junior high school, which meant that my sister and I got free school lunches every day. The cafeteria food was far better than the peanut butter and jelly sandwich, along with an apple, that I'd otherwise bring to school. Still, getting free lunches—and wearing shoes that were too small and clothes that had been bought in bargain basements—often embarrassed me. Maybe that's why, even though I worked up to 30 hours a week in high school, I never had much money in my pocket for long.

At 16, I discovered betting on horse racing. I was working across the street from Bay Meadows Racetrack in San Mateo, California. I found out that, although I was not yet 18, they were happy to let me bet illegally—and usually lose. Over the next five years, I became increasingly addicted to gambling. By 21, I had lost a girlfriend I thought I would marry, was thousands of dollars in debt from legal and illegal 'borrowing,' and was so emotionally and spiritually bankrupt that I considered killing myself.

Fortunately, I got help with my addiction and stopped gambling. I repaid all my debts, got a new job, and slowly began to build a new life. Financially, I was still wobbly. When I got a new credit card, I thought it meant that I had spending money equal to whatever the credit limit was. Annual percentage rates? That was the fine print I didn't need to read as long as I made the minimum monthly payment.

When I met with a friend to review my finances for the first time, he had me track every penny I spent for 30 days. I was shocked to discover that I'd spent $500 more than I planned. No wonder the balance owed on my credit card kept rising.

SUNDAY SCHOOL

I was a financial work-in-progress when I met Kathleen. I was 26, living in a subleased, badly furnished apartment in San Francisco. She was a single mother with a three-year-old son, Justin, living in a new apartment across the bay in Alameda. I liked her and Justin a lot.

The first time I went to her apartment to take them to a movie, however, I almost ran away in horror. Kathleen had a budget stuck to her refrigerator door. It wasn't a general budget, but one that detailed every dollar spent, covering such categories as food, rent, childcare and savings. Amazingly, despite making less money than I did and paying more for rent, Kathleen was able to save money every month. I felt good if I was able to pay $25 over the minimum payment on my credit card. Savings? Not a chance.

Despite my financial defects, she saw enough in me to say yes to my marriage proposal. I had to borrow to buy an engagement ring. But after we married, I learned the Kathleen style of accounting. We set aside money for all our expenses when we got paid, and always included savings as part of our budget. I followed Kathleen's example and joined the 401(k) at my job. I realized I'd been throwing away the 6% company match that had been on offer for the past three years.

Within six months of our wedding, I was promoted at work. We had more money than either of us had ever had before. That helped us not only save for the house we were about to buy, but also allowed us to travel and buy new furniture. We could get used to this, I thought at the time. I started listening to financial shows on the radio and reading financial advice books.

We bought our first house on our first anniversary. We weren't sure we could afford it, but everyone told us they felt the same way when they made the leap. By the end of the next year, Kathleen had given birth to our son, and we were a family of four.

While my financial education helped me understand the difference between an index fund and a savings bond, I found the second step on my road to financial freedom at an unusual place for me: church. Kathleen had been raised a Catholic, but when it came to church, I was barely a 'CEO'—Christmas and Easter only. Friends told us the local nondenominational church was great and invited us to come one Sunday. The community was inclusive and celebrated many paths to divinity and wisdom. We learned a lot, and our kids did, too. Although we were part of that church for only a few years, one lesson there changed our financial lives forever.

Each Sunday before the offering, the minister or a layperson would say something about generosity. One Sunday, a couple around our age, who had a young daughter, talked about the power of tithing. I think I rolled my eyes at first. But as I listened to their story about losing anxiety about money and growing in generosity, I became intrigued.

When we got home and talked about it, my wife said she was intrigued, too. I began learning about tithing, which is the practice of giving 10% to God, a religious tradition or the greater good. There seemed to be something special about giving 10%, apart from making the math easy. We looked at our budget and decided we could afford to give away 10% of our income—*after* we paid taxes, mortgage, food, insurance and contributed to savings each month.

GIVING AND RECEIVING

Kathleen was still keeping a detailed budget. We knew that our version of tithing from leftover funds meant that we would be giving away only about $18 a month. Still, it was 10% of something. Every few months, one of us would suggest giving away a full 10%, before we'd paid for food or insurance or set aside money for savings. Each time we tried it, we'd gulp a bit. But it felt so good that we didn't want to stop.

To our surprise, one year we both agreed to give 10% off the top—even before taxes. Each payday, we'd transfer the money into a special checking account and donate it wherever we thought it would do the most good. That was more than 30 years ago, and we've done it ever since. It is, by far, my most important financial and spiritual practice.

Why? Because when we started tithing, our worries about having enough money slowly melted away. It took a while, but money seemed always to be there when we needed it. We started to believe that we would have enough. Money no longer seemed scarce if we could afford to give 10% away before seeing to our own needs.

Now, some people can find faith without any experience or

evidence. Not me, especially in my younger days. I gained faith through experiences like these that gradually let me trust others, myself or a higher power. I was taking risks and seeing how things played out. That's why we started small with tithing and took a couple of years to build up to giving away 10% of everything.

One experience taught us a lesson that we would never forget, and converted me to a faithful tither for the rest of my days. When Kathleen was pregnant with our son Lucas, our friends and family members threw her a baby shower. I was allowed to drop in just to say hello, but was shooed away so the party could begin. When Kathleen came home, she brought many presents, including some for Justin.

Feeling a bit left out, I decided I wanted more than a two-week vacation when my son was born. This was in the late 1980s, before paternity leave became a workplace benefit. Friends warned me that I would kill my career if I asked for two months off without pay. But I wanted to be there to support Kathleen, to get to know my new baby and to help Justin adjust to having a little brother.

Kathleen was working full time, and she was going to take ten weeks off, using maternity leave plus vacation time. We reviewed our budget and figured out that if I took a two-month leave of absence, we would drain almost all our savings. We decided that it was a once-in-a-lifetime experience and worth the risk.

When I asked my boss for the time off, he eagerly granted my request. He told me he wished he'd taken as much time off when his kids were born more than 20 years earlier. I don't share this story to show what a great dad I was, but to reveal how it helped us progress on our road to financial freedom.

When I went back to work, my boss called me into his office and told me he was giving me a 20% raise. That was unheard of at this Fortune 50 company. Raises were set by human resources using the latest cost-of-living figures, plus perhaps a one- or two-percentage point bump for good work. Two weeks later, I was promoted and received an additional 10% raise. My wife, who had been planning to go back to work the next month, stayed home instead—for the next seven years.

Whenever I tell this story, I need to add a few caveats. Does this mean that once you start tithing, money begins falling from the sky? I don't think so. Perhaps when I was away from work on leave for two months, my value became clearer to my employer. Or maybe someone was impressed that I had my priorities in the right order. I'll never know. The true meaning of this story, for me, is that doing the right thing is always the right thing to do. Even when the finances don't seem to make sense.

Most people will tell you that their road to financial freedom took some learning, some hard work, and some luck or even grace. I believe that luck is far more important than most realize. Factors such as where and when we are born, whether we learn good financial practices or not, and the stock market's performance during our peak earning years are far more consequential to our outcome than our financial expertise. Because we can't control our circumstances, it's important to always practice good values—because, when we have good values, I find that things have a way of working themselves out.

DOING THE RIGHT THING

As a recovering compulsive gambler, I know that my risk tolerance is higher than most people's. My wife and I have learned how to balance each other out. Her tolerance for risk is much lower than mine. In January 1994, we learned both how similar and different we are.

We came home one night to find a message to call Kathleen's doctor. Our worst fears were confirmed when the doctor answered the phone. My wife had been diagnosed with breast cancer at age 36. It was too early to know how bad it was, but we both imagined the worst. That night, as we held each other tight, I told her that I thought this "might be one of the best things to ever happen to us." I cringed, and I still cringe, at having said that, but it was what was in my heart. And it turned out to be pretty true.

The next few weeks were a blur of tests and discussions about so many things we had never considered before. That's what having a potentially terminal illness can do. I had a busy job as a sales manager, so I took some days off to help with everything. I soon realized that a few days off wasn't going to be enough.

Coincidentally, my company was downsizing and offering severance packages to those with more than ten years of service. At 35, with a successful team and a seemingly bright future, I was not the intended target of the offer. After talking with Kathleen, however, we agreed that the eight months of severance pay and the time off would be good for all of us.

She couldn't have dreamt of what I would come up with next. We had recently watched the movie *Lost in America*, about a couple who sell everything, buy a recreational vehicle (RV) and set off to see the country. We both agreed that we wanted to do that—someday. After we learned that Kathleen's cancer was relatively mild, I proposed that we buy a used RV and take the kids on a trip around the country so we could reconnect as a family. I knew that time passes way too quickly, and this opportunity might never come again.

She said what most spouses who have cancer and a jobless husband probably would say: "You are out of your mind. No way!" Fortunately, Kathleen had been part of a support group for mothers for six years. When they heard of my insane idea, they said that she would be crazy *not* to go. So we did.

In April 1994, we loaded our used 27-foot RV with our 13- and six-year-old sons, as well as our nephew, and started down Interstate

5 to see the country. On our first night at a campground, I realized I had forgotten how to clean out the RV's sewer hose. I worried we'd be carrying sewage across the country. Thankfully, we discovered a community of RVers who were happy to help and teach us at every stop along the way. We visited 26 states over the next three months, seeing things we had only dreamed about, while also learning so much about our country and each other.

When we returned home, I got a job in a smaller city, and my wife got her dream job: driving a 25-foot bookmobile for the library. As I said, do the right thing, and the money will work out.

GETTING TO ENOUGH

At my new job, I discovered I was growing tired of the corporate world. After a year, my boss called me into his office. He told me that if my numbers didn't improve, they would have to fire me in three months. I told him that, given changes in the market, I wasn't going to make the goal.

That Sunday, I went to our new church. It was Ministry Sunday, and they talked about the importance of ministry and asked for money to help support seminarians and ministerial training. I thought it must be an annual event. It was not. It had been held on only one Sunday in the previous 30 years.

It felt like God had kicked me in the behind. I had done a little preaching at the first church we had found, and I had been studying spirituality and religions for a long time. Every time I took an aptitude test, the ministry placed near the top of my suitable vocations. I met with the church ministers and applied to enter a seminary.

After three months, my employer did fire me. By then, however, I had been accepted to seminary and had lined up a sales-training job that I could work at full time in the summer and part time during school terms. My wife was willing to return to full-time work. We looked at our budget again. This time, we couldn't figure out how to tithe and save, so we jointly—with some prayer—decided that tithing was more important.

Most of my seminary colleagues were younger than me, and many of them were taking on huge amounts of student debt. Graduate-school debt limits are designed for those becoming lawyers and doctors—not ministers. I was appalled at the naiveté most of my colleagues had about money. I designed a course, 'Financial Management for People Who Don't Want to Bother,' and offered it to my seminary and, eventually, to seminaries around the country.

My money journey had been a long and sometimes rocky road. Sharing my financial lessons and hardships helped deepen my understanding of the basics. It also gave me a way to gratefully share my knowledge in the hope that it could help someone else.

After graduating from seminary, I served congregations for eight years and then became the founding executive director of our ministers' association. Every year, I made a point of preaching about money—not only how to raise it, but also how it affects us and the way we live. Most ministers I know don't discuss money, and especially dislike having to ask for it. Most congregants hate hearing about it, too.

But we have a problem in this country and maybe in the world. We need to ask ourselves: How much is enough? We need to work through the feelings and lessons we learned when we were young. Is a job that saps our spirit worth it just because we can have the newest car or nicest house? How do we reconcile the vast differences in wealth accumulation in our society? How do we teach young people about managing their money for today and for tomorrow, too?

When I was 59, I decided it was time to leave the ministers' association. When Kathleen and I met with our financial advisors, they told us that I probably wouldn't have to work again because we had saved so much. I scoffed and thought there was no way that could be true. After all, it took me more than 20 years to make as much as a minister as I'd made in my final year in my corporate job.

In addition, we were one of the rare couples who had sold a home in California after eight years and only broke even. Since I became a minister, we'd barely cleared a profit on the next two homes we sold. How could we have enough to live on for the rest of our lives?

That was almost five years ago. I have worked only part time since then. It appears the financial advisors were right. All those years of careful spending and diligent saving did indeed do the trick. Through my two-plus decades as a minister, we regularly saved at least 10% of our income, stashing much of the money in stock mutual funds, and that consistency and a rising stock market got us to enough. I won't need to begin taking Social Security until I turn 70. My wife, who is still working, will begin her benefit whenever she decides to retire. That will be when she no longer enjoys her work. Her paycheck won't be a factor in the decision.

I feel extremely fortunate. I still can't believe that I probably don't have to make another dime in my life. I plan to work as long as I can, doing what I want to do, with the people I want to do it with. I wish I had some secret to pass on, but I really don't.

There are some practices, however, that have worked for me: Tithe, save steadily, invest prudently, and pray that luck and love enter your life. I can't guarantee this will result in financial freedom. I can guarantee, however, that you will have a life that others will envy, no matter their net worth. It will feel pretty good, too.

THREE LESSONS

* Marry someone who is good with money, especially if you aren't.

* As much as possible, do what's right rather than what provides the most money. Be grateful for what you have rather than yearning for what you don't have. Count your blessings more often than your dollars.

* Give away at least 10% of your income, save at least 10%, and be as boring as you can with your investments. Index funds and low-cost mutual funds can grow amazingly over the long haul.

FINDING MY BALANCE

BY
WILLIAM EHART

Bill Ehart is a Washington, D.C.-area journalist and an experienced individual investor. Much of that experience has been of the 'school of hard knocks' variety. He enjoys sharing what he's learned to help people cut through the market noise and understand why they should invest, how simple it can be and how to avoid common mistakes.

SUCCESSFUL INVESTING IS about temperament. Keeping an even keel. Knowing your capabilities. Avoiding excesses of ambition or emotion. Having patience and humility. Only a smidge of investment knowledge is needed. But it's critically important to know what you don't know.

Unfortunately, I was not born with such a temperament.

From a young age, I had a desire to learn about investing. I can remember Janie Corcoran turning away from me in eighth grade as I expounded on Schering-Plough or some other long-forgotten company I didn't own stock in or really know much about. I'd been at my father's side, watching *Wall Street Week with Louis Rukeyser* on television.

What was most attractive about investing was the idea of getting something in return for nothing—nothing except the exercise of my supposedly superior brainpower. Put another way, I liked the idea of getting rich by outsmarting others.

Therein my weak character was revealed: For much of my younger years, I assumed I deserved more than others did, that I had been unfairly denied. I wanted what was not mine to have. It was an attitude that went beyond money. It destroyed things beyond wealth. But it did destroy wealth.

To the extent I have anything useful to say to you now, it's because character and integrity have been beaten into me over the decades and because the advance of years has tempered my temperament.

ANY WHICH WAY BUT HAPPY

Leo Tolstoy opened his classic novel *Anna Karenina* this way: "Happy families are all alike; every unhappy family is unhappy in its own way."

To apply to investing: There are numerous labor-intensive, emotionally fraught, overly complicated ways to lose—many of them slickly promoted by Wall Street. I define losing here as trailing the market significantly over many years. That's the almost predictable result of trying to beat the market, and it's a virtually certain outcome of trying to get rich quickly.

Meanwhile, there are some simple ways to win, by which I mean capture the long-term return potential of stocks. That's most reliably accomplished by simply matching the market's return with broad market index funds. Those with the right temperament could follow this passive approach, accept somewhere around 9% a year and be happy. But that was boring to me. I made myself unhappy in a variety of ways until I fully absorbed those kindergarten lessons: Patience is a virtue. Slow and steady wins the race.

A foreshadowing of my future ego-driven investing miscues was my penny hoard. Some people collect coins. As a young teenager, I hoarded them. A whole $23 worth, in one of those bags from the bank that you see robbers carrying on TV. I had read that pennies— then made out of solid copper—cost the government more than one cent to make. That meant my rolls of pennies were worth more than $23, right? Melted down or… whatever? Who knows what I was thinking as I fancied myself outsmarting other people. As would be the case for decades to come, I had a wildly inflated view of my ability to understand world events and profit by anticipating them.

Perhaps I was minted from the same stuff as my late father, who kept South African Krugerrands in his sock drawer. I often faulted him for not investing more in the stock market in the early 1980s after he sold his business. But the truth is, I would ultimately do far worse for my family.

I would also do much worse than my late mother. I thought she knew little, and that her financial advisor—with whom I clashed— knew little more. But Mom had absorbed one lesson from her mother: Never sell.

She simply held on to good funds such as American Balanced, Income Fund of America and Vanguard Wellington for decades without worrying much about what the supposed gurus said on *Wall Street Week*. Thirty years after she inherited investments from her mother, and 20 years after she inherited more from my father, my siblings and I inherited them from Mom in 2021. She never sold.

It was I who had to do some selling for her to pay the huge expenses for her care in her final years. Her home care cost more than $200,000 in the last year of her life. Yet she still had a substantial estate to leave to her heirs.

DIARY OF FUTILITY

Sadly, from my early days gaming what the U.S. Treasury would do about pennies, my investment wisdom advanced fitfully—and my ego fended off all efforts to contain it.

In my 20s, I dabbled in Vanguard Group's gold and energy sector funds—completely missing the tremendous performance of its healthcare fund. See a pattern? Copper, oil, gold—I sought riches in tangible things. Which, in the disinflationary boom of the 1980s and '90s, was the wrong place to look. I imagine I avoided the healthcare fund in part because it was already popular with other investors, its portfolio manager lionized by the press.

I also invested in Vanguard's STAR and Windsor II funds, which bored me. What do you mean it's only up three cents a share? I wasn't going to watch paint dry. Little did I realize that I was positioned for great success with those funds. I was contributing to my retirement nest egg from an early age, as encouraged by my father, and those dollars were going into solid, low-cost funds.

Neither STAR nor Windsor II became the stuff of legend like Fidelity Magellan Fund. I looked back recently, however, and was stunned by the wealth I had forfeited by failing to simply continue contributing to those funds over 35 years. There's that word again: *simply*.

I was dating my future ex-wife when the sudden bull move hit in 1991, and I was seized by the prospect of doubling my money in a year in an aggressive growth fund. Never mind whether the fund was already popular. This time, I wanted in. I was chasing performance now. Many funds had posted eye-popping returns that year, but—like lightning—such good fortune rarely strikes in the same place twice. Instead, most of 1991's biggest winners went on to disappoint—or to crash and burn.

I still recall that nearly ten years later, my then-wife was beckoning me for some alone time, but I put her off to keep poring over my spreadsheets. I had to get rich *for the sake of the family*. We didn't get much richer, if at all, although I weathered the dotcom bust reasonably well. But it wasn't long before my family was broken.

Blaming myself, I took a brief hiatus from my investing obsession. But my investment knowledge, such as it was, was still just a dangerous tool in the hands of my ego. By my late 40s, during and in the aftermath of the 2008–09 financial crisis, I had lost almost everything through a stomach-churning series of horrible decisions. It was like a perfectly choreographed dive. I couldn't have fallen faster if I had tried.

I had virtually nothing left with which to ride the market back up. Then, at the end of 2009, I was laid off from my newspaper job. It would be a year before I could make 401(k) contributions again.

HARD LESSONS

You're not here for my personal tale of woe. Suffice it to say, there was divorce, excessive drinking, illness, two jobs lost, a home that plunged in value, spending well beyond my means and investing with borrowed money—with predictably disastrous results.

I thought I knew the risks of investing on margin—that is, borrowing money against your stocks—and I thought I was doing so within safe limits. But I didn't realize that the broker has the right to declare that some of your holdings no longer qualify as collateral for your margin debt. They are no longer marginable. When that happened to my substantial investment-bank holdings in 2008—I was bottom fishing like a genius, you see—my margin gig was up.

Being forced to sell near the market low of 2009, I even lost the money I had mentally set aside for my kids' college expenses. It all culminated in 2010 with my bankruptcy filing.

Slowly, I learned to live with myself again. Even more slowly, through better spending habits and by keeping my nose clean at work, my finances began to rebuild. The long bull market helped.

Though I was more responsible—and sober—still more investment lessons were to come. I hadn't fully embraced indexing, although I admired index-fund pioneer Jack Bogle, founder of Vanguard, and learned a lot from his books and interviews. Contrary to Bogle's advice, for much of the 2010s, I listened to the siren song of those who said market-cap indexing is blind, dumb and risky. I have a value bent, so that notion appealed to me. I was back to seeking gains anywhere except where other investors already had made them. Forget the FAANGs, I said to myself, as Facebook, Apple, Amazon, Netflix and Google continued their historic run.

My portfolio was chock full of value funds and foreign funds. Anything but substantial exposure to a U.S. market-cap index fund. I dabbled in faddish exchange-traded funds (ETFs), such as those seeking to profit from the growth of consumer spending in developing countries. Emerging markets were cheap, the experts said. I revisited my favorite themes with gold, agriculture and energy ETFs. I can't tell you how much of the bull market I missed in such vain pursuits.

I knew that only a handful of investors can beat the market with skill, so I tried to find them. My last two big hopes were famed value investors Carl Icahn and Dan Loeb, both of whom have publicly traded investment vehicles. These investments languished for years while the market soared. Even as I eventually gravitated toward indexing, I didn't give up on Loeb and Icahn until early 2020, when I replaced the last position with a total market index fund. (Loeb's offshore fund has outperformed the index since I sold it—just goes to show—but still has lagged over the seven years since I bought in.) I ultimately had to fire not just two billionaire portfolio managers, but also demote myself as manager. No more trying to get rich by outsmarting other people.

BACK ON TRACK

Of course, because I'm mainly tracking the market now, my results are closer to the index's return. That may not feed my ego, but it feels right, like I'm a good steward of my capital. Realizing you have lagged the market by a mile year after year feels like hell. Not knowing how much you're lagging is irresponsible, so I monitor my performance closely with a spreadsheet.

I'm still engaged with investing in a way that I enjoy. I still make decisions in which I find my experience and lifelong learning helpful. First, we all have to make fundamental asset-allocation choices based on our risk tolerance, time horizon and diversification preferences. Mine have been fairly steady for years, but I reevaluate them once in a while.

I have set trigger points for rebalancing and buying market dips. I make decisions about Treasury bond funds versus corporates and Treasury Inflation-Protected Securities. I also allow myself little side bets—satellite positions around the core of broad index funds and the balanced funds that I inherited from Mom. Those side bets are within preset limits, so I avoid dragging my whole portfolio down if I make a mistake.

I maintain an investment spreadsheet and investment journal tracking my stock-bond and U.S.-foreign mix, my satellite positions and other decisions, and my performance. Yes, I actually enjoy that. I'm happy with my recent batting average on the side bets. But I require accountability and I need guardrails—established limits on my investment opportunism. You could, of course, skip all this effort and just use balanced, asset-allocation or target-date retirement funds.

My system is likely to change soon because I've decided to seek professional financial help. With the inheritance from Mom, my circumstances have changed. And at my age, probably about ten years from retirement, I need to know more than just what to invest in.

BUYING ADVICE

I've learned the value of financial advisors. Proponents of doing everything yourself can turn self-sufficiency into a fetish, arguing that advisors' advice is not worth the cost. But you will recoup those fees many times over if the advisor keeps you away from foolishness.

In 2016, when it came time for me to take over my mother's affairs, I met with her retiring advisor, Joan, with whom I had bickered 16 years earlier, and her successor, Casey. They were prepared for the worst, but I was a changed man.

Casey, along with an estate lawyer, helped us create a family trust with a portion of Mom's assets. I don't expect market-beating advice from advisors any more than I expect it from the most illustrious investment gurus. I consider a financial advisor mainly a guide, a check on my worst impulses, and a source of counsel on broader personal finance issues. Casey wasn't infallible, but she did redirect me on two occasions. The resulting profits more than covered her fees.

Now that Mom has died, I have retained Casey's colleague Danine as my advisor—the first time I've had one for myself—and I have persuaded my brother to do the same.

I'm no longer trying to get rich by outsmarting other people. But I just might amass considerable wealth and leave my children a decent inheritance—if I don't outsmart myself.

──── THREE LESSONS ────

* Check you have the patience and humility needed for long-term investment success. Lacking the necessary temperament? Build guardrails for yourself, limits on what you can do beyond holding a core position in index funds. Or seek—and listen to—professional advice.

* Don't go for the big score. Efforts to get rich are almost certain to disappoint. Over time, the money you can earn tracking the market is just too good to jeopardize with self-defeating schemes.

* Don't invest with borrowed money. Mr. Market tends to exact his toll when you can least afford it.

COURSE CORRECTION

BY
JIM WASSERMAN

Jim Wasserman is a former business litigation attorney who taught economics and humanities for 20 years. He's the author of a three-book series on how to teach elementary, middle and high school students about behavioral economics and media literacy. He's also authored several educational children's books. Jim lives in Texas with his wife Jiab, who also has an essay in this volume.

F OR MUCH OF my life, I only had to deal with financial issues in the abstract, the result of being born into an economically comfortable family that worried little about spending choices. But like all good privilege stories, I had my comeuppance and resurrection.

I grew up with just about every privilege a person could want. My family was as stereotypical a nuclear, suburban, well-to-do group as any seen on a TV sitcom. I never wanted for food, shelter, top-flight schooling or the latest comforts. I was born wealthy, male and white in America. The road to success was flat and freshly paved.

Budgets, paying bills and other pragmatic aspects of finance were discussed in our family. But I kept all this knowledge at arm's length. Money was, for me, a valued but undefined resource that didn't necessarily need management, like living in a forest and never worrying about running out of timber.

My father was self-made. He had taken a money-losing curtain, drapery and bedspread company and turned it into the country's leading producer of such goods. He was hands-on with everything, overseeing all the manufacturing plants and making personal sales trips to JC Penney in New York and Walmart in Arkansas.

He was also pragmatic. I remember excitedly showing him one of my comic books that was, according to a collector's guide, worth $50. My father smiled and asked, "Do you know anyone right now who will pay you $50 for that comic?" When I sheepishly said no, he put his arm on my shoulder and said, "Then it's not worth $50."

If Pop had a fault, it was that he was too generous with his kids. He wanted us to be free of money worries so we could pursue our dreams. But there was a cost. While I learned to stay mostly within my allowance and spend reasonably, there was no harsh penalty for blowing the budget once in a while. I learned about stocks and watched interest rates—I grew up during the inflationary 1970s—but I also knew I had a safety net if I made a bad choice. My privilege told me that money took care of itself. I needn't worry about paying for college and law school, so I didn't.

One good lesson I learned from watching my father—though it didn't immediately stick—was that just because we could afford the best didn't mean we should spend that much. If a salesman tried to talk my father into buying the high-end deluxe model, my father would point-blank ask, "Tell me what exactly makes this version worth so much more than the other one, and then I'll judge." We learned that the basic version of things, like a car, was almost always enough.

I came out of law school ready to take on the world and, with a good job in hand, I again didn't need to worry about money. I had plenty to live on and even invest. I bought stocks and municipal bonds. I won't say I bought wisely. It was pretty much hunches supported by a little research. Despite being mid-20s and having spent almost all my life in school, I thought of myself as an advanced investor because I was using the latest high tech, in the form of a 640 KB RAM personal computer, as well as programs like Quicken, to monitor it all. In truth, I was like a novice driver in a Ferrari.

When spending, I resisted buying big-ticket items, except, of course, those that I 'needed,' like expensive designer suits to play power litigator in court. Where I was most undisciplined was day-to-day expenses. I usually ate at good restaurants. If I needed something, I opted for convenience, rather than spending time shopping for a better deal. Also, at this point, in my haughty 20-something-knows-everything mind, I opted to counter my father's example and buy more expensive versions of everything from tires to furniture to wine. That way, in my naïve thinking, I knew I was getting quality.

I married another lawyer and we moved to Dallas, each working for a different law firm. We bought a starter home and began a family with the birth of our son. We each saved and invested, but we kept our investments mostly separate, except for shared things like the mortgage.

MY RUDE AWAKENING

For the U.S., the 1990s was a time of strong growth. For me, it was my crash. I came to realize what I had felt intuitively for a long time: I hated being a lawyer. It was what society said was 'success,' but it wasn't for me. I was raised with a sense of *noblesse oblige*, that my privilege not only *allowed* me to give back to society, but that I had a *duty* to do so. As a business litigation attorney, I was giving little back, instead simply moving piles of money from one rich party to another, while also keeping a chunk for the law firm. I hated the monotonous day-to-day grind. It showed in my work and attitude. I was paid well, but I put on weight and had chest pains.

I quit law. Lawyers don't have a lot of transferable skills—that's why they're usually the first chosen to be eaten in surveys of people told to imagine they were marooned. I looked around for what I could do to both serve humanity and still serve my son food. I found it in teaching. I put together a résumé and sent off letters to schools, saying I was a lawyer who wanted to teach and please give me a shot. I substitute-taught to see if I liked it and could handle being in a classroom. I loved it.

During this time, I had a long lunch with my father, discussing my career transition. He just wanted me to be happy. For my part, I told him I owed him an apology. Growing up among elite kids, I was somewhat embarrassed that my father was so bourgeois as to make money by manufacturing curtains and bedspreads. I now realized that he made a tangible product that improved people's lives and, in the process, he and Mom created a wonderful environment for their kids to grow up in. I'm glad I got to say this before his passing.

At around the same time, my marriage fell apart. My now ex-wife and I were friends who had the law in common, but we weren't good as a couple. For one, I had already lived with privilege, and didn't really desire club memberships and the latest doo-dads. Been there, done that. My ex had grown up modestly in a rural town where young girls were told the best they could do was marry the local seed salesman. Law and the lawyer lifestyle were her vehicles to self-reliance and to prove her worth.

Neither of us was right or wrong, but we had different aspirations. Now that I wasn't a lawyer and could no longer afford to spend without thought, the marriage crumbled. She retained primary custody of our son, so she got the lion's share of our assets. I put most of the assets I had to give her into a college fund for our son.

Luckily, I proved good at teaching and managed to get a great job and remain employed for the rest of my career. The problem: I was pretty much starting over. My savings were gone in the divorce. I had the spending habits of a lawyer, but a teacher's salary. I was forced to limit how often I ate out and care whether something was on sale. I had one fancy leftover bit of bling, a shiny red convertible with a $450 monthly lease payment. I broke the lease, paid a large penalty and bought a plain PT Cruiser. My toddler son was disappointed that we could no longer jump in and out of the convertible, but he loved the Chrysler emblem on the Cruiser because it looked like Harry Potter's golden snitch. It was a reminder that it isn't things that bring meaning to our lives. Rather, it's the meaning and appreciation we invest in them.

I tried to live within a budget, but having never done so, it took a long time to corral my spending. Still, I maxed out my contributions to my 403(b) plan. Our school's retirement services manager, TIAA-CREF, made it easy to do basic research and pick funds. I was finally able to join the rest of the country's rising 1990s portfolios by buying global funds, tech shares and some adventurous gambles on small-cap funds.

Even as I invested, though, the credit card was my best friend and worst enemy. I had, of course, endless offers for new cards, with assurances I only had to pay the minimum each month. I never bought big, but the "what the heck" instances were like body blows to my credit score.

I had two weaknesses. First, I tried to keep up with my ex. If she took my son on a great vacation or bought him tons of gifts, I feared he would prefer her, so I acted like a third-world economy trying to keep pace with a first-world one. Eventually, I had to look for shortcuts and freebies. Instead of vacations, we did "buddy hikes" and made secret buddy caves in the woods. We saved cardboard, and built forts and other things.

My other big money leak was dating. I was fixed up with lawyers, businesswomen and other professionals. The expectation was to "do the town." Flowing cash would supposedly make the evening flow better. I was even told by a dating consultant to lie and say I was still a lawyer because "no woman wants to date a teacher."

Ironically, while I was watching my debt rise, I began teaching economics and started seeing a disconnect between theoretical economics—which presumed buyers and sellers made rational decisions—and real life. I had irrational spending habits and often made bad purchases that I figured I could worry about later.

My classroom textbook explained that a credit card was like a temporary loan from the bank. But I came to realize I was actually borrowing from my future self, with the expectation that the debt would be easily repaid because inflation would make the debt worth less and because I would supposedly have more money. Being a teacher paying off a lawyer's debt, I saw the folly of it all. Meanwhile, my high school students were reading about how to spend rationally "when they become consumers in the future," only to immediately run to the mall after school.

I began studying behavioral economics, especially the psychology of consumerism, which would become popular ten years later with the publication of Steven Levitt and Stephen Dubner's *Freakonomics*. I became fascinated that consumers, starting as children, get 'nudged' into irrational spending choices and habits by the media and those around them. I fancied myself a Holden Caulfield of economics, becoming a pioneer in this new field of media literacy. I wrote articles and eventually three textbooks on the subject.

This academic foray helped me to reassess and cut back my own spending. I shopped at discount stores for clothes. I'd make a vat of chili and then eat it for the next week, rather than going to restaurants every night. I was still a tech-loving geek. But I began looking at the features offered by computers and other devices—the ones advertisers said I had to have—and asking if I actually needed the upgrade. Dating became more fun, as I no longer posed as a high roller but could relax and say, "This is me and where I am. If it works, great. If not, nice to have met you."

Along with hikes, my son Ben and I had a regular outing for burgers and shakes, during which we rolled out a chessboard and I taught him how to play. One time, I even heard a sigh and looked up to see several single moms smiling and even giving me the once-over.

MEETING JIAB

Redirecting a ship from its nearly 40-year course is tough, and better done with help. I found the right co-captain in January 2002. I'd been using what was then seen as the new 'weird' system of online dating. I actually liked it because I could look over profiles and decide if a woman might be a good fit. If we had different core values, such as she only wanted men of a particular faith, or didn't want to be a parent, or wanted a high-end lifestyle, I knew it wouldn't work.

I won't get into all the things in Jiab's profile that attracted me, but there is one facet that sums up our different financial attitudes. I had bought a year's online dating subscription but would ignore it for a month at a time. I just liked having it there when I needed it. Jiab, by contrast, signed up for the 30-day free trial and wasn't going to subscribe—read 'pay'—after that. I happened to catch her during the trial period. Lucky that I did, because it was magic.

We met for coffee after she had done yoga. So enamored was I that I immediately and impulsively offered to buy her dinner, going back to my old spending habits. Unable to resist a freebie, Jiab accepted. I went home and immediately wrote her an email. I apologized for not playing it cool by waiting a few days to then casually ask if she wanted to get together. I said I didn't want to risk losing an opportunity with a great woman by playing games. It worked.

I was also lucky that we met after I had started to right my financial ship. If it had been earlier, I don't think Jiab and I would have jibed. But as things stood, we agreed on our general outlook on money management. We both believed in saving as much as possible and maxing out our retirement accounts. We also—and this is essential—believed in the greater value of experiences, especially varied ones, over the power of owning things.

For example, we did the obligatory family Disney World vacation. Even then, Jiab and I sat through a time-share presentation to get free tickets. If you ask our two children—Jiab also has a son from an earlier marriage—more fun was had on the family trip done on the cheap, where we backpacked through New York, Philadelphia and Washington, D.C., staying in hostels, taking trains, walking and, yes, carrying all our stuff in backpacks.

Jiab and I differ in two ways. First, she's detail-oriented. She knows every dollar we have, where it is and what it's doing for us. She has her head down micromanaging to make sure we have the quantity of money necessary for a good life. Jiab has earned a reputation on three continents for her reluctance to spend. Meanwhile, I focus more on the quality of life and advocate for judiciously releasing our grip on funds to get all we can from an experience. For example, having a pet really makes no sense financially, but my joy at having cats got Jiab hooked and we have had a houseful ever since.

I don't need her to tell me I was right on those occasions. Her smile at enjoying a rare carefree-about-money moment is enough. Some of my old habits are still hard to shake. Sometimes, I don't bother to look at prices or shop around much when I feel something is a necessity, like food or a home repair. To this day, when I start to say, "Just get it," Jiab will give me a not-so-subtle hint by asking,

"But how much does it cost? Is there another place we can get it cheaper?" For us, tipping remains a negotiation.

The other area we differ on is the tradeoff between time and money. Jiab will spend hours looking to save just a few more dollars, but—and I'm sorry, honey—is terrible about wasting time. She's always surprised at how late the hour is and how behind she gets. I, on the other hand, am stingy about time. I want to "get 'er done" and move on to the next thing. It's a product of managing a classroom for so long, or perhaps my ADHD. Jiab spends time to get money, and I'll spend money to get time.

The key to us is that we don't counter, we complement. At the heart of our marriage, and even when we disagree financially, there's a mutual respect and willingness to reexamine our beliefs and maybe trust the other's view. We aren't either-or. Rather, we're like the yin-yang that's completed by the other's viewpoint.

When we take family vacations, Jiab will plot the travel and find the best places to stay, all maximizing savings. Once we get there, I'm in charge of finding that cool attraction, like a weird museum, a great hiking trail or a haunted spot. Our reciprocal respect often comes out in good-natured teasing. Jiab refers to "Wassernomics" when I say we "made" money because something was cheaper than we anticipated, or when I contend that a videogame the boys and I want to purchase will be made cheaper every time we play it.

Our differing styles influenced how we raised our two sons. Jiab rightly thought that the boys were getting too many gifts for Christmas, so I found Heifer International, through which 'Santa' delivered two goats, named after the boys, to a remote village in Africa. The only problem: The day after Christmas, the boys excitedly demanded we visit the goats.

When they were older, we had a Salvation Army Christmas, where everyone agreed to only buy gifts at thrift stores and not spend more than $10 per gift. The hit was the mug with a battery-operated fan that kept chocolate milk mixed. If there was a key to instilling an appreciation for saving money with our sons, I would cite two factors. First, we never presented spending less as a sacrifice, but more as a lifestyle choice to avoid consuming so many resources. Second, we were all in it together and enjoyed it as a fun event.

GOING PLACES

When the boys went to university, Jiab and I began downsizing. There was no sense in paying a mortgage on empty rooms that were rarely used. We sold our larger suburban home and moved to a nearby townhome. Without fully realizing it, we were also taking small steps toward the retirement door.

The idea of exploring the world, something we'd always loved doing, crept into more of our conversations. We both liked our work, but had become increasingly bothered by the administrative roadblocks and workplace politics. For years, I could just sit and smile through every staff in-service meeting that proclaimed that a rebranded version of something from a dozen years ago would purportedly revolutionize pedagogy. More and more, however, irritation lingered after the meetings. I more openly proclaimed my skepticism, probably as an unconscious first step toward announcing that I was done.

The moment of clarity is different for everyone. For me, it was a meeting with a TIAA financial advisor. Retirement was one of those 'someday' states of mind—until the advisor said he ran our savings through a Monte Carlo analysis and determined that the odds our money would be enough for the rest of our lives was over 99%.

Done.

The entire drive home, I kept thinking, "We did it." By the time I got home, however, my thought was, "We now do… what?"

We began planning our life's next phase. True to our roles, I dreamt and read, Jiab crunched. We wanted to travel, but we'd always favored rubbing elbows with locals and living like them. Rather than taking glamorous cruises and vacationing behind resort walls while devouring Americanized versions of local fare, we preferred staying in modest hotels and eating street food. To us, it's a more authentic experience. To our wallets, it's more cost-effective. We wanted the same experience now, just more extended.

We settled on relocating ourselves to a place from which we could explore the world. Once our boys graduated university, we knew we had a window of time between then, when they wanted to be on their own, and when we might get the call that we were to be grandparents and once again needed.

We first considered Costa Rica. It had great expat reviews, a relatively low cost of living and was only a two-hour flight from the U.S. Soon, however, we were looking farther afield. We discovered that for about the same cost as Costa Rica—$30,000 per year—we could live in southern Spain. That would give us easy access to the rest of Europe.

We looked into Spanish visas and, the next thing we knew, we were in Houston getting them. We chose Granada, in Andalusia, as our initial landing spot, but ended up asking the flat owner if he was willing to make it a year-long lease. Of course, Jiab handled the paperwork. I added color commentary, encouragement, made coffee and looked for Spanish language courses.

Once we reached Spain, there were further hurdles, such as having to set up financial accounts and learning that many aspects of official business seemed stuck in the 1500s, when Spain was the world's dominant empire. Most everything, from government interactions to banking, was still best done in person and on paper.

For all the annoyances, we only had to take a walk in the mountains, or on the beach, or have tapas and wine followed by a siesta, to remind us that annoyance was the price of choice and privilege.

We remained grateful for having both. When not wandering and wondering, we strove for the Hemingway-like writer's life abroad. The house full of entitled cats was a good start.

Three years later, we returned to the States. We had family matters to attend to. We also missed the boys. COVID isolation brought that point—and us—home. We're still secure in our savings and enjoying what is the essential power of money, which is the power to choose.

America was founded to give people the right to pursue happiness, but the pursuit is not free. There are charges all along the way. As a young man, my pursuit was prepaid. I didn't really learn how to play the game until my 1990s wipeout.

Much of my good fortune has stemmed from the luck of the birth lottery and the help of others. But I also helped myself with some good choices and some key adjustments made by my younger self. To that, I keep hearing the words of an old tae kwon do teacher who would—on the rare occasions I adjusted my sparring strategy to take advantage of an opening—drop his scowl, nod and offer his highest praise, "Not bad, Wasserman."

THREE LESSONS

* Think of spending not as a sacrifice, but as a lifestyle choice that frees up money for other options. The base model car, computer or gadget is often the best buy, particularly if you want money left to save and invest. Life is full of financial decisions. A bias toward value can save you a fortune.

* Experiences provide more joy than things. Many of the best experiences are free, or nearly so if you think creatively. Building a cardboard fort in the yard may be a more cherished memory than a Disney vacation.

* When you travel, stay in modest places and eat street food. Checking into a four-star resort and dining in elegant restaurants tends to seal tourists in a bubble, and rob them of the rich experiences offered by another culture.

INVESTING in MYSELF

BY
CATHERINE HORIUCHI

Catherine Horiuchi—now professor emerita—recently retired from the University of San Francisco's School of Management, where she taught graduate courses in public policy, public finance and government technology.

M Y FIRST ALLOWANCE was a nickel a week. I was five years old. I can't recall how I spent it, but I vividly remember visiting cousins and discovering they received a quarter.

It was a shocking introduction to a world where people might have much more, for no clear reason. My access to capital amounted to 52 nickels a year, or $2.60. Added to that was $1 reliably tucked in my Christmas stocking, as well as a little something from grandparents. Once my allowance rose to a dime, my total annual haul climbed to $10.

In my early teens, my parents divorced. Mom moved to the city where her sister lived, rented a duplex and got her first job. She'd gone to college, even graduate school, but had been a stay-at-home parent for 20 years. She had limited employment options. She wasn't young and pretty, knew almost nobody in town, had two kids to watch over and no work history. Few jobs met our family's constraints.

She ended up working the swing shift as a nurse's aide in a rest home. That way, she could see us off to school each morning and be there when we returned each afternoon. Then she'd leave for work. As I saw how she—and we—struggled financially, I became determined to fend for myself and avoid low-paying jobs.

By then, Mom gave me $3 a week in allowance, so my income was about $150 a year, mostly spent on records and books. I sewed my own clothes, aside from T-shirts and jeans, while also raiding and deconstructing my mom's vintage outfits for new looks. I had a passbook savings account with pretty much nothing in it.

A young couple moved in next door and we became friends. One was a graduate student who'd served as a Peace Corps volunteer somewhere in Africa. My eyes were opened to a much wider world, and I wanted to see it. The journey that followed might seem meandering. Still, I ended up in surprisingly good financial shape, in large part because my needs and wants have almost always been modest. This is an underappreciated source of financial freedom—one available to almost everyone.

COLLEGE ON THE CHEAP

When I graduated high school in the early 1970s, many kids I knew received fancy presents like cars and trips to Europe. I was envious but I had a plan: Go to college and see the world. My graduation presents—a dictionary and the complete works of Shakespeare—have served me well. I still have both books.

I turned down admission to a prestigious out-of-state school because its financial aid package wouldn't cover my expenses. Instead, I enrolled at the local university, where I had a scholarship. I moved in with three friends who'd gone straight into the workforce. In that bygone era, I lived on $100 a month, which came from my dad plus whatever I could earn from college work-study jobs.

My share of the monthly rent for that two-bedroom apartment was $28.50, plus a quarter of the utilities. We each put $5 a week into a food kitty for suppers together. We also had dinner out once a week. I walked the two miles to campus or rode the bus.

If I didn't have enough money to buy a textbook, I'd read it on reserve at the university library. I lived just five miles from home, so I could visit often for a home-cooked meal, to do laundry and for help typing term papers. I graduated from college completely debt-free, but with little savings, possibly $100 in my bank account.

My career plan? Become a high school Latin teacher. Once I got into a classroom, however, I felt uninspired. I needed a new idea. My roommates helped me get my first full-time position, an office job. That lasted maybe a year before I returned to college for a master's degree, something my bosses encouraged.

I didn't pick a major in a particularly rational way. Instead, I asked myself, of all the professors I'd met in my undergraduate classes, who seemed to be having the most fun? I settled on a master's degree in linguistics. My plan from there was to get a job where I could travel and see the world.

I got by on scholarship money, a teaching assistant's stipend and a $1,000 student loan. It would take me six years to pay off that debt, the first of several small debts that left a lifelong distaste for borrowing. People I respect have argued that using debt can be valuable, and I've seen them do so successfully. But it's not for me.

SENSITIVE COMPUTERS

Before graduating, I applied to serve in the Peace Corps, but my paperwork got snagged. I thought about going on immediately for a doctoral degree and maybe becoming a college professor. Instead, in 1978, I moved to the city where my brother lived.

I needed work, so I looked for something with lots of openings, where they might hire just about anybody. I hoped to land a job whose skills would be useful for my future. I didn't want to get stuck like my mom in a dead-end, minimum-wage job. I'd learned that men earned more than women, and read about why that happened. I couldn't battle those causes head-on, so I focused on applying to male-dominated positions where few women workers had been hired and salaries were more equal.

I took a position as a computer operator, tending an oversensitive machine. It was an early networked time-sharing system that supported remote corporate clients who could access their data 24 hours a day. I worked a crazy schedule, nights and weekends, as well as days. There were just four or five computer operators providing customers with 24/7 coverage.

At night, I'd work alone. I'd backup data and reboot the computer with a length of paper tape after every electrical disturbance, such as a lightning strike near our building. During slower hours, I'd read computer manuals and write code for data reports. This work paid the princely sum of $700 a month.

After a while, I got a raise to $850. That meant I'd crossed over to earning $10,000 a year, a symbolic milestone that changed almost nothing. Those were years of high inflation, so rising costs gobbled up the spending power of my raise. I barely got by and didn't save anything. I was a lousy cook and ate a lot of fast food, devoting my off hours to pizza, beer and music with friends. I gave absolutely zero thought to my financial future.

FARAWAY LANDS

I took an exam to qualify for a federal job but didn't score high enough to advance above others who had received preference, generally those with military service. I thought about joining the military, but first I contacted the Peace Corps again. They found my missing paperwork and invited me to join. I bid the balky computer farewell and boarded a plane to a country I'd never heard of before.

The Sultanate of Oman is a Kansas-sized, comma-shaped desert kingdom to the southeast of Saudi Arabia, beginning at a naval chokepoint, the Strait of Hormuz, and stretching from there around the Arabian Sea to Yemen. I would earn little money over the next three years, but this was my dream come true. I was seeing the wider world.

I've often been asked what it was like living in a country in the early stages of modernization. I was based in a small town far from the capital city of Muscat. My home was a cement-block house, essentially the same size and construction as a typical one-car garage. It had electric lighting and a ceiling fan in the main room. Electricity was purchased monthly from the neighborhood grocery store, the cost dependent on the number of installed lightbulbs. The grocer owned a portable generator that ran a few hours daily to keep meat and soda cool in the store, his expenses defrayed by sharing the output with those who lived nearby.

There was no such thing as trash day. People burned garbage to reduce its volume. We had no heat or air-conditioning in a climate where temperatures ranged from the low 50s in winter to above 115 degrees in summer. It was simply impossible to replicate my comfortable American life with its nearly infinite choices of food, entertainment, friends and jobs. I lived on a monthly $300 allowance, which covered rent, utilities and food.

I met almost everyone in the village during those two years

teaching school, before spending a third year in the south of the country as a traveling health worker. Despite hardships, people seemed no less happy than everyone back home. Each family had hopes and ambitions similar to mine. They worried about their teenagers, exhorted their little ones to do well in school, and took care of one another when sick. They traveled to visit friends and family, and came back with pictures and stories to share as they whiled away their evenings with social calls.

There were personal tragedies and petty rivalries and party nights and holiday traditions. It was the same as my world back home, except each household had to manage all their essential human activities and expectations with very little money.

Repeatedly over the following decades, whenever I faced a major setback or my life situation became precarious, I would recall my years in Oman and other places I'd visited. I'd remind myself that almost everything that creates happiness, that makes life worth living, is possible at all price points. I'd stop obsessing over whatever I wanted, what I thought essential for my happiness or success, and look for an alternative that would fit my current station.

I'd also remember that others had much less, and see if there was something I could do to improve their lot for a while, by word or deed. Over my life, this has saved me a mountain of grief and a pile of money.

STARTING TO SAVE

I didn't yet have the vocabulary for what I was doing, but over that first decade after high school I was building human capital. It increases an individual's opportunities, including his or her earnings potential. These early investments in myself—and my dreams— have carried me through life.

Not long after I returned from Oman in 1982, and after another two years of graduate school, I took a second computer-related job, this time as a programmer. I was nearly 30 years old and had accumulated no savings. As part of its culture, the company where I worked taught employees how to plan for the future. I finally got serious about saving for retirement and began contributing to a 401(k). My annual salary rose from $19,000 to $35,000. I earned a few thousand more from freelance projects, a practice encouraged by my employer, who thought everyone ought to have a side gig.

I made plenty of financial mistakes. For instance, I was more focused on saving for retirement than preparing for unexpected expenses. As a result, when my father got a terminal cancer diagnosis and asked me to come see him, I didn't have the cash or credit to buy a plane ticket. My boss suggested I loan myself money from my 401(k). I borrowed enough for two trips and signed an agreement to pay myself back with 7% interest. An adequate emergency fund would have been better.

Here's another mistake I made: I worked at government agencies for 12 years, three years in the Peace Corps, two years at city hall, and seven with our local electric company. Technology workers earned tens of thousands more in the private sector, so most didn't stay long in government. Yet I remained.

Why? One advantage of the public sector was having a defined benefit pension plan. Plan rules permitted me to buy three years of service credits for my time in the Peace Corps. I delayed purchasing them until long after the end of my public service career, which cost me a small fortune.

My cost for the pension credits followed a formula based partly on salary and partly on imputed returns. Though I'd received little income as a Peace Corps volunteer, buying three years of pension credits cost me $58,000. This was many multiples of what it would have cost when I first started my city job. My income had risen from \$30,000 to \$90,000 over those nine years of employment, and 20 years had passed since I started at the city. Still, the credits I purchased contributed substantially to my small, inflation-linked government pension.

Each year, I'd estimate how much I could expect from my pension and I'd review my Social Security statement. I'd consider whether that would meet my retirement needs. I remember at one time thinking that \$15,000 a year would be plenty, and that my pension would almost equal that. But I also assumed I might be overlooking potential retirement expenses, so I carried on working and saving.

My parents had died at age 57 and 62, so I never counted on getting to retirement. If I didn't make it to old age, I didn't want to regret the way I spent my life. I regularly reviewed how well my current work suited my life and whether the job made good use of my abilities. If it seemed a bad fit, I'd look for a promotion or seek a new job that could be more satisfying. I had continued to add to my technical and managerial skills, and so kept my talents in demand.

At age 40, I thought I'd retire at 55, leaving plenty of time to spend with my husband before one or the other of us died. As has happened before, my plan went one way, my life the other. Over the decades, I had married twice. One marriage ended when my husband left. The second ended when my husband died following a brief, unexpected illness.

I have raised five children across two separate generations. I still have one in high school. Through it all, I paid my bills when due, and made cuts elsewhere to balance my budget. Childcare and college bills have cost me as much over the years as houses and cars. Only rarely, and for as short a time as possible, did I stop saving for retirement. When things turned around, I started saving again—and doubled down if I could.

BACK TO ACADEMIA

In the late 1990s, I saw large numbers of in-house information technology staff and managers replaced by contractors and temporary workers from abroad with H-1B visas. As a manager, I didn't want to have to replace good workers or get caught in the turnover, so I looked for an exit strategy of my own.

I called a family meeting to discuss how everyone felt about me leaving my government job to try another career. If my family said no, I would have stayed in my job forever, perhaps. But I had completed most of a doctoral program on the excellent advice of a mentor, and so had just a few credits and a dissertation remaining. My family was enthusiastic in their support that I finish my degree and pivot to academic life.

I graduated debt-free, thanks to education subsidies from my employer, along with some savings and money made from part-time college teaching. I took a full-time academic position and ultimately earned tenure. I also served as an associate dean for three years. I politely declined invitations to apply for dean or senior university leadership positions.

In my last years at the university, my annual income topped $100,000, not by much and not for long, but a marker of prosperity for sure. I maxed out my 401(k) contributions, including catchup contributions allowed after age 50. I also saved the maximum in a nondeductible IRA and even added a little money to my regular taxable accounts.

I wasn't saving all this money in case I lived to 95. Rather, I was saving in case my spouse lived to 95, and to make sure the youngsters in our house wouldn't be left in financial difficulty if something unfortunate happened to me. I like the good things in life as much as anyone, but I also have frugal habits from long practice.

Much that brings me joy is really cheap. For instance, listening to my teens laugh as they talk about their lives. Walking the family dog. Chatting with neighbors. Watching people picnic in the park. Can I admit it? I've joined city council meetings on Zoom, just for fun and out of curiosity about what's important in our city.

MY RETIREMENT

It's been three exceptionally difficult years since my husband died. I had a freak accident. Early retirement. Then, weeks after clearing out my campus office, the pandemic shut schools for over a year and hijacked my twins' college preparations. But we carried on. Now, they're finishing their freshman years.

I have concerns about spending my old age alone. I had planned to enjoy this time with my husband of 30 years. I feel bad that, of all my friends, I'm the first to lose my life partner. I don't want to be a burden on my kids. They're starting their journeys now, not so different from the adventure I began so many years ago, and I don't want to stand in their way.

My retirement is not filled with carefree activities, new friends and travel—yet. That's why, looking back, I value more than ever the choices I made when spending time and money. It's how I ended up with a large family and lots of friends, and it's allowed most of my fanciful dreams to come to fruition. To understand what I mean, consider three memorable trips.

My dad died in 1988, months after my first marriage failed. I was in low spirits, adjusting to a single salary while most of my expenses were unchanged. Coming back from my dad's funeral, my brother suggested that we sign up for a mountain climbing trip in South America. Not that we knew much about mountain climbing or had ever been to South America. He said it would cheer me up, and that the months I spent developing the required physical conditioning would keep me busy. I agreed, imagining I might meet a nice guy on the trip.

I cut out all other discretionary spending for the entire year to pay for that trip. In December, I flew to Ecuador. We spent Christmas Eve at a climbers' hut so full that I had to sleep outside under the stars. Before dawn, we started our hike to the summit of Tungurahua, an active volcano. The precise peak we summited no longer exists, wiped out by a later eruption. A few days after that summit, I climbed to the top of Cotopaxi, the world's highest active volcano.

Remember Y2K, when the world's computers were supposed to crash? At the beginning of 1999, I requested vacation leave for the end of the year. It was easy to get in January. By December, my bosses were sweating and asking me to cancel. But I had prepaid for a cruise and I knew my computer systems were in order. My husband and I celebrated New Year's Eve dancing our way into the new millennium on a promenade deck in Panama, while my colleagues spent a boring night at the office.

One of my twins qualified for the U.S. team for the World Baton Twirling Federation's 2019 International Cup. Six months after my husband died, the two of us flew to Limoges, France, for her competition. It was a quick trip, because I had to arrange alternate activities for her brother and sister back home, and I didn't want to strain the kindness of friends and family any more than necessary.

At the end of the meet, we had one glorious, rainy day of sightseeing in Paris before our return flight. My daughter was bone-tired and I was getting about with a cane after my accident. Still, there are so many memories from that trip, such as cutting short our visit to the terrace atop the Arc de Triomphe as a hair-raising electric storm approached.

Some adventures are no longer possible. At this point in our lives, neither my brother nor I would feel safe hiking in crampons above 15,000 feet. I don't have my husband to cruise with anymore. My teens will soon spend their holidays with other young adults on their own adventures, without me in tow.

Today, I'm a single parent with three young adults still to care for. We're getting by financially on Social Security and a pension, supplemented with withdrawals from savings. I've lived in the same house for nearly 30 years. I paid off the mortgage long ago, and owe no one money.

Looking at my peripatetic path through life, with some good luck and some bad, I'm doing far better than I might have expected in terms of my net worth and annual income. That's because I started saving and investing while relatively young, choosing to spend less than I could have, even in years when I had more money than usual.

My life is full of purpose, and I'm grateful to have the financial wherewithal to meet its challenges. I've learned to tolerate myself, and channel my quirks and preferences in ways that improve my financial standing. Right now, I'm simplifying my accounts, and spending more on myself and on causes I've contributed to for decades. As my children mature, I share with them bits and pieces of my financial picture, so—in due course—they won't have unpleasant surprises.

I don't have unreasonable expectations of continued good health or good fortune. Instead, I'm a realist, grateful for any week that shows nothing worse than gradual decay and delighted with any week where things seem slightly better than expected. I'm insured for the worst. And I never forget that, despite my age and stage in life, I still have three teenagers to launch. The adventure continues.

THREE LESSONS

* Earn as much as you can in jobs that you like as best as you can. Save a meaningful sum each payday so you'll have enough later on. After each month's saving and giving are set aside, spend as much as you wish on yourself, leaving a little for inclement weather.

* Unless you're born to high wealth and class, and can count on someone escorting you into the most lucrative and powerful positions, figure out a way to make money and gain personal autonomy. Learn about the work world so you can find your place in it. The Bureau of Labor Statistics' *Occupational Outlook Handbook* is a treasure trove of information.

* Invest in financial products you understand. The simpler your investment strategy, the less chance you'll be tricked and the less time required to manage it successfully. Buying a total market index fund is easier, and comes with a greater likelihood of success, than choosing and managing a portfolio of individual stocks.

GETTING BY

BY
MATT TROGDON

Matt Trogdon is a financial planner with Craftwork Capital, LLC. He's based in Washington, D.C., and has a special interest in helping Gen X and Gen Y families. He also serves as a workshop instructor for the Babson College Financial Literacy Project.

I T WAS SUMMER 2021. I was working a job I didn't like. The salary was solid, but I dreaded Monday mornings and lost sleep at least twice a week. This had been going on for months. Finally, I'd had enough.

I looked at my portfolio one last time. I didn't need to, of course. I've been an almost obsessive tracker of my investments for 20 years and, indeed, acutely aware of money since I was a child. I knew I had more than enough saved up to take the leap.

"The only reason I'm in this job anymore is because I haven't found another job," I told my fiancée, Sarah. "But I can afford to live off my savings for a bit. Are you okay if I quit?"

"You're miserable, and we'll be fine," she answered. "You'll get by."

I left in August 2021 and haven't looked back. By October, I was back to work, having joined a couple of friends who started a small investment and financial planning firm. While I'm technically an employee, I'm building my own practice and essentially working for myself. My goal now is to continue working for myself for the rest of my life. I've never been as professionally fulfilled as I am right now.

Lots of people would be thrilled to have a steady, well-paying salaried job. To be able to walk away from a job and not worry about making ends meet? That's a privilege, no doubt.

But I also have lots of experience with learning how to 'get by.' It's been the core motivation in my life for more than 30 years. The idea of leaving a salaried job to jump into something riskier was never that scary for me.

Where did this mindset come from? My financial journey began with tragedy. My mother died three weeks before I turned age six. My father died the day before my eighth birthday. I went to live with my maternal grandmother—the only grandparent I had left.

I could write a whole book on how losing my parents at a young age affected me mentally, emotionally and psychologically. I've spent many years trying to peel back the layers. The devastating loss also affected how I think and feel about money. It might be somewhat predictable that it provoked a sense of scarcity that I still deal with today. Still, some time after losing my parents, I developed a keen sense of knowing what I needed to survive. I think I'm more dialed into that sense than most people.

FINDING MONEY

On a happier note, I grew up in a big Greek family, with plenty of uncles, aunts and cousins. I recall having to create a family tree in grade school. Mine only had one branch, but I put so many cousins in my tree that it made up for it. I got an A.

My family talked about money quite a bit. One of the first things my grandmother did when I went to live with her was open a savings account for me at the local bank. She deposited $50 and told me I was going to receive something called "interest." She also told me to look out for the mail at the end of the month. The bank would send me something called "a statement," and I'd find out how much interest I'd earned.

I don't remember the exact amount, but I think I received about 45 cents that first quarter. When I reflect on that now, I realize that 45 cents annualized on $50 would be a 3.6% return. I'd be thrilled with that from a savings account today. But as an eight-year-old, I wasn't impressed.

We had enough money. There was always food on the table. But my grandmother never let me think we were anything other than getting by. She sent me to a private school that was walking distance from our house. That's when I first realized what 'rich' looked like. I had classmates whose parents were doctors, lawyers and successful business people. I'd visit their homes and note how much bigger and more lavish they were than ours.

School is where I honed my 'getting by' techniques. I got very good at asking for favors. My grandmother didn't drive at night, so I always needed a ride home from baseball or basketball practice. I would rotate my requests so the same friend's parents never took me home more than twice in a row.

My grandmother also taught me how to balance a checkbook. We had a separate account for all my expenses, and we wrote three checks each month: one for private school tuition, one for health insurance and one to my grandmother for my "room and board." I received a Social Security survivor benefit each month, and that was the main source of income for the account.

I was age 11 or 12 when I realized that we had more money going out of my account each month than coming in. I marched up to my grandmother and pleaded that we needed to do something to fix our monthly shortfall. Deeply religious woman that she was, she just said, "Don't worry, God will provide."

I could debate all day about whether God was actually involved or not. But on a practical level, our monthly shortfall wasn't a problem because there was another account I didn't know about until I became a teenager. This was an account that was managed by my aunt, who was the executrix of my father's will and later the trustee of his estate. She would supplement the required funds when necessary. She would help us get by.

I soon learned that there was something called "a trust," and that it would be mine when I turned 25. My aunt, unlike my grandmother, was a fountain of transparency. She opened the books and showed me exactly what was happening behind the scenes. Was God pulling the strings? Or was it my aunt? At the end of the day, I'm not sure there was much of a difference.

The trust wasn't massive. It held some brokerage accounts and a couple of rental properties of questionable investment value. Once the books were opened, my aunt gave me the job of collecting all of the investment account statements as they arrived and putting them in a filing cabinet. I successfully executed my job about 40% of the time—I was a teenager, after all.

In the late 1990s, I couldn't help but notice that the investment account balances were growing quickly each quarter. Again, I didn't know what I didn't know, but I figured there might be more to my position than I'd previously thought. I left for college in August 2000. On my fall break, I went with my aunt to meet with our accountant.

"Your father left you a nice nest egg, Matthew," he said. "As long as you don't spend it frivolously, you could be set for life. The way things are going, you could be a millionaire by 30."

That was October 2000. Two years later, I was home from college for the summer and decided to check my investments to see how things were going. I was appalled. Like everyone else, we suffered significant losses in the tech crash. There was still a rump portfolio left, but becoming a millionaire by 30 was no longer in the cards.

That summer was when everything changed. I dove into my investments head first. Even as a beer-drinking, math-despising history major, I realized that I still held an ace in the hole. As long as I learned about what I had and protected it, I'd be able to get by financially no matter where my life led.

One cousin explained the rule of 72 to me—how you can divide 72 by your expected annual investment return and thereby learn how many years it'll take to double your money. "Just don't spend that money," my cousin told me. "Even if you never save another dime, you'll be absolutely fine."

FINDING MY WAY

In retrospect, that money was a bit of a double-edged sword. It allowed me to be less serious and less career-focused than I probably should have been. I had lots of friends who'd studied business or economics. Many of them got investment banking jobs and set off on successful career paths. I had other friends who studied history or government. Many of them went to law school.

Meanwhile, I flitted in the wind during the first few years out of school. I worked as a full-time reading tutor for a year. I spent two years as a history graduate student. Eventually, I went to work at *The Motley Fool* investment website, where I did a number of different jobs over a period of 12 years. I enjoyed my time there, but I never advanced much in any specific role. Of course, I knew I could get by if I just protected what I had, so how much more did I actually need to achieve?

Fortunately, the Fool was a great place to work. Being around people who wrote about investing and personal finance helped deepen my interest and understanding of those topics. The company provided a generous 401(k) matching contribution and offered some great education on how to invest the money. I regularly contributed to the 401(k) throughout my time there, always heeding my cousin's advice to keep my spending below my income. My financial position improved along with the market.

I finally got serious about my career in 2016 when I decided to try financial planning. I enrolled in Certified Financial Planner coursework and passed the exam in 2018. In 2019, I left the Fool and joined a local firm in Washington, D.C. I took a pay cut to do so, but I didn't much worry about that. Adjusting my expenses to meet my new, lower income wasn't a problem.

Today, three years later, my financial situation is one of constant calibration and measurement. My income is uneven as I work to build my planning practice. I know I have a couple of years ahead of me when things will be lean. But I also know how much I need to make each month to avoid dipping into savings. And I can estimate how things will look in the future, depending on different assumed investment rates of return.

Despite knowing the math, I'm not sure I'll ever get over the sense of scarcity that lives deep within me. It's laughable how frugal I am about some things, given how stable my financial situation is. The best example of this: How I keep my car running instead of getting a new one.

The car is ten years old. It has so many things wrong with it that I have trouble remembering them all. The alignment is off. The driver's side door has an unsightly dent. The air-conditioner doesn't always work. I had to get a waiver just to pass the inspection last year. The pièce de résistance: I can't take the key out of the ignition without using 'the flick trick.'

I drove my friend to a basketball game recently. When we arrived, I told him I can't pull my key out of the ignition normally. He asked me what I do and I showed him. I pushed the key further forward into the ignition and then released my fingers. The ignition flicked backwards and spat the key out. My friend keeled over laughing.

"How'd you learn how to do that?" he asked.

"I Googled 'can't get key out of Volkswagen Jetta ignition.' The comments said it would cost $6,000 for a new ignition column. Then I saw this 'flick trick' video and tried it. It works like a charm."

He kept laughing.

"Look, if you ever need someone to tell you how to do things the right way or how to pick out the nicest stuff, don't waste your time calling me," I continued. "But if you need someone to tell you the trick to making something last just a little longer, I'm your guy."

My car will get by for another year or so. I have no doubt that I, too, will continue to get by.

THREE LESSONS

* Examine the money experiences you had as a child, and try to figure out how those affect you today.

* If you come into a significant sum early in life, you may be set for retirement—provided you leave the money to grow rather than raiding it for spending money.

* When bequeathing assets to children, consider a trust arrangement that pays out the money over time, rather than all at once at, say, age 21. That way, they're more likely to be motivated to study hard at school and perform well at work.

FOLLOWING MY MUSE

BY
RAND SPERO

Rand Spero is president of Street Smart Financial, a fee-only financial planning firm. He provides comprehensive financial services to help clients organize, increase and protect their assets through life transitions. Rand teaches personal finance and strategic planning classes at universities in the Boston area. He also contributes articles to the *HumbleDollar* website, and hosts the podcast series *Financial Crossroads*.

WHEN I WAS a young boy, my grandmother kept telling me, "You must go into the family warehouse business." She was a product of the Great Depression. To her, this well-established business represented security. Many people would crave an offer of financial stability and a career roadmap. But I hated the feeling that my life path was being dictated by my family.

Maybe my financial journey was complicated by two competing influences—my father and my mother. My businessman father, who had gone into his own father's warehouse business, made life choices based on their financial return. He had enjoyed going to college in California, but succumbed to family pressure and returned to Youngstown, Ohio, to join the warehouse business.

Meanwhile, my cosmopolitan mother, who grew up in Manhattan, had a more expansive worldview. She valued ideas and diverse experiences, and encouraged me to find my own voice and remain curious. Perhaps influenced by my mother, I wondered how intellectually stimulating it would be to run a warehouse in northern Ohio.

During my high school years, our struggling steel-mill town saw its main industry start to collapse. It never recovered. Even though our family enjoyed a comfortable lifestyle in a leafy suburb, the region was marked by poverty. My family's home was worth $100,000 in 1970. If you simply adjusted for inflation, the house should be worth more than $725,000 today. Instead, it's currently valued at less than $150,000. Working in the family business would have meant living in this declining community.

GETTING EDUCATED

While attending Vassar College in New York's Hudson Valley, I became intrigued by psychology. My college advisor suggested I pursue a doctorate in clinical psychology, but that sounded too narrow to me. Instead, I was more interested in social psychology and the influence of group dynamics. My favorite economics professor stressed that human emotions can distort financial choices. It was the beginning of a lifelong interest.

Even though I felt pressured to go into the family business after graduation, I delayed any career decision. I half-heartedly took the Graduate Management Admission Test and applied to business schools, even though I had no real-world business experience.

I was fortunate that my parents had paid for my undergraduate education. But I knew I'd have to foot the bill for graduate school.

That's why I chose the MBA program at the University of California at Los Angeles, where tuition was lower than at top-rated private schools.

While attending UCLA, I concentrated on strategic marketing, while also working as a teacher's assistant for two organizational behavior classes. I was still unsure about pursuing a business career and considered becoming a full-time academic. Despite more than 300 business recruiters coming to campus, I graduated without signing up for a single job interview. The only definitive career decision I made during the two-year program was to reject going into the family business.

Not pursuing job interviews and seemingly forgetting about my pending MBA debt was out of character. I wanted to be financially responsible. Yet I felt so stressed and ambivalent about working for any business, I became stuck. At age 24, younger than most of my MBA classmates and with no significant work experience, I needed to find a sense of purpose. I was convinced things would fall into place once something got me excited.

THE FUTURE FORETOLD

While many of my fellow business school classmates took the summer off before starting their new jobs, I devoted that time to regrouping. I found temporary work to pay bills, swam and biked to clear my head, and spent time in the library exploring career ideas. Within a month, I was inspired by reading Alvin Toffler's futuristic book *The Third Wave*, which argued that the developed world was moving from an industrial age to an information age. He predicted that the information and entertainment world would become decentralized, and new cable services would lead to a social transformation. My interest was piqued.

I attended cable industry conferences that summer and diligently studied future trends. I targeted a specific company, Continental Cablevision, known for its high-quality and innovative management team. Thanks to the knowledge and insights I'd picked up through my research, my interview at the Boston headquarters went well and, in the fall, I was offered the position of director of corporate marketing.

My new bosses gave me a fair amount of autonomy. The work offered variety and the growing company granted flexibility. The CEO and co-founder, a brilliant and successful Harvard Business School graduate who went on to become a billionaire, shared his philosophy with me. He hired bright people and gave them leeway, which he hoped they could handle.

I was grateful that no one tried to make me fit the corporate mold and that the company encouraged creativity. I had market research and customer service responsibilities. I also designed and taught company workshops that encouraged employees to buy into new corporate initiatives.

From a purely financial perspective, I knew I should stay with this thriving private firm, which would eventually be bought out for mega-bucks. After four interesting years, however, my academic itch had only gotten stronger. To the surprise of company management, I informed them of my plans to go to graduate school at Harvard to study organizational behavior. My boss wanted me to stay, and offered me a generous raise as an inducement.

Instead, I left on good terms to focus on my academic interests. The missed financial opportunities—leaving before Continental Cablevision's eventual buyout—mattered less to me than the chance to be more intellectually stimulated. Having the opportunity to study with world-famous professors felt liberating. I used personal savings from my corporate job to pay for the one-year master's degree program. My plan: Find a decent paying job with a company shortly after graduation.

SOME LIFE-CHANGING ADVICE

The lesson that made the biggest impression on me—and which changed my life—resulted from a paper I wrote for an instructor whose own book recommended using certain organizational techniques to create a strong company culture. In my critique, I praised the book's insights. But under each section, I added comments from my own perspective. I explained that I personally would feel too constricted working for an organization that used his techniques.

He wrote on my paper, "Great insights, you SHOULD DEFINITELY work for yourself!" This shocked me. I invited the professor to lunch and he graciously accepted. He explained that in class I appeared comfortable when presenting my point of view. Working for myself would require marketing ability, which he felt wouldn't be a problem for me.

I was a bit intimidated by the professor's suggestion. My financial goals had evolved as I turned age 30, and now included owning a home and supporting a future family. I had concerns that being self-employed came with some financial risk, such as not qualifying for a mortgage due to unsteady cash flow. Still, the idea of working for myself got me excited, and I began to envision what services I could offer my network of contacts.

My transition to self-employment went smoothly, thanks to my connections at Continental Cablevision. Right after graduation, my old employer—plus other managers who had left to work for other firms in the same field—hired me for numerous consulting projects. Working on a variety of marketing and organizational projects proved stimulating and financially rewarding. Had I not been lucky enough to have worked for an industry leader like Continental, which was respected by other firms, breaking in as a business consultant would have been more difficult. Within a few years, the steady consulting earnings allowed me to qualify for a mortgage to purchase my first home.

Most of my consulting projects involved marketing research and strategy, but my background in organizational behavior and teaching also allowed me to offer instructional workshops. Many managers find thick reports full of analysis boring. I tried to make my research and strategic reports come alive, and to encourage managers to reexamine their assumptions.

Rather than simply presenting research findings, the workshops I led encouraged managers to challenge their current plans. What research findings concerned them? Where was their firm most vulnerable? How would they attack their firm if they were a competitor? No challenge to accepted beliefs was considered off-limits. As one executive commented, "The sessions were exhilarating by allowing us to let go of assumptions, and terrifying to see how unprepared we were in key competitive areas."

Complementing my consulting work, I taught strategic marketing part time as an adjunct lecturer at a Northeastern University Graduate School of Management evening program. But what I found most enjoyable was instructing older adults in a community college program.

Financial necessity had forced the best of these students to get full-time jobs right after high school. If they hadn't been economically constrained, they would have thrived in college. Now, heading back to school later in life, they were passionate and driven. I volunteered to review some students' business plans, which were often impressive. Several went on to run their own successful companies.

Over time, the entertainment and telecommunication industry consolidated. Many of my consulting clients became business whales gobbling up smaller companies. My little fish clients, which were often the most innovative, felt an imperative to sell out. I found myself secretly rooting for the underdogs to stay independent.

THE ACCIDENTAL PLANNER

This new business environment felt confining and forced me to reassess my consulting career. Around the same time, I was asked to sort out the financial mess created by my parents' late-in-life divorce.

The warehouse business ownership split up after their divorce. My parents had owned half the company, which was divided between them. My older cousin—who managed the warehouse—owned the other half. My parents wanted someone they could trust on the company board. They asked me to join it to represent my mother's interests and to assist my aging father. I wasn't at all pleased by their urgent request, but I felt obligated to help. The warehouse business, which I had long ago rejected, still haunted me.

Participating in a family business sounds appealing to many people. But in this case, the relationship dynamics made everything more difficult. Upon joining the contentious board, I found out the building roofs and infrastructure needed substantial updating. Obtaining major bank loans for these unbudgeted capital expenditures, and redirecting management's focus, became a time-consuming imperative. I wanted to disengage from this quagmire and have the company, or at least my parents' shares, sold, so I could concentrate on my full-time career. But there was no existing provision for buying out an owner's stake, so everything became a difficult internal negotiation.

Meanwhile, after my parents' legal separation, my mother hired a broker who constantly churned her bond account, while charging high trading commissions. When I challenged this slick employee from a well-known financial firm, he claimed to have unique market-timing insights. Outraged, I compared his performance to Vanguard Group's intermediate-term bond index fund. I found he underperformed this benchmark by more than ten percentage points a year. It became apparent why older people—and others—

need a financial advisor they could trust. The self-serving hype of many financial providers motivated me to become a more educated investor.

My background in research statistics proved useful as I reviewed evidence-based studies. Nobel Prize-winner Harry Markowitz explained the value of portfolio diversification. John Bogle, the founder of shareholder-owned Vanguard, stressed the value of low-cost index investing. Eugene Fama, the renowned portfolio theorist, demonstrated how small-cap and value stocks could enhance performance.

The investing books that I found compelling highlighted why investors had great difficulty beating the market. I became a do-it-yourself investor, relying on well-diversified, low-cost U.S. and international stock index funds. I had slight tilts toward value and small-cap stocks, and I also invested in quality short-term bonds to limit volatility. To these, I added a few speculative stocks picked using my knowledge of information and entertainment companies.

Creating a low-cost diversified portfolio didn't seem too difficult. What proved more challenging was managing my own emotions and ego. Keeping up with current events and the latest market trends may have helped in my consulting work. But the financial markets were too complex to forecast, and overconfidence when investing can be treacherous.

I nevertheless found myself predicting where the market might be heading. It was all too easy to find confirming articles or have discussions that reinforced my opinions. Fortunately, I heeded the warnings of experts who criticized market-timing. Obeying John Bogle's maxim to "stay the course"—rather than act on market forecasts—saved me lots of money.

Advising families and other individuals about their personal finances seemed like a career possibility. I enrolled in Boston University's financial planning evening program, while continuing to consult during the day. I had concerns about business models that depended on commission-based brokerage fees and insurance sales. That led me to embrace a fee-only financial advisory model that followed the fiduciary rule—clients' interests come first.

A FORK IN THE ROAD

My background in strategic planning and psychology seemed well suited to financial planning. Yet I questioned whether it made financial sense for me to give up a solid 20-year consulting practice. Perhaps I should keep consulting and gradually add personal finance clients?

Then, unexpectedly, a longtime consulting client offered me a chance to dive in. This wealthy entrepreneur had worked in the cable, entertainment and search engine businesses. By age 50, he was set for life and had been able to provide his children with substantial trust funds.

He offered to jumpstart my financial management career by providing me the opportunity to oversee these trust accounts. He made a stipulation, however, that I must stop all business consulting. He insisted personal investing and financial planning would require my full attention. I contacted other prospective clients and found a receptive audience. Since I no longer found consulting especially satisfying, I agreed to focus on my new career.

What bothered me most about the financial services industry was its emphasis on generating investment buys and sells. I wanted a practice that instead cultivated long-term relationships. Would a potential client be a good fit over time, regardless of her financial value to my practice? Rather than maximizing my advising income stream, like my traditional father might have suggested, I favored my mother's orientation toward quality connections with people.

As an advisor, two behavioral finance insights have proven invaluable. The first revolves around loss aversion. Studies show that people feel the loss of money much more intensely than an equivalent gain. I suggest to some clients that they may want to temper their aggressive investing approach. What, I often ask, about the potential impact of substantial losses on their lifestyle? Might they sell in a panic during tough times?

My second insight is that many clients' career choices have a big effect on both their finances and life satisfaction. Maintaining the status quo—staying in one place rather than considering career options—can prove limiting. This, of course, is a lesson I've learned myself. The path ahead can seem murky and changing course is often difficult. Professional and family commitments may weigh you down for an extended time. In my case, my father passed away three years ago. Last year, my cousin's son bought out my mother's and stepmother's warehouse shares. Finally, after reluctantly sitting on the board of the family business for two decades, I was free.

At this point in my journey, at age 66, I continue to enjoy working with clients and teaching, but I've expanded my approach. Now, I teach personal finance courses at adult education centers for senior citizens, while also guiding medical school residents at Boston-area teaching hospitals. I write blog posts and articles that cover financial behavior and planning topics.

Since I remain curious about other people's financial quests, I started a podcast series called *Financial Crossroads* that explores how people handle career and lifestyle transitions. My goal is to interview a range of people willing to share what's worked for them. A surprising bonus: My 93-year-old mother listens to—and comments on—my episodes.

What about my own journey? Managing my human capital hasn't meant making the most money possible, but I have earned a comfortable living. When I think about the people I admire most, it's those who feel they have *enough* and who enjoy giving back. I remind myself that success and failure have never been totally in my control. My goal: Follow my passion—and be grateful when things happen to go my way.

THREE LESSONS

* To have the life you want, sometimes you need to sacrifice the highest possible income.

* Don't let others dictate your career and financial path. A fulfilling life may require balancing practical requirements with following your curiosity and passion.

* Get to know yourself. Allow your goals to evolve over time rather than sticking to a rigid roadmap.

RISK AND RETURN

To earn high returns, we need to take high risk. But will that risk be rewarded? Sometimes, it is. But often, the results aren't so great, as you'll learn from some of the essays in this section. And frequently, the better strategy is to focus less on boosting returns—and more on managing risk, another topic tackled in the pages ahead.

FACING DOWN RISK by Adam M. Grossman

A BAD BUSINESS by Juan Fourneau

FIVE TIMES LUCKY by Charles D. Ellis

A DAY TO REMEMBER by William Bernstein

MY EXPERIMENTS by James McGlynn

A COSTLY EDUCATION by John Lim

LEARNING BY ERRING by Michael Flack

FACING DOWN RISK

BY
ADAM M. GROSSMAN

Adam M. Grossman is the founder of Mayport, a fixed-fee wealth management firm. He advocates an evidence-based approach to personal finance. Adam has written regularly for *HumbleDollar* since 2017, penning almost 300 columns.

IN REFLECTING ON his life, Apple founder Steve Jobs noted that, "You can only connect the dots looking backward." When we're the authors of our own story, it's all too easy to connect those dots in a way that's most flattering to ourselves. But to be useful to the reader, a narrative must be honest—and it should start at the beginning.

My first money memory dates to the early 1980s. I was maybe ten years old and sitting at the kitchen table with my father, who was looking over some papers. It was his office's new retirement plan, he said. My dad was a lawyer. He explained that, with this new plan, employees were going to be allowed to choose their own investments. That sounded interesting and like a good idea—for about one second.

Then my dad described how difficult it was for each person to be his or her own investment manager, picking and choosing from among all the options. Especially after the 1970s—a dreary decade for stock investors—it was hardly clear that the right move at that time would be to invest heavily in the market. With the benefit of hindsight, of course, that was the perfect time to jump into stocks with both feet. But no one knew then that a two-decade-long bull market was just getting started.

At the time, I didn't even have a savings account. But I could understand the challenge my dad was describing, suddenly being put in the position of being his own investment manager. It was no different from asking an investment manager to become his own lawyer. It didn't make a lot of sense. The same was true for my father's colleagues—fellow lawyers, secretaries, IT folks. All were experts in their respective fields, but not in investments. The task seemed difficult, if not completely unreasonable. But that was only part of what made it difficult.

In every family, there are subjects that aren't talked about very much. They aren't necessarily secrets, but they simply aren't anyone's favorite topic. That was certainly the case in my family. The story goes back to the 1890s, when my great-grandfather emigrated to the U.S. Soon after arriving, he began selling odds and ends off a horse-drawn wagon. Over time, that evolved into a chain of stores selling lumber and building materials. All went well until the late 1960s, when the family decided to sell to a larger retail chain.

What happened next was unfortunate: Like a lot of acquisitions, the larger company paid mostly in stock. In the doldrums of the 1970s, the larger company's stock lost much of its value. If I had to guess—and I'm only speculating—that unpleasant experience factored into my dad's thinking that day as he considered how much risk to take in his new retirement plan.

This early memory from the kitchen table has always stuck with me. It was the first time I had learned anything about the stock market, and it didn't seem like a lot of fun. Over the years, I've learned much more, and it's now part of my job. But to be honest, I still view the market as a hall of mirrors—and that's on a good day. I'm probably giving my ten-year-old self too much credit, but it may have been on that day, at the kitchen table, that I started getting interested in investments.

Aside from that experience, I didn't think a lot about financial matters as a kid. I did start a business in high school—selling sunglasses via mail order. But the years up through college were otherwise uneventful from a financial point of view. College tuition was high, but it hadn't yet reached today's absurd level, and I was able to graduate with no debt. For that, I'm eternally grateful to my parents.

Things changed, though, when I finished college. Instead of pursuing a traditional job or going to grad school, I instead decided to start a business. I had enjoyed the experience in high school of creating something from nothing, and I wanted to try it again. Thus started the next phase of my financial life, which couldn't have been more different from the tranquil financial life I had enjoyed up until then. It was a roller coaster.

LEFT WITH A NAME

The business I started was a software company—a sort of internal social network for large companies. It was a reasonable enough idea, and I had some success selling the product. Customers included law firms, hospitals and companies like Johnson & Johnson. In the late 1990s, I raised one round of financing. But in the end, I wasn't able to build it into a large enough business before the 2000 dotcom crash.

Being in my 20s, this wasn't a big deal. I'd learned a lot from the business and I was happy to try something new. There was just one problem: At the moment when I wanted to lean on my savings, they evaporated. What happened? During the 1990s, I had started working with a stockbroker. He seemed like a good choice. He was a family friend. He worked for a well-known firm. He seemed experienced. And he had a DeLorean in his driveway, which seemed to indicate success.

For a time, I thought things were going well. He had built a portfolio of stocks for me and, through the late 1990s, it grew. What I understood only later was that it was barely diversified. The bulk of it was invested in a handful of technology stocks, which all dropped at the same time. On top of that, because the broker had suggested I borrow against my stock holdings to buy a car, the whole portfolio went, more or less, to zero.

From a financial point of view, this was a disaster. I wondered why this experienced financial professional had stacked the cards this way. The silver lining: It helped plant the seed for my later career as a financial planner. It motivated me to want to help others in all the ways that my stockbroker had not. In fact, in my work today, I mostly just do the opposite of what I experienced as a client back then. I work to understand a client's needs in detail before designing a portfolio. Instead of picking stocks and building a concentrated portfolio, I diversify with funds. Instead of using high-cost funds with sales charges, I stick with low-cost index funds. Instead of betting too heavily on a rising stock market, I'm always preparing for a rainy day. And I'm wary of leverage.

It's a cliche to say that, when one door closes, another opens. But sometimes, that happens right on cue. In the aftermath of the dotcom crash, as I was reassessing my business, I received an inquiry. It turned out that this other startup wasn't that interested in my company. Instead, it wanted to buy my company's domain name. We almost had a deal—for an amount that might have paid for a (modest) new car. But the prospective buyer backed out when he found that another startup had filed a trademark application that would have posed a conflict.

On the advice of a quick-thinking lawyer, I reached out to the other startup using the contact link on the company's website. The email I received in response came from the young company's founder, who turned out to be a college student. It took some time, but we eventually reached an agreement. Because his company was just getting started, he didn't have a lot of cash to offer. At the same time, his early results seemed promising, so we agreed that the deal would include some stock.

For a time, that stock was no more meaningful than a piece of paper in the back of a file drawer. But over time, the company enjoyed impressive growth and eventually it went public, making its early employees and their backers very wealthy. Ironically, this was the sort of bet that my old stockbroker was pursuing—buying tech stocks and hoping to catch lightning in a bottle. In a funny kind of way, it validated his strategy. But I draw the opposite conclusion: I view the startup that bought my domain name as the exception that proves the rule. Sure, there are stocks that go to the moon. But the number is small compared to all of the companies started each year, and it's small even compared to all the companies that are currently public.

DECISION TIME

For a variety of reasons, I'm not going to name the company involved and, in any case, it's not that important. What is important: The decision I had to make. What did I do with the stock after it went public?

The data say that investors are better off, on average, going with index funds than trying to pick stocks. At the same time, I have a healthy respect for the entertainment that stockpicking can provide. It's far more fun to pick stocks than to invest in index funds. But it's important to separate entertainment from investing, and to recognize the odds associated with each. I don't look at individual stocks as poison, to be avoided at all costs—just as I don't look at the occasional Powerball ticket as completely reckless. That's why my recommendation to the families I work with is this: If you want to pick stocks, do it in a separate account, with a fixed—and small—percentage of your portfolio.

So what did I do with the stock after the startup went public? The answer: I took my own advice. I sold a lot of my shares and diversified. Because I'm still working, with a number of years until retirement, I kept most of the money invested in the stock market. But instead of one stock, I chose a set of Vanguard Group index funds that cover most of the world's markets. In the U.S., this includes the S&P 500 and the extended market index. The latter includes everything outside of the S&P 500. Together, these are the equivalent of a total stock market index, but I bought them separately so that I could control the mix, tilting toward mid- and small-caps. Also in the U.S., I chose Vanguard's large-cap value and small-cap value index funds. In overweighting small-cap and value stocks, I'm acknowledging their record of long-term historical outperformance.

Ten years later, what's been the result of this effort to diversify? There's no doubt that, if I'd just held the one stock from the IPO, it would have been a better move financially. Still, I don't regret diversifying. In fact, I don't think investors should ever regret spreading their investment bets widely. The reason: Even with all the antacid in the world, it's simply too nerve-racking to have the majority of your net worth tied to the fate of any one company. As I write this, the company's stock is down almost 50%. Because I sold most of my shares, I haven't lost much sleep over the decline. That, I think, is how it should be with any investment portfolio. Harry Markowitz, father of Modern Portfolio Theory, once described diversification as the only free lunch in the world of investing. Others have observed that the optimal portfolio isn't the one that has the greatest growth potential. Rather, it's the one you can live with. I agree with both sentiments.

MEASURING SUCCESS

My grandfather, who ran the family's retail business, was an unconventional guy. One side of his business card, which was bright orange, included just the word "SMILE" in large block letters. On the other side, it carried this quote: "Success is never final, failure is never fatal." That line is sometimes attributed to Winston Churchill. It certainly applies to personal finance.

As I said at the outset of this essay, we're each the author of our own story. We can connect the dots in any way we wish. The story I've presented here is factual. But I've probably left out a few of the less flattering detours along my financial journey. The reality is, anyone who has ever been involved in a startup can romanticize the experience and later laugh about the financial gymnastics required to keep things going. But I'm sure I have more gray hair than if I'd taken a more conventional road.

Research has shown that, once a family's annual income exceeds a threshold of around $75,000, happiness doesn't necessarily continue increasing along with income. I have to agree with this. At a certain point, many people reach what the late Jack Bogle, founder of Vanguard, called "enough." That's why the investment benchmark I use isn't the S&P 500. Instead, it's a concept that's more fundamental: contentment and peace of mind. That may not sound very rigorous, but I believe it's true.

What brings people happiness? Here's what I've observed among folks later in life: It's things like living within walking distance of adult children. Taking grandchildren for bicycle rides. Taking a camper up to the mountains or loading the kids in the car for a trip to the beach. Training for a marathon. Working part time, just for the enjoyment of it.

I know that when I say this, I run the risk of sounding like an idealist. I'm not suggesting that we all become ascetics. There's no doubt that more money in the bank carries many benefits. Among them: the option of early retirement, the chance to explore the wider world and the opportunity to engage in philanthropy on a grander scale. In the end, of course, it's a balance. As the title of this book suggests, it's a journey. And that's probably as it should be.

THREE LESSONS

* The optimal portfolio isn't the one that has the greatest growth potential. Rather, it's the one you can live with.

* Highflying stocks catch our attention and make winning seem easy. But these highfliers are a rarity—which is why the prudent strategy is to avoid trying to pick the next hot stock and instead diversify broadly.

* What's the best measure of financial success? It isn't beating the S&P 500. Instead, it's the degree to which your financial life brings you contentment and peace of mind.

A BAD BUSINESS

BY
JUAN FOURNEAU

Juan Fourneau, who is married with two children, recently retired from the ring after spending 25 years on the independent wrestling circuit. He wrestled as a masked Mexican Luchador under the name Latin Thunder. When he isn't at his manufacturing job, he enjoys reading about personal finance and investing.

I F YOU ASKED me about my financial life, I could regale you with stories about working the swing shift at the local chemical plant, or the rental properties I've invested in, or my efforts to make a living as a professional wrestler. But instead, I'm going to tell you about the coffee shop—so perhaps you can learn from my biggest financial blunder.

In 2009, as the financial world was falling apart around us, I saw a classified ad describing a small business for sale. A drive-through coffee shop had recently closed. The owner of the equipment and the landlord were both trying to find a buyer who would operate the business. I was intrigued.

At the time, I already owned a fourplex apartment and two single-family homes, and was renting them out. Thanks to my forays into rental real estate, I felt I could accurately evaluate business deals. Indeed, I'd also looked at laundromats, small apartments, foreclosures and other small deals—and didn't bite on any of those.

Still, I was looking for my next business challenge. I had married in 2007, and our daughter was born in 2008. I'd held off buying anything during that first year as a parent, as I adjusted to the change. But after a while, I felt that—between my rental properties, my job at the chemical plant and my young family—I was managing my time well.

As I got details about the coffee shop from the landlord, huge red flags emerged. Books I had read over the years about Warren Buffett's teachings, coupled with my experience as a landlord looking at properties, were warning me: "Danger ahead."

The biggest red flag: The landlord was a fantastic local lawyer and business mogul, and yet he told me he couldn't provide the shop's sales figures. I was looking at buying a business despite lacking key data and knowing nothing about the industry. But hubris led me to ignore such warning signs.

I sat down and did some back-of-the-envelope math. The shop's rent was modest: $300 a month plus utilities. It was solely a drive-through, with no inside seating. It was in the industrial part of our Iowa town. I drove by it every workday, and I knew that the level of passing traffic was tremendous. It was one city block from the Hardee's franchise where I had worked as a teenager. I had been employed at Hardee's on and off over the years, becoming an assistant manager, so operating a restaurant-type business didn't intimidate me. I felt that this was within my circle of competence.

Boy, was I wrong.

My wife was supportive of buying the equipment and trying to make a go of it. She had worked in retail, and done some bartending and waitressing. We felt confident that we could operate the shop. It would only be open from 6 a.m. to noon, so it wouldn't take up our whole day. My basic numbers said that sales of $100 a day would produce a profit.

I knew that the previous owner had done well with the shop for a few years when it was on the north end of town, the site of most of the city's restaurants and stores. Development by the local mall had forced the owner to move, however, and the shop reopened on the south end of town. Why the previous owner had given up the shop wasn't clear. We were told that it might have been personal reasons, not necessarily that the shop was losing money.

We settled on a purchase price of $9,000 for the equipment. We bought a few more items that we felt we needed, such as an industrial blender, as well as some inventory. Because we didn't know how to operate the espresso machine, we hired a trainer who had owned a shop in Canada. She was fantastic, and trained my wife and me on the ins and outs of making great lattes. It's embarrassing to recall now that I had had a latte only a handful of times. I had never visited Starbucks in the nearby bigger cities. Despite having driven by the shop on my daily commute, I had stopped to try it just once.

LEARNING THE BUSINESS

On the first day, I handed a lovely customer a caramel latte. She was so happy that we were open, and I was proud of our drinks. After completing her order, I had a moment of dread, though. I could see why the previous owner had done so well on the north end of town but struggled at the new location. This woman was clearly an affluent professional, our target demographic. But I also knew from my five years of working at Hardee's that affluent, professional women were scarce in the neighborhood. Almost all the passing drivers—and we saw lots of them—were men on their way to the nearby factories. There, they drank regular coffee, not lattes. For many of them, that coffee was provided free by their employer. Those men also worked shifts, in some cases starting before we opened each day.

We had a few promising Fridays and Saturdays when we broke $100 in sales. One Saturday, during fantastic weather, we took in $153. I realized our prices were too low, but changing them would have required paying for new menu signs.

As days of operation turned into months, we began to learn the business. We found a good roaster of excellent espresso and drip coffee. We made a deal with a local grocery store to buy half-and-half and milk at low prices. We cut out supplies that I had thought we would need but that turned out to be unnecessary. For instance, our espresso machine filtered our water, so I didn't need to pay for filtered water.

Also, I thought I was buying a coffee shop, but what I bought was a latte shop. Lattes were 90% of our business, and I had been blind to that when I purchased the equipment. If I had worked two weeks at a Starbucks, I would have known so much more about the coffee business and how it operates. In short, I wouldn't have bought the shop—or, at a minimum, I would have had the knowledge and experience needed to have some chance of success.

Within three months of opening, we were bleeding money. My wife wisely suggested that we cut our losses and eat the monthly rent on the one-year lease we had signed. That way, we wouldn't lose additional money every month, and we wouldn't be tied to the shop seven days a week. We had been trying to have another baby, and we got the good news that my wife was pregnant. But my stubbornness couldn't get past the money we had invested. I didn't foresee the business improving dramatically, but I wanted at least to finish the lease.

That was a mistake. The business was doomed. Our target customers weren't in our part of town. Even if the business had been more successful, the time we were spending at the shop wasn't worth the small profit we might have made.

As my wife's pregnancy progressed, her time at the shop dwindled and then ended. All the while, sales declined as summer ended and cold weather arrived. I had assumed that people drink more coffee in the winter, but the opposite is true. It was no different from my days in fast food: Summer was the busiest time. By contrast, my buddies who worked for grocery stores said winter and holidays were their biggest sales periods.

Meanwhile, thanks to the 2008–09 financial crisis, my 401(k)—which had performed so well—plummeted from a high of $147,000 in spring 2008 to $90,000 by the time I bought the shop in May 2009. I had a sizable portion of my 401(k) in my employer's stock, and the company was hit that summer by bad news and Chinese competition. My 401(k) sank further, to $75,000.

Just as my retirement portfolio hit a low, my wife's pregnancy became challenging. She developed kidney stones. My losses from the coffee shop meant I couldn't pay all our bills. I was falling behind on the groceries, my electricity bill and my mortgage payment. I had no choice. I took money from my 401(k) at the worst possible time, when its value was down. I was confident that my investments would rebound, but I didn't have the luxury of time—because the bills kept piling up.

When my son was born in January 2010, we knew that we would sell or close the shop when our lease ran out at the end of April. We were fortunate to find a young buyer who was willing to pay half what we had paid. I was honest about the shop's failure to turn a profit in the year we operated it.

LONG ROAD BACK

My wife sees the positives in our year of owning the coffee shop. We met some wonderful people. But to me, the financial repercussions seemed to last for the next decade. I've come to terms with the fact that almost everyone who launches a business suffers setbacks and failures. Still, being humbled by your mistakes, ignorance and blind spots is tough. It's painful to know your family and loved ones suffered because of your poor judgment.

In 1965, before I was born, my mom and dad had moved to Iowa. Every Hispanic family we knew in the area had the same story: Head north to a cold city where little to no Spanish was spoken. Most arrived from South Texas or Mexico. All were seeking a job and an opportunity to improve their family's future. Many in our community had found that opportunity in Iowa—opportunity that had been kept from their families for generations. They bought homes, raised families and lived the American dream. Now that I was a husband and father, I marveled at all of them and the hardships they must have endured. Now, I also had to accept my share of hard times.

During this period, I often thought of my father and the example he set. "Keep moving forward," he would tell us. I tried to focus on what I had going for me. Though I had gained 30 pounds from neglecting my workouts and diet, I had my health. My wife had fully recovered from delivering our son a month early. Alex was healthy and doing well. I had my steady, good-paying job at the chemical plant, which I now appreciated more than ever. If I worked an hour, I got paid for an hour. Regardless of my company's latest quarterly results, I got paid for my work.

Time would be my friend as I licked my wounds and ate my humble pie. "I could dig myself out of this," I would tell myself as I went to work.

Slowly, my 401(k) recovered. I try not to think of where it'd be today if I had left it alone during the depths of the Great Financial Crisis. I remember reading somewhere that it's too bad that losers don't write books because you learn a lot from mistakes. I'm not a loser. But I feel the same way about the coffee shop that I feel about my professional wrestling career. I didn't 'make it.'

For 26 years, I competed in wrestling matches across the Midwest, hoping to hone my craft. But during the first two decades, I never put myself in a position to learn from a mentor and consistently practice my trade. Then, in 2019, I asked WWE (World Wrestling Entertainment) superstar Seth Rollins if I could train at his wrestling school in Davenport, Iowa. Finally, I had a ring, talented young wrestlers to work out with and an atmosphere that drove me to get better. But at age 49, that hard ring and my aging body were letting me know the journey was ending. I never got that WWE contract but I had a better career than most independent wrestlers.

By contrast, the beauty of the money game is that you can play for as long as your mind stays sharp. Make a mistake? Learn your lesson and keep going. Today, I define my circle of competence narrowly. I recently drove by a carwash that was for sale and kept driving. My job is my main source of income. We now have a good real estate business consisting of a fourplex and eight single-family homes. I don't manage any of my properties, allowing me to focus on my family, my job and enjoying my workouts. My property managers are far more skilled and have a better temperament for the job. We own two of the rental homes free and clear. My long-term goal is to have six paid-off rental homes to help fund our retirement.

I hope to retire from my job at the chemical plant six years from now, at age 55. In addition to my 401(k), I have a Roth IRA and a brokerage account. These two accounts should help pay for my early retirement years until I claim Social Security. We'll also have the rental income, which should provide around $3,000 a month, and my pension, which will amount to $800 a month.

If I hadn't blundered with the coffee shop and had to tap my 401(k), I would have been able to retire even earlier than 55. On the other hand, I'm certain that if I hadn't made that foolish investment, my arrogance would have led me to make an even bigger blunder, one that might have wiped me out. We all make missteps. I'm grateful that my financial fall came earlier rather than later—and that I learned from my costly mistake.

THREE LESSONS

* When you realize you've made a financial mistake, move quickly to cut your losses—before a small financial hit becomes a large one.

* Stocks are a great long-term investment that can have horrendous short-run results. Try to avoid putting yourself in a position where you need to sell your stocks and stock funds at short notice.

* When you succeed financially, resist becoming overconfident, or you may find yourself making risky investment bets that come back to haunt you.

FiVE TiMES LUCKY

BY
CHARLES D. ELLIS

Charles D. Ellis is the author of 20 books, including *Winning the Loser's Game*, which is now in its eighth edition, with 650,000 copies sold. His two most recent books are *Inside Vanguard* and *Figuring It Out*. Charley has taught investing courses at both Yale and Harvard business schools, and he served for 17 years on Yale's investment committee.

L UCK HAS BEEN a key element in my financial journey. My good fortune has come in stages, beginning with my parents teaching me the lessons of saving and moderate spending. They valued education, supporting me as I attended first Yale for my undergraduate degree and then Harvard Business School.

After business school, I was fortunate to be hired as a junior analyst by the Rockefeller family office. This got me into the investment world, that most interesting line of work. In the early 1960s, there were no courses on investing at Harvard Business School. Obviously needing to get educated on investing, I was delighted that my employer would pay the cost of courses at New York University night school.

Over the next several years, I worked on my PhD. My timing was fortunate. Older professors taught traditional securities analysis, while younger faculty taught modern portfolio theory and efficient markets. I also studied to become a Chartered Financial Analyst. This three-way education gave me a unique opportunity to learn advanced best practices in investment management.

Meanwhile, I had moved on to Wall Street, taking a job with Donaldson, Lufkin & Jenrette, a leading research-based stockbroker. I was assigned to cover major clients in Boston, New York and Philadelphia. Each client had a stellar team of bright, hard-working, highly competitive analysts and portfolio managers, and each of these teams had its own concept and process for winning the battle for superior investment performance.

With several dozen clients, I was blessed with an extraordinary opportunity to learn from each. I was also able to see that as smart and hard-working as each group was, they were competing against each other. They all read the same research coming out of Wall Street and they all had access to the New York Stock Exchange, where corporate filings required by the Securities and Exchange Commission were available.

Two things seemed clear: Not all could win every year, and those who won this year seldom won again next year. As performance measurement firms were soon able to document, over the long term, many investment managers were falling short.

CASE CLOSED

The next phase of my good fortune was a series of annual three-day seminars I was privileged to lead, eventually for 30 years, in which the leading portfolio managers came together to discuss investing. This 'best of the best' assemblage made it even more clear that the competition in *The Money Game*—as George Goodman, writing under the pen name 'Adam Smith,' dubbed it in his bestselling book—was superb and intense.

During a break in one of the seminar's sessions, my friend Jay Sherrerd, co-founder of the investment firm Miller, Anderson & Sherrerd, said, "Did you know you can get Neff at a significant discount?"

John Neff, widely recognized as one of the all-time best mutual fund managers, had recently launched a dual-purpose closed-end fund named Gemini, after the mythological twins. Half the money in Gemini got all the dividends and half got all the capital gains—and all the losses. A severe bear market was particularly punishing to the value stocks in which John specialized, so Gemini's capital shares had taken a terrific beating. Because Gemini was a closed-end fund rather than a regular mutual fund, its shares traded on the stock market. At that time—1974—the capital shares were selling at a steep discount to the value of the fund's already-depressed portfolio.

Lucky me, I knew John well. He had a strong record of outperforming the market, and was unusually focused on understanding and managing risk. This presented me with a special opportunity. Believing the market was seriously oversold, particularly for the value stocks that John specialized in, I made an assumption that the market would not go down more than an additional 20%. Then, with maximum margin, I put all I had into Gemini's capital shares. In a few months, the bear market turned into a bull market, and value stocks outperformed the overall market. John's picks beat value stocks generally, and the double leverage of the duo-fund structure—and my hefty use of margin—multiplied one another in a most wonderful way. It was my first notable investment win.

My second winning experience came with Greenwich Associates, the consulting firm I founded in 1972. The firm had a profit-sharing retirement plan. Each year, the firm contributed 15% of each person's earned income. Added to this was the 2% to 3% left behind by those employees who didn't stay five years and so missed full vesting. And added to this was our early years' practice of investing in closed-end mutual funds that were likely to go open-ended. These open-endings—or conversions to regular mutual fund status—had the effect of eliminating the gap between the fund's share price and its higher underlying portfolio value. As Senator Everett Dirksen once said, "Pretty soon, it can add up to real money."

MEAL TICKET

My third winning experience was the best. I was pleased to be invited to lunch by Sandy Gottesman, the much-admired senior partner of First Manhattan and one of Greenwich Associates' clients. I hoped this would give me an opportunity to get him to adopt our recommendations for the firm's stockbrokerage business.

As we sat down at his regular table at his club, Sandy said, "We are not going to renew our engagement with you in stockbrokerage this year and I'd like to tell you why. Our research is focused on creative investment ideas, but your research shows that institutions want us to organize around coverage of whole industries. We don't want to do that. You also show that clients want us to get into block trading, which we also do not want to do. It's too risky for us."

I was about to offer Sandy our program on investment management for large corporate pension funds, but he said, "I know you have a great program on big pension funds, but that's not our market. We focus on smaller funds."

The conversation was effectively over and our lunch orders hadn't yet come. To fill the void, I said, "Sandy, thank you for being so open and courteous with me about your decision." Then, knowing Sandy was a very successful investor, I asked him to share his experiences with great investments.

He replied with one word: "Berkshire."

I had heard about Warren Buffett and the Buffett Partnership, so I asked, "How long have you invested in Berkshire Hathaway?"

"A long time."

"How long would you expect to continue owning it?"

"Forever."

While we ate our lunch, Sandy told me the Berkshire story, about how Buffett took control of an ailing New England textile company in 1965 and turned it into the vehicle he used to make a slew of extraordinarily successful investments, with an early focus on insurance. He then used the insurance company 'float'—the money earmarked for possible future claims by policyholders—to make further investments, eventually building what today is one of the world's largest companies.

Lucky as Sandy's recommendation was, it was actually perfectly matched by a fortunate situation. My partners and I had agreed to create a reserve fund in case our small firm ran into a bad earnings situation, so we wouldn't have to each scramble to put up more capital if we had an operating loss. The fund was only $100,000, but we thought that would be enough, if and when an emergency developed. The money was raised by simply slow-paying our year-end bonuses by a few months. We had agreed that the money would be invested in safe stocks and that I would recommend the portfolio. By the time Sandy had finished his reasoning for holding Berkshire Hathaway forever, the obvious move was to invest the whole fund in Berkshire. The result over nearly five decades has been superb—more than 300 times our cost.

EMBRACING AVERAGE

My fourth winning experience in investing: not losing the money I had made. I accomplished this by investing in index funds at Vanguard Group. Over the past 20 years, nearly 90% of actively managed stock mutual funds have fallen short of the market averages, often by large amounts. I believe indexing has saved me from considerable grief and losses. Indexing has also saved me time and concern. Other than Berkshire, my investment program is and has been simple: index.

I was so convinced by indexing's virtues that I became a proponent even before I could invest that way. In 1975, for the *Financial Analysts Journal*, I wrote an article entitled "The Loser's Game," where I argued, "The investment management business (it should be a profession but is not) is built upon a simple and basic belief: Professional money managers can beat the market. That premise appears to be false." More than a decade later, that article turned into a book that's now entitled *Winning the Loser's Game* and which has gone on to sell more than 650,000 copies.

My fifth winning experience in investing may surprise readers, but it's the one part of my experience that others might enjoy including in their overall financial strategy. I certainly recommend each person give it careful consideration. It's been a big win for me.

Scholarships for talented young people, that enable them to get first-rate educations and make the most of their talents, are a wonderful way to strengthen our society. It can also lead to unmatchable personal satisfaction. For me, providing scholarships for exceptional young people has been a joy. The importance that my parents put on education, and the steps they took to ensure I got the best available, has been a huge part of my success. It's a gift that I am more than happy to share with others. What a wonderful investment!

THREE LESSONS

* Most of us get so caught up in Mr. Market's short-term antics that we fail to recognize the great importance of Mr. Economy's long-term powers. Result: We end up paying high fees and high taxes, and changing investments far too often.

* Stock prices are driven by countless complicated factors. Chances are high that we don't know all that's going on— and what we do know is already known by the experts and already incorporated into share prices.

* Successful long-term investing rests on three key strategies. First, make saving a priority. Second, set realistic goals and settle on an investment policy most likely to achieve them. Third, have the discipline to stick with your investment policy.

A DAY TO REMEMBER

BY
WILLIAM BERNSTEIN

Bill Bernstein is a recovering neurologist, author and co-founder of Efficient Frontier Advisors. He's contributed to peer-reviewed finance journals and has written for national publications, including *Money* magazine and *The Wall Street Journal*. Bill has produced several finance books, including *The Four Pillars of Investing*, and also four volumes of history, the latest of which is *The Delusions of Crowds*. His life's goal is to convey a suitcase full of books and a laptop to Provence for six months—and call it "work."

JUST AS ANYONE around on September 11, 2001, November 22, 1963, or December 7, 1941, remembers where they were when they first heard the news, one date resonates for investors of a certain age: October 19, 1987.

As a young practicing physician, I was just finishing up the day's charting when I took a call from one of my colleagues: "Did the Dow fall enough for you today?" Indeed it had, by 508 points, or nearly 23%, and 36% off its peak of some weeks before.

Gulp. My net worth had plunged nearly six figures in just a few hours. In my unhappy state, though, it occurred to me that if I was comfortable owning stocks at Dow 2700, shouldn't I be even more comfy owning them at Dow 1800?

And so I held my breath and increased my stock exposure. This one salutary move, though, did not exactly herald a full flowering of financial wisdom. I continued to make mistakes: reading market-timing newsletters, trying to pick both stocks and active fund managers and time the market, and allowing my spirits to rise and fall on a daily basis with share prices. I even got taken in by 1989's spurious cold fusion excitement and went long palladium futures.

Fortunately, my financial journey got better from there. Not long after, I came across the books of Burton Malkiel and Jack Bogle, and began to immerse myself in the world of academic finance, particularly Eugene Fama and Kenneth French's work on market efficiency and factor investing. I taught myself to spreadsheet, which was far less ubiquitous back then than it is now. My portfolio, whose stock exposure now consisted entirely of low-cost passively managed funds, prospered. Perhaps most fortuitously, in the early 1990s, I came across Charles Mackay's *Extraordinary Popular Delusions and the Madness of Crowds*, which immunized me from the dotcom bubble that blew up a few years later.

Even so, I could have done things better. Here are two lessons that took me decades more to learn—and which could have made my financial journey far smoother:

First, a suboptimal portfolio you can execute is better than an optimal one you can't. Yes, it's true that, over most long periods, the more stock-heavy a portfolio, the higher its returns will be. The problem is that we humans are overconfident about most things, and none is more deadly to financial success than overestimating our risk tolerance. It's one thing to fire up a spreadsheet and simulate losing a large chunk of assets, but quite another when it happens in real-time. A good analogy is how experiencing a plane crash in a simulator compares with the real thing.

Never forget humorist and financial journalist Fred Schwed's famous injunction: "There are certain things that cannot be adequately explained to a virgin either by words or pictures. Nor can any description I might offer here even approximate what it feels like to lose a real chunk of money that you used to own."

Over the past four decades, I've learned that the prime prerequisite for a successful portfolio is that it *survives*. One occasionally comes across newspaper articles about a recently deceased janitor, secretary or kindergarten teacher's estate that surprises a charity with a multi-million-dollar bequest. Such stories always feature two common elements: first, the departed's frugality (anecdotes involving bus and subway transport are mandatory journalistic elements); and, second, that they invested over periods of around half a century.

By the same token, it's not uncommon to read about star money managers who flame out after a few years of shooting the lights out. The difference between these two narratives? The first group made sure their portfolios survived long enough for compound interest to work its magic. The best way of ensuring that is to have a portfolio that can be held through the inevitable episodes of economic and financial excrement hitting the ventilating system.

To wrap this first lesson up, I'll risk one more analogy. The financial markets are a car that conveys your assets across town from your present self to your future self. The roads are slick with ice and studded with giant potholes. If you drive fast, you might indeed get to your destination a lot quicker. But it's usually a bad idea.

Second, mentally compartmentalize your portfolio. For decades, whether it was my money or that of clients, I hewed to the conventional academic and financial practitioner wisdom of designing a single overall portfolio encompassing all assets. I still go through that exercise, and it still drives the security purchases and sales we make for ourselves and for our clients.

But here's what I'm doing behind the scenes: I'm mentally

dividing a given portfolio into two completely separate pools, the safe assets necessary to sustain body and soul—more on that in a bit—and the risky assets aimed at consumption decades hence. This mental shortcut is commonly called the 'two bucket' approach to asset allocation. You have a retirement bucket for your basic needs, along with a risk bucket earmarked for your aspirational desires—think BMW or first-class travel—and for future generations.

Investment guru and writer Charles Ellis observes that you can win the investment game in one of three ways: by being smarter, working harder or being more emotionally disciplined than the other participants.

The first two are clearly impossible. Wall Street is packed with folks with 175 IQs working 90 hours per week. But winning the emotional game is doable. The secret is to be able to say to yourself after share prices have halved, "I don't need to tap my stocks for decades. In fact, if I manage my portfolio well enough, in the long run that money will be going to my heirs and charities." If you can do that, you'll sleep soundly, your stocks will eventually recover and, when they do, you just might sell some and fatten your safe portfolio a bit. Remember, your portfolio's prime directive is *to survive*, and there's no better portfolio longevity tonic than a nice pile of 'sleeping money.'

The implications of this strategy are manifold, and apply differently at different ages. The young person might say, "Wait a minute. My portfolio is tiny. My safe assets won't even last me three months." While that's literally true, she still owns a large amount of bond-like assets in the form of her human capital, which dwarfs her retirement portfolio. What does it matter if her portfolio craters today? Three or four decades from now, it'll be fine, and the money added to it at today's low prices will likely be some of the best investments she'll ever make.

The retiree, because she has no human capital left, is in a

completely different place, and she had better have a nice pile of safe assets to see her through the hard times. How big should that pile be? Consider the following graph, which shows the peak-to-trough drawdowns for the broad U.S. stock market.

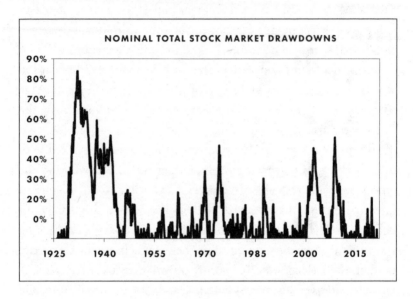

NOMINAL TOTAL STOCK MARKET DRAWDOWNS

These losses weren't always quickly recouped, especially once inflation is factored in. If you had owned stocks, the spending power of your stocks fell significantly over ten years on three separate occasions—by about 25% in the 1930s, 35% in the 1970s to 1980s, and by 45% during the 2007–09 global financial crisis. Further, despite the fact that overall long-term U.S. stock returns have held up well over the past century, the inflation-adjusted drawdowns seem to be getting worse.

Why is this? At the beginning of the 20th century, each dollar invested in stocks yielded about five cents in annual dividends. Even if stock prices fell, that 5% yield nicely cushioned the loss in share prices. Over the decades, that yield has fallen to well below two cents, which is a much thinner cushion.

Almost a century ago, economist John Maynard Keynes said this about owning stocks: "It is from time to time the *duty* of the serious investor to accept the depreciation of his holdings with equanimity and without reproaching himself." (Italics added.) Think you can time the market and avoid these drawdowns? Guess again. There is now almost a century of academic research demonstrating that no one has consistently done so, and the boneyard of Wall Street is littered with the remains of those who gained fame with one lucky call and then made spectacularly lousy forecasts for decades thereafter.

Now, let's see what this all means for the young investor and for the retiree.

Theoretically, even if the young investor puts 100% of his savings into stocks, those savings are so small relative to his bond-like human capital that his overall stock allocation is still quite small. Even knowing all that, our young investor with 100% stocks in his 401(k) plan may not be able to emotionally handle half of it disappearing for some years. Our young investor, then, needs to discover his real-world risk tolerance. Start with, say, a 50% stock-50% bond retirement portfolio, and see how you respond during a bear market. Were you able to buy more and up your stock allocation to, say, 75% stocks-25% bonds? If so, then great. Wait until the next time, rinse and repeat. Did you just barely hang on? Then 50-50 is probably about right. Did you panic and sell? Then even 50-50 is too aggressive.

For older investors like me, things are a bit more complex. Let's start with the simplest, and most felicitous, case. There are likely millions of retirees who have won the retirement trifecta with income from Social Security and an old-style corporate pension whose monthly payments meet or even exceed their living expenses and taxes. Their investment portfolio, then, really doesn't belong to them. Rather, it's destined for their heirs, charities and maybe even Uncle Sam. (Which applies, as well, to the essence of estate planning:

You can piss the money away, your heirs can piss the money away or the government can piss the money away. Your job is to pick the pisser.) The stock allocation of these fortunate individuals really doesn't matter at all to them and, by the time they're retired, they should have a good idea of their risk tolerance. If they've hung on in the past with 100% in stocks, then God bless.

The same is also true of retirees who need, say, less than 2% of their portfolio to meet living expenses. Since the dividend flow on their stocks should provide this, and since dividends do not decline very much for very long even in severe bear markets, then even a nearly 100% stock allocation with a small sliver of cash for emergencies, if tolerated emotionally, is fine, too.

Below that level of assets, things are a little dicier. For the retiree, holding ten years of living expenses in safe assets is barely acceptable, 15 years is better and 20 years' worth is optimal. Once you've filled your retirement safe-asset bucket, you can begin filling and growing your risk-and-aspirational bucket. Never forget, if you're going to survive retirement, your portfolio first has to survive. If you play portfolio Russian roulette, by taking more risk than you can handle during a frightening economic and investment crunch, you'll inevitably pay the price.

Thirty-five years after my 1987 baptism by fire, this is how I've come to view the great lifetime financial endeavor of amassing and then spending money. I often tell people that, when you've won the game, stop playing with the money you really need. Perhaps all would be fine if I kept 100% in stocks. But I'm now in my 70s and more interested in financial survival, which is why today I keep at least 20 years of living expenses in bonds and cash investments. That won't make me rich. Instead, I've done something more important: minimize my odds of dying poor.

┌─────────────── **THREE LESSONS** ───────────────┐

*   The best portfolio isn't the one that delivers the highest return, but rather the one that you can stick with through turbulent markets, so you enjoy the long-term benefits of investment compounding.

*   Once you've won the financial game, the goal isn't to get even richer but rather to avoid ending up poor. To that end, stop playing with money you really need.

*   Think of your portfolio as two buckets—the bucket that'll cover your spending a decade or more from now, and the bucket that'll carry you through the intervening rough spells.

└───┘

MY EXPERIMENTS

BY
JAMES MCGLYNN

James McGlynn, CFA®, RICP®, is chief executive of Next Quarter Century LLC in Fort Worth, Texas, a firm focused on helping clients make smarter decisions about long-term-care insurance, Social Security and other retirement planning issues. He was a mutual fund manager for 30 years. James is the author of *Retirement Planning Tips for Baby Boomers*.

I WAS BORN AT Carswell Air Force Base in Fort Worth, Texas, to a Canadian mother and a father who was raised in a Catholic orphanage. My mother and father both had civil service jobs. I was fortunate that my father was, by then, retired from the military, so I never had to move while growing up. I benefited from a stable home life, loving parents and good public education.

In high school, my only brush with business was taking four semesters of bookkeeping—a head start for accounting classes. My father taught me how to play tennis and I made our high school team in the Jimmy Connors–Bjorn Borg era. My high school minimum-wage jobs were as a dishwasher in a seafood restaurant and as a heating and air-conditioning assistant, mainly wrapping fiberglass insulation around air-conditioning ducts in attics. These jobs were motivation to go to college and earn a business degree.

When I began college in 1977, I was undecided between accounting and finance as my business major. One path was the field of public accounting and the 'big eight' firms. Another was finance and investing. I took many accounting classes but eventually was drawn more to investing, even though the stock market had been moribund for years, with the Dow Jones Industrial Average languishing below 1000.

My final class at the University of Texas at Austin was Modern Portfolio Theory. I did well enough that my finance professor suggested I apply for a job with the university's endowment fund after graduation. This proved to be excellent advice. It started me on a 35-year career as a money manager, the first of my two professions.

GETTING DOWN TO WORK

In 1980, at age 21, I was hired as a junior analyst at the Permanent University Fund, one of the largest college endowment funds in the country. The fund was initially seeded with enormous amounts of Texas scrubland, some of which turned out to be above huge oil deposits. The fund's substantial assets drew brokerage-firm analysts to our Texas offices. During these visits, they would educate us— and try to persuade us to buy and sell stocks through their firms. Their employers would earn commissions from us and, in exchange, we would get investing advice over meals at high-end restaurants.

When I began my career, trading costs and interest rates were high, and retirement accounts were relatively easy to understand, unlike today's bewildering array of choices. My first retirement investment was $2,000, which I invested in an IRA soon after the accounts became available to all workers. Since interest rates were so high, I invested in a Fidelity Investments' money market fund paying more than 15%. Meanwhile, in my taxable account, I remember my first individual stock purchase was John Deere. I bought 50 shares and paid $1 per share in commission to purchase them through a full-service broker.

I have been a lifelong learner. In addition to studying the investing business at work, I earned the Chartered Financial Analyst (CFA) designation, which takes a minimum of three years to complete. The CFA was starting to become a mandatory designation for those in the field of institutional investing. In 1983, I was one of the first 10,000 to receive the CFA, and it helped propel my career through several job changes with increasing responsibilities. Today, there are more than 175,000 CFA charter holders.

With my CFA freshly in hand, I took a job as a senior analyst at American National Insurance Co. in Galveston, Texas. I assisted in managing both the insurance company's stock portfolio and its mutual funds. Mutual funds were not as common then, and our funds charged a 7% front-end load, or commission.

The load was waived for employees, however, so I started investing both my taxable and tax-deferred money in the mutual fund I was helping to manage. I also began managing an equity-income mutual fund for my employer just months before the October 19, 1987, stock market crash, when the U.S. market plunged more than 22% in a single day. The weekend after the crash, I went to the office and made a buy list of the names in the portfolio that had declined to absurdly low levels. My assumption: If the market continued to decline, I'd lose my job anyway—so why not bet that stocks would recover? Fortunately, at the time, CNBC didn't exist to whip investors into an even greater state of panic. The abrupt loss was a shock, but the market quickly rebounded, recouping almost all its losses by year-end. With the market on the mend and now that I was established as a portfolio manager, I felt confident to embark on family life. In 1988, I got married.

A few years later, I parlayed my investment experience and CFA into a new job, which took me to Oklahoma City, where I worked for the state's largest money manager. When I left my home state with my pregnant wife in 1991, my only connection in Oklahoma was a coworker from Galveston who recommended me for the position. My daughter was born later that year and my son in 1995, just six months after the Oklahoma City bombing, which took place a few blocks from my downtown office.

After I became the lead manager for a newly launched mutual fund, I once again transferred my investment account into the fund I was managing. I guess you could say I was eating my own cooking. But I did diversify my holdings a bit. When the firm set up a SEP-IRA, I began dollar-cost averaging into an S&P 500-index fund for my retirement.

After eight years in Oklahoma, I took a new position with broader responsibilities at another insurance company, this one in Cincinnati. I was the firm's head of equity investing and managed more mutual funds. My move coincided with the beginning of the lost decade for stocks, which started with the dotcom bust of 2000 and ended with the 2008–09 financial meltdown. From 2000 to 2009, the S&P 500 turned in a cumulative total return of -9.1%.

Not only was the market unforgiving, I also missed my home state of Texas. I wanted to raise my Oklahoma-born children there. In 2006, I kept my job with the Cincinnati insurer, but returned to the Dallas-Fort Worth area and became a pioneer in the 'work from home' movement. I had hoped to work from home for perhaps two years. Nine years later, I called it a career and stopped working in active stock management. The stress of working from home and telecommuting was exacerbated by the 2008 financial meltdown, and my marriage ended in 2012. While I had witnessed setbacks like

1987's Black Monday and the 2000–09 lost decade, it had overall been a great era for investors. I had seen the Dow rise from under 1000 to over 17000 during my time in investment management. Amazingly, the Dow has doubled again since then.

SWITCHING GEARS

When I retired from money management, I was age 55 and felt I still had more to do, so I decided to set myself up for an encore career in retirement planning. My initial motivation: I was interested in researching retirement strategies and products that I might use myself.

To prepare for my encore career, I hit the books again. I researched the retirement planning certifications available and chose to pursue a Retirement Income Certified Professional (RICP) designation. I had to pass a three-part exam that covered all things retirement, including Social Security, Medicare, long-term-care insurance, annuities and portfolio withdrawal strategies. I soon realized I needed to become a licensed insurance agent if I wanted to sell the financial products about which I had just learned. I passed the health and life insurance exam, which allow me to sell life insurance, annuities and long-term-care insurance. All this education helped me to better analyze the investment and insurance offerings available to retirees.

What did I want to achieve with these products? Like many looking ahead to retirement, I had a handful of financial concerns. I didn't want to outlive my savings. I was worried about the potentially crippling cost of long-term care. I wanted to leave behind some money for my heirs. I was concerned that I could face steep taxes in retirement, especially once I turned age 72 and had to start taking required minimum distributions from my retirement accounts.

To address these worries, I began experimenting with a host of products and strategies, using myself as the guinea pig. My first foray was to purchase a whole-life insurance policy, which gave me a promised death benefit twinned with a tax-favored investment account. I wanted to create a pool of money that would pass tax-free to my heirs upon my death. I overfunded the policy with the maximum legally allowed, so I would get the greatest benefit from the tax-free cash buildup. Today, seven years later, the policy's cash value is growing at 3.5% annually. I tried to add a long-term-care rider to the policy, so I could tap the policy's value to pay for at-home care and similar costs, but I was deemed too risky by the insurer. I suspect it was because my medical records included three different surgeries—on my rotator cuff, hip and neck.

My second experiment: purchasing qualified longevity annuity contracts, or QLACs. These deferred-income annuities were appealing to me. I could use money from my traditional IRA to hedge against the risk of outliving my money. For a comparatively small investment, these annuities provide guaranteed lifetime income, with the payouts beginning relatively late in life—potentially as late as age 85. I already had a life insurance policy to benefit my heirs, so I opted for annuities that simply paid income for as long as I lived. These annuities potentially kicked off the highest monthly benefit but left no residual value for my heirs and there's a risk that even I won't receive anything, should I die before the payment period starts.

This made my next decision crucial. At what age should the annuity payments begin? I hedged my bets by buying three policies, each starting payments at a different age. It was a bit like putting chips down on three different numbers on a roulette table.

I invested $25,000 in a payment plan that starts at age 85. This investment would give me a high potential payout. The $25,000 I invested will kick off $18,000 a year for life—provided, of course, that I live until 85.

I invested in a second policy that begins paying out when I'm 76.

I wanted to generate $1,000 in monthly income from the policy. It turned out that could be accomplished if I invested $50,000.

With my third choice, I invested $50,000 to buy payments beginning at age 80. This will pay me $18,000 annually, should I live to receive it. That is the same amount of income I'll potentially receive from the policy that begins paying out at 85, and yet I had to invest twice as much to guarantee the same amount of income because it's scheduled to start paying me income five years earlier. After seven years, these QLACs are effectively worth twice what I invested, as interest rates have declined and there are seven fewer years before I start collecting.

TAKING CARE

My next retirement experiment came about almost by happenstance. As part of my information gathering, I would often go to hear sales pitches for various retirement products. I received an invitation for a presentation in Dallas on Medicare products and long-term-care (LTC) insurance. The presentation centered on hybrid LTC insurance, which involves twinning either a tax-deferred annuity or a life insurance policy with an LTC benefit. These policies involve making a large upfront investment, with the potential to receive some multiple of that sum as an LTC benefit, should you need care.

I left the meeting intrigued, though also dubious about the presenters' claims. Traditional LTC insurance has a terrible reputation, thanks to frequent and large premium increases. But according to the presenters, hybrid LTC was different. There would never be price increases. In addition, the presenters said that—if I changed my mind—I could get a full refund of the sum invested at any time. And they said insurers would accept candidates like me, whom a provider of standard long-term-care coverage would likely deny.

I felt I owed it to myself to investigate further. I took continuing education classes on traditional and hybrid LTC insurance. I questioned fellow professionals about the product. I even contacted former coworkers who worked for insurance companies that were offering hybrid LTC insurance. All this research eventually convinced me to purchase a joint policy for myself and my girlfriend. The "retirement smile," made famous by retirement researcher David Blanchett, posits that spending through retirement steadily declines until—late in life—steep medical costs kick in and retirement expenses climb again. Now, I feel prepared for that possibility.

Thanks to the LTC policy, I also feel free to spend at a higher rate from my portfolio earlier in retirement. I don't have to maintain a 'what if' LTC contingency fund to pay for my possible long-term care. I have even written a short ebook about hybrid policies, which discusses different examples and benefits. The policy designs are, I'll admit, a little confusing.

I now have multiple insurance policies in place: a whole-life policy, three QLAC purchases and a hybrid long-term-care policy. The next step in my experimenting was to decide how to maximize my Social Security benefits. I would receive the largest monthly payout if I delayed benefits until age 70.

I had read financial-planning expert Wade Pfau's article about building a Social Security "bridge," which is designed to replicate Social Security payments until benefits begin at age 70. I could use cash, a ladder built using certificates of deposit, or buy a period-certain annuity. It turned out the highest return would come from a so-called period-certain annuity, which could provide me with monthly checks from age 62 to 70.

After spending $125,000 from my trusty IRA for the QLACs, I withdrew another $200,000 for the period-certain annuity. It will provide me with $30,000 annually for eight years. I purchased the annuity four years before I turned 62 to lock in a higher payout rate.

Now, at age 62, I've begun receiving payments. When they end at age 70, my Social Security benefit will begin.

There has been one other key element to my retirement plan. At age 55, I converted $1,000 from my IRA to my Roth IRA for one simple reason: I wanted to start the five-year clock on my Roth account, so I would be eligible to take tax-free withdrawals—if needed—at age 60. I subsequently converted more assets to my Roth account, thereby reducing the size of my traditional IRA even further. This will ensure smaller required minimum distributions starting at age 72, leading to lower tax bills in my 70s and beyond.

I wanted to get these Roth conversions wrapped up by age 62. Why? When Medicare benefits start at age 65, the premiums can be higher—sometimes much higher—if your income is above certain thresholds. The tricky part: These Medicare premiums are based on your income from two years earlier—the year when folks turn age 63.

What's left on my retirement timeline? My next move will be to file for Medicare three months before I turn 65. I also plan to purchase two other insurance policies: a Medigap Plan G policy and Part D prescription drug coverage, which will supplement the coverage provided by Medicare. At age 70, of course, I plan to file for my Social Security benefit. Under current law, I will need to take distributions from my traditional IRA after 72. While I have reduced its balance substantially by purchasing insurance policies and through Roth conversions, I still have money in a traditional IRA. I may take advantage of so-called qualified charitable distributions to contribute that money directly to charity after age 70½ or, alternatively, leave part of the balance to my children.

Having spent seven years planning my retirement, I'm now turning my attention to enjoying the fruits of that planning, especially travel. Even though my grown children now live in Colorado, I enjoy taking them on adventures. So far, my children and I have been to the Amazon, Thailand and Egypt. I have taken my girlfriend to Aruba and to a coffee farm outside Medellin, Colombia. I have also traveled solo to Germany, the Czech Republic and Poland, where I taught English as a second language. My other retirement passion is playing pickleball, which is like the tennis I learned in high school, but easier on the knees. I've begun playing in pickleball tournaments and even volunteered at my local pickleball facility to be the pickleball commissioner.

What about the retirement planning business I launched? What began as an encore career morphed primarily into designing my personal retirement plan, while also advising friends and family on Social Security, Medicare, annuities and LTC insurance. I plan to continue helping others through my articles and books—and sometimes, in between games, on the pickleball court.

THREE LESSONS

* Consider delaying Social Security until age 70 and, in the meantime, build a "bridge" consisting of, say, bonds, certificates of deposit or a period-certain fixed annuity that will generate income until benefits begin.

* To ensure you don't outlive your savings, you might invest in deferred-income annuities, which involve handing over a large sum to an insurer today in return for guaranteed income later in retirement.

* If you can't qualify for traditional long-term-care (LTC) insurance, investigate hybrid policies, which couple cash-value life insurance or a tax-deferred fixed annuity with an LTC benefit.

A COSTLY EDUCATION

BY
JOHN LIM

John Lim is a physician, author of *How to Raise Your Child's Financial IQ* and a frequent contributor to *HumbleDollar*'s website. He's passionate about economics and finance, with a special interest in behavioral finance. John's hobbies include running and classical music.

THE PUNGENT ODOR of formaldehyde filled our nostrils. Rows of cadavers lay before us on cold metal tables. The class was gross anatomy and we were nervous first-year medical students. That day marked the beginning of our long, arduous journey to becoming physicians, lasting anywhere from seven to 13 years, depending on the specialty.

Money was the furthest thing from my mind that day. But for many of my peers, financial worries cast a long shadow. They had begun to amass a mountain of debt that would average more than $200,000 by the time they earned their medical degrees. That was on top of any existing debt carried over from college. Though blissfully unaware, I was at a huge advantage because I was unencumbered by student loans, thanks to the generosity of my parents.

I didn't exactly excel in medical school. Memorizing hundreds of muscles, bones and nerves just wasn't my cup of tea. I was more comfortable around numbers, which explains my passion for finance. But I'm getting ahead of myself.

After four years staked out in the library and hospital wards, I finally graduated medical school. Unfortunately, a medical degree hardly prepares you to practice medicine. That's the function of residency and fellowship, which come after medical school and often last longer than medical school itself. I chose to follow in my father's footsteps and pursue radiology, which meant another six years of training. I completed my radiology residency in San Francisco and fellowship in Palo Alto, which is where I married my medical school sweetheart. Despite the long hours and brutal nights when I was on call, I relished those years. I finally felt like I was making a difference in the lives of my patients.

One night, while on call as a resident, I read a scan of a young girl with suspected appendicitis. The appendix looked okay to me, but the girl's ovary had an unusual appearance—one which suggested possible ovarian torsion, a twisting of the blood supply to the ovary. This was unusual for a girl of her age. I immediately performed an ultrasound, which seemed to confirm my suspicions. I'll never forget the tears in her parents' eyes as I explained what I saw and the emergency surgery that would be required to salvage their child's ovary. That my actions could send a child to surgery—or send her home and cause her to lose an ovary—left an indelible impression on me. As a physician, I was entrusted with something both sacred and priceless—people's health.

Over the next six years, I pored over radiology textbooks and learned alongside some amazing radiologists. From a purely financial standpoint, it was an investment in human capital, and a sizable one at that. It cost my parents hundreds of thousands of dollars in medical school tuition, room and board, and it cost me ten years of my life. But ultimately, the investment would pay handsome dividends, both financially and vocationally.

In 1997, I earned $32,000 a year as a radiology resident. After contributing $9,500 to my 403(b) account and paying payroll taxes, my take-home pay was $1,500 a month. It wasn't a lot, but I never felt poor. I had plenty to eat and a roof over my head. Besides, most of my time was spent either working in the hospital or studying textbooks at home, and I was surrounded by peers who were doing the same. While my official training was in radiology, I was subconsciously learning a financial lesson of immense value—that you can lead a very satisfying life on a modest income.

Then it happened. A decade after that class in gross anatomy, I finally became an 'attending' or full-fledged physician. I landed a job in Southern California with a medium-sized radiology group and started working in earnest.

The transition from trainee to attending physician is absolutely pivotal in the financial journey of any physician. When a trainee becomes an attending physician, his or her income skyrockets. A fivefold or greater bump in income isn't uncommon. In some cases, this is followed by a second, albeit more modest, boost in income several years later, when the doctor becomes a full partner in the practice. Many physicians immediately grow into their attending salary. Imagine delaying gratification for a decade or more, spending most of your life in the library and hospital. The urge to splurge is powerful. Moreover, you're surrounded by colleagues who drive fancy cars, live in upscale neighborhoods and go on exotic vacations.

I'll confess, as a newly minted attending physician, I did my share of splurging. I replaced my beaten-up clunker with a brand-new Toyota Camry, and my wife bought a Lexus SUV. We moved into a two-bedroom apartment with a community pool and tennis courts—a big upgrade from the hole-in-the-wall we inhabited in San Francisco during residency. We also ate out and traveled more.

But on the whole, we were slow to upgrade our lifestyle. This meant we were able to save prodigious sums. Our savings rate ballooned, ranging between 40% and 60% most years. Living modestly on a physician's salary is a financial superpower. More than anything else, this paved our path to financial freedom. What's more, our relative frugality hardly diminished the joy we experienced. As researchers have discovered, the happiness we derive from money is subject to sharply diminishing returns.

HATCHING PLANS

A turning point in my financial journey occurred a few years into private practice, when I was asked to serve as a trustee for our group's retirement plans. At the time, our radiology group had a traditional 401(k) plan, a profit-sharing plan and a cash balance pension plan. As trustees, we were responsible for overseeing the three plans.

Our cash balance plan was a lot like a traditional company pension. Participants contributed pretax dollars to the plan. They were guaranteed a future payout based on their contribution history and the plan's investment returns. Since many of my partners made large contributions every year, the plan quickly grew to a substantial size. While the trustees didn't directly manage the investments, we oversaw the financial advisor who did.

By the time I became a trustee, our group had been working closely with the same advisor for many years. Many of my coworkers also hired him to manage their 401(k) investments. But I became increasingly disillusioned by what I saw. For example, the DoubleLine Total Return Bond Fund had been a staple of the cash balance portfolio for years. We had a few million dollars invested in that one fund alone. I noticed that the fund had two classes of shares, retail and institutional. For some reason, we were invested in the pricier retail shares. Those shares had a 12b-1 fee equal to 0.25% of assets, while the institutional fund didn't. This fee went to brokers who sold the fund.

Given our sizable investment in the DoubleLine fund, we were needlessly paying thousands of dollars in extra fees each and every year. When I asked our advisor why we weren't in the institutional share class, he promised to look into it. Months went by and we heard nothing. After more prodding, he moved us into the institutional shares without so much as an explanation.

On another occasion, our advisor proposed we make sizable investments in a nontraded real estate investment trust and a variable annuity, both inside our cash balance plan. Though our advisor never mentioned it, I discovered that both investments paid generous commissions to the selling broker—namely, our advisor. How much of our cash balance plan did he suggest we put in the annuity? "Just" 50%.

We ended up firing the advisor. These experiences reaffirmed my belief that no one cares as much about your money as you do. Don't get me wrong: There are many upstanding advisors who do good work, and they can add great value outside of portfolio management. But it's my view that once you know enough to separate the wheat from the chaff, you should consider managing your own investments. Don't underestimate the power of compounding: Saving 1% or 2% in fees over a lifetime can really add up.

While I was a trustee for our cash balance plan, I was also an investor. One of the most important decisions I had to make: whether and how much to contribute. Participants could choose their annual contribution amount up to a limit, as determined by their age and years with the group. The amount of money at stake was considerable. The more senior members, for example, could make tax-deductible contributions of $200,000 or more per year. In a high-tax state like California, this was very appealing.

But since a cash balance plan is a pooled account with a

guaranteed rate of return—for years, the 30-year Treasury yield was our benchmark rate—it had to be invested very conservatively. If the portfolio sustained a sizable loss, we would have to make up the shortfall. By "we," I'm referring to the participants in the plan, which was nearly everyone in our group. Because of this, the plan typically kept about 70% in bonds, with the remainder in stocks. Such a conservative allocation was destined to generate modest returns.

The consensus among my partners was that the tax benefits far outweighed these limitations. I wasn't convinced. Given the enormous money at stake, I ran some numbers. My fundamental question: Should I save large sums in the tax-deferred cash balance plan with its low expected return—or should I pay taxes on my earnings and then invest in a taxable account with higher expected performance?

If I went all-in on the cash balance plan—as many of my partners did—I'd likely retire with a huge 401(k) balance. That's because, when partners retired or left the practice, their portion of the cash balance plan was rolled into their 401(k). On the other hand, forgoing the cash balance plan meant taking a large tax hit today and investing the after-tax savings in a taxable account. Despite that big tax hit, my spreadsheet showed that the taxable account might beat out the cash balance plan on an after-tax basis. This was chiefly due to the higher expected return for my more aggressively invested taxable account. Ultimately, I decided to hedge my bets, contributing some money to the cash balance plan but also saving significant sums in a taxable account.

Toward the end of my tenure as a trustee, I lobbied hard to add another type of retirement account: the Roth 401(k), which would offer participants tax-free growth but no initial tax deduction, unlike the traditional 401(k) plan we already had in place. Here, we dragged our feet. Though the Roth 401(k) was born in 2006, our group didn't add a Roth 401(k) option until 2014. I believe this was a serious mistake. While the cash balance plan was popular, given its obvious tax benefits, the lack of tax diversification it encouraged was a major downside. To get a sense of the problem, imagine the following scenario: You're a high-earning physician who is also an aggressive saver. You're able to contribute more than $60,000 a year to a traditional 401(k) and profit-sharing plan, plus another $200,000 or more to a cash balance plan, depending on your age and years with the group. Now imagine doing this consistently, year after year. By the time you retire, you'll have built an enormous tax-deferred nest egg, with income taxes owed on every dollar withdrawn.

Many of my partners did just that. But they probably saved little to nothing in a taxable account or a tax-free Roth account. This lack of tax diversification could come back to haunt them in retirement. The assumption that they would enjoy a lower tax rate in retirement could prove badly wrong, given the substantial required minimum distributions that must start at age 72. Should income tax rates rise from today's historically low levels, that would only compound the problem. Roth 401(k) accounts—coupled with Roth conversions— could provide some tax relief in retirement.

CHOOSING BADLY

Our practice's 401(k) plan was entirely self-directed, offering the sort of choice found in a traditional brokerage account. Participants could buy and sell what they wanted, when they wanted. The commissions were relatively low—later to disappear altogether—which reduced the frictional costs of trading. Complete freedom to invest as one pleased, combined with near zero commissions. Investing nirvana, right? Not so fast.

Some physicians hired financial advisors to manage their 401(k) investments—including the less-than-scrupulous advisor mentioned earlier. About half were self-directed. Without an iota of formal financial education or training, many saw fit to manage their retirement nest egg completely on their own, me included. It was like giving a layperson a scalpel and forceps, maybe throwing in a surgery textbook or two, and saying, "Take out the patient's appendix."

The results were predictable. Although I joined the group in 2002, I heard stories of fortunes made and then lost during the late 1990s technology stock bubble. Some portfolios held just five or fewer stocks. Others languished 100% in cash. By the looks of the hyperactive trading in some accounts, you might have guessed we were running a hedge fund rather than a medical practice.

It's clear to me now that most of us would have been far better served by a menu of fewer but smarter investment options inside our 401(k)—things like target-date funds and index funds. If I could go back in time, I would have made age-appropriate, low-cost target-date funds the default investment within our plan. Smart defaults and free choice can coexist. If plan participants don't like their default target-date fund, they could switch into other investments. But my guess is that many of my coworkers would have appreciated a gentle nudge in the right direction. The federal Thrift Savings Plan, which I would encounter later in my career, is a model in this regard.

Physicians are a proud and confident lot. Years of academic success and being addressed as "doctor" can go to our heads. Add to that generous compensation and you have the makings of a toxic brew. Physicians—especially male physicians—suffer from supreme overconfidence. We fall prey to the specious notion that we can beat the markets, in our spare time, no less.

I, for one, should have known better. Fairly early in my career, I'd read some of the investing classics—*A Random Walk Down Wall Street* by Burton Malkiel, *Common Sense on Mutual Funds* by John Bogle, and *The Four Pillars of Investing* by William Bernstein. The message was loud and clear: Markets are efficient. Passive investing was the way to superior results. But pride and overconfidence intervened, whispering,

"Surely you, John, are not an *average* investor." Unfortunately, I believed the lie. Here's just a sampling of my investment mistakes:

- Amazon.com. I bought the stock, along with other internet darlings, during the dotcom craze of the late 1990s. Most went to zero. After getting back to even, I sold Amazon for a split-adjusted $2.50 a share. Talk about selling too soon: Even after getting roughed up in early 2022, Amazon's shares were still trading above $100.
- XM Satellite Radio. After reading a bullish article in *SmartMoney* magazine, I invested in this growth stock. Not long after, the stock began to plummet. After doubling down several times, I managed to turn a small loss into a sizable one.
- Sears Holdings. Here I followed in the footsteps of wunderkind investor Eddie Lampert, who some were calling the next Warren Buffett. This was by far my largest investing blunder. When Sears finally filed for bankruptcy, I had lost about a year's wages on this investment alone.

Now that you've lost all respect for me as an investor, let me say that I've also had my share of investing successes. Amid 2008's global financial crisis, I made large investments in the big banks that paid off in spades. More recently, I bought aggressively during the COVID-19 bear market of 2020, investments that have paid off handsomely so far.

But on the whole, I sincerely doubt that my investments have outperformed a simple index-fund portfolio. Even if I had marginally outperformed the averages, it wasn't worth the cost. As any economist will tell you, there are opportunity costs to every decision. How do you place a price tag on the hundreds of hours spent researching stocks and poring over the market, time which could have been spent in other, more fulfilling endeavors? Time is the one commodity that can't be recouped.

LEAP OF FAITH

About four years ago, my life took an unforeseen turn. Our children were approaching their teen years, but we had yet to find a suitable high school for them. This was not for lack of trying. Public school, private school, homeschooling—we had tried them all. The ideal school seemed an elusive dream.

Our parenting philosophy may seem extreme to some, but providing our children an opportunity to thrive academically was our highest priority. My own parents sent me to boarding school in the seventh grade. It was a major sacrifice for them—and a rough few years for me—but, in retrospect, I benefited enormously. Now, it was time to do the same for my children.

Eventually, we found what seemed to be the ideal school—one that grouped students by ability rather than age. There was just one problem: It was located in another state. While our children's education was of paramount importance to us, we weren't willing to break up the family so they could attend. If our children were to go to this school, we were moving as a family. By this point, I had been with my Southern California radiology group for nearly 16 years. It wasn't the perfect job—no job is—but it was an incredibly stable and desirable one by most criteria. On top of that, I had toiled four long years just to become a full partner. Moving meant giving all that up and starting over from scratch.

A preliminary job search had come up empty. Still, I assured my wife that we could afford to move even if I didn't find a job right away. Years of saving aggressively had put us in a position to make a difficult choice based on our values rather than our finances. While we weren't financially independent at that point, we were financially secure enough to make a leap of faith. I took great solace in Ecclesiastes 3: "To everything there is a season, and a time to every purpose under the heaven." It was the season to invest in our children's education.

Having no job leads, I sent my CV to as many radiology practices as I could find through the internet. I also tried cold-calling. Nothing. Either radiology groups weren't hiring or they were only considering people they knew through personal connections. It seemed like I might be unemployed for the first time in my life.

One day, as I was dictating cases alone in the "reading room"—the term radiologists use to refer to our dark, computer-packed work area—a thought occurred to me. What about a Veterans Affairs (VA) hospital? As a radiology resident in San Francisco, I'd spent a few months training at the San Francisco VA. Rotating through the VA was a godsend for sleep-deprived residents since the patient volume was far lower than at other hospitals. But working for a VA hospital as a full-time attending physician had never before crossed my mind—until now.

A quick Google search returned an immediate hit. There was indeed a VA hospital where we planned to move. Feeling an invisible nudge, I picked up the phone and placed a call. After being transferred to the radiology department, I asked the person on the other end, "May I speak to one of your radiologists, please?" After what seemed like an eternity, a man picked up the line. It was the chair of the radiology department. Trying to hide my trepidation, I introduced myself and explained, "My family is moving to your town in a few months. I was wondering if you have any job openings for radiologists."

I heard a pause and then a quiet chuckle. My heart sank. Was my desperation so obvious? "That's funny," said the voice on the other end. "Just last week, one of our radiologists gave notice that he plans to leave. So, yes, we have an opening." He gave me his email address and asked for my CV.

As I put down the phone and sat in silence, goosebumps rippled over my body. What had led me to make that phone call at that moment? Had I called a few weeks earlier, I would have been rebuffed. Had I searched the official government job website, I would have come up empty—the job hadn't yet been posted. Was it an amazing coincidence or had I just witnessed a miracle?

Over the next month or so, I interviewed for the position and was offered the job. In becoming a government employee, I took a very steep pay cut. But having a job was infinitely better than the alternative—being unemployed. I soon learned that there are wonderful benefits to being a federal employee: an inflation-adjusted pension upon retirement, access to an excellent defined contribution plan—the aforementioned Thrift Savings Plan—with generous matching contributions, and amazing health insurance benefits, to name just a few.

But it turned out that the greatest benefits were nonfinancial. After joining the VA, I channeled my passion for finance into spreading financial literacy. I developed a curriculum for healthcare staff and trainees, giving monthly talks on personal finance and investing. Later, I taught an elective on personal finance to fourth-year medical students at a local university. It was also around this time that I started writing for *HumbleDollar* and I finally published my first book, *How to Raise Your Child's Financial IQ: The Most Important Things*, which was years in the making.

This latest phase of my life and financial journey are replete with lessons. The first one is immortalized by Robert Frost's beautiful lines in 'The Road Not Taken':

> Two roads diverged in a wood, and I—
> I took the one less traveled by,
> And that has made all the difference.

Giving up a secure, well-paying job in midcareer was viewed by many as financially irresponsible. But what I discovered was that the road less traveled is often the most scenic. The educational benefits for our children were well worth the move. But the risk we took also paid off for me both personally and professionally.

The second lesson is that financial security opens up doors. One reason we were willing to leave California was that our financial house was in order. Had it not been, I wonder whether we would have taken such a large risk. In the end, financial freedom is about far more than retiring early and hitting the proverbial golf course. It's about being free to make difficult choices and follow your true north.

Finally, I've learned that we are in far less control of our finances and lives than we imagine. Instead, life is filled with randomness and chance. In investing, these forces can easily conspire to make or break an investment. But they can also bend the course of our lives in unpredictable ways. How many blessings in my life—financial or otherwise—were the result of dumb luck or divine grace? Plenty.

THREE LESSONS

* As your income climbs, don't let your living costs rise quite as quickly. That'll allow you to save even more each year—with little or no impact on your happiness.

* Tax-deductible retirement accounts are attractive, but there's a price to be paid—in the form of higher tax bills in retirement. To ensure those tax bills aren't too high, consider putting part of your retirement savings in Roth IRAs and Roth 401(k) plans, which offer tax-free growth but no immediate tax deduction.

* Beware overconfidence. Just because you're successful in one area of your life doesn't mean you can also successfully pick investments. Most folks would fare far better with a simple index-fund portfolio.

LEARNING BY ERRING

BY
MICHAEL FLACK

Michael Flack is a former naval officer and 20-year veteran of
the oil and gas industry. Born on Long Island, New York, and
trained as a nuclear engineer, he tries to write with a New Yorker's
skepticism, an engineer's sense of logic and hopefully some humor.
Now retired, he enjoys traveling, blogging and spreadsheets.

I MAGINE AN AGE long ago, before the internet. Not only that, it
was so long ago that it was before most Americans cared about the
stock market. Unimaginable? Well, it isn't to me.

When I came of age in 1987, the stock market was a fantasyland. It
was a place inhabited by your dentist, a friend's father who was a lawyer,
or that banker your dad knew from the Knights of Columbus. People
like my parents, a janitor and a secretary, lived in a different world of
passbook savings accounts, certificates of deposit and—if they were
lucky—pensions. It was so long ago that if, for some bizarre reason,
you wanted to know the price of an individual stock, you had to look it
up in the newspaper's business section—one that was printed on paper.

Most people's knowledge of the stock market was limited to
hearing that "the Dow closed up 12 points in light trading" on the

11 o'clock news. The market was such a non-story that when, on October 19, 1987, the S&P 500 dropped 20.5% in the largest one-day percentage decline in its history, it passed me by nearly unnoticed. The only vague recollection I have is a fellow student asking if I'd "heard what was happening with the stock market." I hadn't and went back to studying or, more likely, watching *General Hospital.*

All that changed in the spring semester of my senior year, when I took engineering economics, an elective taught by Dr. Joe McNeill, P.E. I give his name this way because I remember him walking into the classroom and writing his name on the chalkboard in exactly that way. I think the good doctor was proud of his P.E.—professional engineer—license. When my fellow students subsequently spoke about him, we always called him "Dr. Joe McNeill, P.E."

Dr. Joe McNeill, P.E. taught a course that consisted of three parts:

- Economic fundamentals, which included terms like 'net present value', 'internal rate of return' and 'weighted average cost of capital.' He taught us how to calculate the value of today's dollar at some future date. Like most people, I realized that time was money, but the theory was eye-opening.
- Saving and budgeting, because setting aside a significant portion of your income could lead to wealth, career options and early retirement.
- Stock market basics, because this was where you needed to invest your savings. By doing so, you could become rich. It all seems so commonplace now—invest and grow rich—but back then, to the son of blue-collar parents, it was a revelation.

Using a special student rate, he made us subscribe to *The Wall Street Journal.* In a way, the *Journal* was better than the internet because, while it contained a wealth of information, it left out much of the nonsense that the internet now reports as news.

You also have to realize that the *Journal* had a very different look and feel than it does today. First, the news stories did not contain any photos. If you were born in this millennium, this may blow your mind. No photos? Instead, the *Journal* used stylized black and white drawings that it called hedcuts. Second, it was only published on days when the stock market was open, not holidays or weekends. The idea was that whatever happened didn't really matter—until the stock market opened.

The front page had a very regimented look, with six vertical columns. Each one covered a specific topic like global news, story summaries, human interest and weekly reports. I can still recall Dr. Joe McNeill, P.E. teaching us how to read the *Journal*, highlighting what to read first and where to focus our time. He also mentioned that the fourth column was about human interest, adding, "You don't need to waste your time on this."

I have two distinct memories of my time with Dr. Joe McNeill, P.E. One was that, as a reward for having the highest grade in the course, I received a six-month subscription to *The Journal* and a plaque. This was given to me with my proud parents in attendance. The second was the realization that I needed to start saving as much as possible and invest it in the stock market.

BUYING PAST PERFORMANCE

The course required that I research a specific mutual fund. The one I picked was the hottest mutual fund then in existence, Fidelity Magellan Fund, managed by the hottest mutual fund manager then in existence, Peter Lynch. At that time, Lynch was possibly the most famous investor in the world due to the outsized returns he produced at Magellan, averaging 29.2% annually over the 13 years he managed the fund.

His secret, as he explained in his bestselling investment books, was working long hours, rigorous fundamental analysis and following his wife to the store. For example, he bought shares of HanesBrands based on the recommendation of his wife, who—while food shopping—came across the company's egg-shaped plastic containers, called L'eggs, which held women's stockings.

She purchased a pair and raved about them to her husband, who promptly bought shares in Hanes for Magellan. It was among those investments that increased 1,000% in share price, or "ten-baggers" as Lynch called them. He had plenty of ten-baggers—over 100—and he made successful investing seem like the easiest thing in the world.

As soon as I graduated, I started investing in Magellan and quickly learned a valuable lesson about active mutual funds, namely that "past performance does not guarantee future results." In this case, Lynch retired soon after I'd invested, as the stress of trying to beat the market was becoming an issue—another drawback of active investing.

His replacements didn't have his magic touch. I soon realized that, while I didn't mind paying Lynch an outsized expense ratio for his outsized returns, I didn't see the benefit of paying his successors the same expense ratio for their underperformance. I started to look around for other places to invest my savings.

FOOL'S GOLD

In the mid-1990s, while living in Hawaii, I attended an investment seminar in a hotel conference room given by a man named Harry Bellefontaine. The whole affair lasted about an hour and it was quite obvious that this was *not* the first presentation Mr. B had given. He mentioned that he thought both the stock market and Hawaiian real estate were overvalued. Indeed, he'd sold most of his stocks and his house. Because inflation was coming, he said that gold and silver were the way forward. Not just any gold and silver, though, but collectible coins—which he sold.

It was most likely the historic allure of gold coins, along with greed, but I bit and bit hard. Among other coins, I bought 20 half-ounce uncirculated 1991 American Gold Eagles. I can still remember leaving Mr. B's offices slightly paranoid, carrying my treasure in a special case that he gave me free of charge. I immediately took the coins to my bank, where now I had the added benefit of paying $100 a year to rent a safe deposit box.

Everything went along swimmingly, with Mr. B sending me monthly statements indicating the steady Madoff-like rise in the value of my collection. Then, one day, I was watching TV and heard a teaser for the local nightly news that went something like, "Local financial advisor scams gold investors, news at 11." Well, that had my attention.

When I tuned in at 11, I almost cried. There was the station's investigative reporter saying numerous locals may have been scammed by investing in rare coins. In the background, they ran grainy undercover footage of guess who? Mr. B. It appears they couldn't interview him, as he had fled Hawaii on a boat to parts unknown. I almost crapped my pants.

A few weeks later, I was contacted by a different coin dealer, who offered a complimentary review of my collection. He was a nice enough guy and appeared to be a straight shooter. He informed me that, while my collection was genuine, I had overpaid for each coin and, for some pieces, grossly. He tried to let me down easy. But my mood wasn't helped when, at the conclusion of the consultation, he asked if I'd ever considered investing in U.S. Mint commemorative coins, as they were sure to increase in value.

BUILT TO LAST-MAYBE

Soon after my Gold Eagle gambit ended, I read a fascinating book titled *Built to Last* by Jim Collins and Jerry I. Porras. It was the must-read business book of the 1990s and detailed an exhaustive study proving that some companies were just plain better than others.

The idea was that these select companies were "built to last" because they all followed similar paradigms, such as setting "big hairy audacious goals"—called BHAGs—like Boeing betting the company on the 747. Or by creating "cult-like cultures"—like Nordstrom providing dazzling customer service. Or by promoting "homegrown management"—like Procter & Gamble, which developed such a deep bench of talent that it never went outside to hire its CEO.

I thought it obviously followed that, since these were great companies, they would be great investments, too, and make a perfect recipe for a stock portfolio. That worked fine for a few years. But it turned out my recipe also included a few unappetizing ingredients—once-great companies that soon fell on hard times. Like Citibank, a penny stock amid the Great Recession of 2008–09. And Fannie Mae, mentioned in the follow-up book titled *Good to Great*, which was placed in conservatorship in 2008. And GE, whose long slide ended in near-bankruptcy in 2008. And Motorola, which was deemed irrelevant by the market in the late 2000s after the introduction of smartphones.

MASTER INVESTOR-BRIEFLY

In 1999, I read an article written by Paul Sturm in the much-missed *SmartMoney* magazine. It was a comprehensive review of a security I'd never heard of before called a master limited partnership (MLP).

An MLP is a publicly traded company that has the tax benefits of a private partnership. Its income is taxed but not its distributions. That meant investors like me could defer taxes owed, sometimes almost indefinitely. Due to the vagaries of the tax code, MLPs are mostly limited to oil and gas pipeline companies.

To me, they seemed like the perfect security: tax-deferred distributions, rich cash flow, inflation-protected and high-yielding. We're talking companies like Suburban Propane, NuStar Energy, Kinder Morgan and TEPPCO Partners. I felt like Yankees' manager Miller Huggins reviewing his lineup card for the 1927 World Series: every player a heavy-hitter and reliable. Would you say no to investing in Babe Ruth and Lou Gehrig—on a tax-deferred basis to boot?

I bought my fill of MLPs and was rewarded richly, even though the K-1 partnership forms were a pain when it came time to file my taxes. But who am I to complain? For ten golden years, I felt like a youthful Warren Buffett, consistently outperforming the S&P 500 with less volatility.

But alas poor Yorick, no security is perfect. I came to realize in time that *every* publicly traded company will borrow to the limit of its cash flows. I won't bore you with the details of the painful deleveraging and subsequent MLP selloff by retail investors, but it was death by a thousand cuts. Since the Great Recession of 2008–09, my MLP lineup has reliably underperformed the S&P 500. Worse, one of my beloved "Babe Ruth" investments was restructured, sticking me with a Ruthian-sized tax bill, plus its distributions were reduced and the share price cut in half. As Job said, "The Lord giveth, and the Lord taketh away"—and then some.

WAIT, THERE'S MORE

In 2000, I bought stock in a company that used the latest technologies to revolutionize the way multiple business lines did their business. A company that only hired the smartest people to work on cutting-edge projects that would change the world. Led by an even smarter CEO who claimed that many existing businesses were dinosaurs and would soon be extinct.

Unfortunately for me, this company wasn't named Amazon. It was called Enron. Soon after I made my investment, then-CEO Jeff Skilling resigned to "spend more time with family." Within months, Enron declared bankruptcy—the largest in U.S. history until then. I hung on for a little while because, as my mother used to say, "hope springs eternal." But I eventually sold to harvest some very large tax losses.

The subsequent fraud convictions of Enron's CEO, CFO and the chairman of the board—along with the collapse of its complacent auditor, Arthur Andersen LLP—were of little consolation. Enron not only shook my faith in the decency of man, but also in the wisdom of picking individual stocks.

This mood only grew on me with the subsequent significant devaluation of other 'can't miss' investments that I owned. Like Thornburg Mortgage, which went bankrupt in 2009. Or Medallion Financial Corp., which was such a stinker that it changed its ticker symbol from TAXI to MFC to hide. And International Business Machine—but at least I wasn't alone in that gradual meltdown.

All the lemons that I'd chosen made me start to doubt my stock-picking ability and realize that *maybe* it was impossible to beat the market. The outperformance of my MLPs early on had made me believe that I possessed superior analytical skills. The subsequent underperformance by the same MLPs—plus all the other lemons I'd picked—disabused me of this notion.

While losing money on my clunkers was bad enough, it also filled me with an amount of anxiety and shame that wasn't offset by my few-and-far-between winners. Because there were some in my portfolio, even if I eventually realized they might be due more to good luck than financial acumen. These included:

- Genzyme. I purchased shares based on my wife's orthopedic analysis, which was in turn based on the injection of a Genzyme-produced drug called Synvisc into her bad knee. Synvisc is a natural joint lubricant and cushion, synthesized from the cockscomb of a rooster—the feathers on the top of his head. Chicken feathers, I thought. I knew that Peter Lynch would approve, so some shares were purchased. A few months later Sanofi bought out Genzyme and I received a 37% annualized return.

- Monarch Cement. I purchased 100 shares at $28.50 based on a reverse stock split arbitrage opportunity offered to owners of record. The stratagem had the company buying back stock at $30 a share for a quick $1.50 gain. But it turned out that, due to a grammatical issue, I was not an 'owner of record,' so the company didn't buy back my shares. It all worked out in my favor, though, as my unsold shares subsequently tripled in value, leading to an annualized return of more than 20%.

- Sysco. In 2009, my mother gave me some money for Christmas. I used it to buy stock. I decided to invest it in a company she would be able to understand, so I picked the food distributor Sysco. I thought it could be a way we could share my interest in the stock market. I wrote her a "thank you" note, including specifics about the company, and mentioned I would update her now and then on its performance. She may not have completely understood what I said, as she subsequently informed me that she "didn't need any stock tips." Since purchasing it in early 2010, Sysco has easily outperformed the S&P 500. Unfortunately, my mother had only given me $25.

ROAD TO INDEXING

Over time, I started to lose interest in doing the deep research that was required to invest in individual stocks. I found I would rather spend my time working out, reading about the Second World War, and traveling. Since it was obvious that I previously hadn't spent *enough* time researching, common sense told me that reduced research would not lead to better results.

All this led me, slowly but surely, to shift my investments from hand-picked stocks to low-cost index funds like the Schwab Total Stock Market Index Fund, iShares Select Dividend ETF and Fidelity 500 Index Fund. These were added to a portfolio that already contained a fair amount of low-cost index funds as, thankfully, my 401(k) didn't give me any other options. While low-cost index funds weren't as sexy as Amazon or Apple, they were easier on my blood pressure and, more important, my ego.

When I retired a few years ago, I looked back at how I did. What kind of grade, I wondered, would Dr. Joe McNeill, P.E. give me? I think he'd be proud of my ability to save. As I tell fellow investors, the size of my portfolio is proportional to the size of my frugality.

He'd probably be disappointed, though, in many of the clunkers I'd invested in. How could I explain away Enron? He might, however, be proud that I'd learned from my mistakes and subsequently invested enough in low-cost index funds to allow for my early retirement.

Dr. Joe McNeill, P.E. was a tough grader. Still, I think he'd give me a "B." But maybe not a plaque.

THREE LESSONS

* The markets are full of wonderful stories, some of them true and some of them lies. Exercise extreme caution when told of a can't-miss investment by a stranger in a hotel conference room.

* It's hard to beat the return of a low-cost, broad-based stock index fund. Many learn this lesson eventually—after first owning more exciting investments like gold coins and Enron.

* Time is your most valuable asset. A dollar invested today can be worth several later on. It follows, then, that there's never a better moment to begin saving and investing than right now.

CONCLUSION:

WHAT'S YOUR STORY?

BY
JONATHAN CLEMENTS

F YOU'VE DILIGENTLY read *My Money Journey* from the very first page—rather than jumping to this conclusion—you've now had a peek into the financial lives of 30 people. But what does your own money journey look like? My challenge to you: Start writing.

I think there's great virtue in committing our stories and ideas to paper. Writing forces us to organize our thoughts, to express what we believe, to recall long ago events that shaped who we are today. It can help us to think more clearly about our life, what we've achieved, what's yet to be done and what the path forward should look like.

And we aren't the only potential beneficiary. How much do you know about your great-grandparents? Wouldn't it be wonderful to read their account of their life? When we write about our money journey, we inevitably describe our life journey—a journey that, I strongly suspect, future generations will find fascinating. Our only immortality on this earth is the memory of others. Want to be remembered? It's time to begin typing. Here are five suggestions:

- **Less is more.** Try to limit your story to 3,000 words and preferably less. If your essay is too long, your family simply won't read it.
- **Don't boast.** Nobody likes a braggart. Your successes likely came grudgingly, and there were probably plenty of failures and mistakes along the way. Luck—both good and bad—no doubt played a huge role in your life's journey.
- **Be candid.** Why not mention your income and net worth? Why not mention your most embarrassing blunders? Very few of us are honest with others about the state of our finances, and we're poorer for it.
- **Go for the good stuff.** Nobody wants to know all of your life's gory details, financial or otherwise. Instead, readers want the highlight reel—the triumphs, the turning points, the terrible mistakes.
- **Take your time.** Good writing takes multiple revisions and many days. Once you have a first draft, set it aside and then look at it with fresh eyes a few days later. Have friends and family review your essay. Ask them which sections were most interesting—and which were boring or confusing. Ask them which parts left them hankering for more—and which stuff they simply didn't need to know.

Happy with what you've written? If you're interested in seeing your essay published, send it to me at jonathan@jonathanclements.com. I'm not offering any guarantees. But if I like what I see, maybe I'll publish your essay on *HumbleDollar's* website.

Another great title
from Harriman House

The Laws of Wealth
Psychology and the secret to investing success
Daniel Crosby

"Should be read by all those new to investing."
—JAMES P. O'SHAUGHNESSY, AUTHOR OF
WHAT WORKS ON WALL STREET

Available from all good book stores

Another great title
from Harriman House

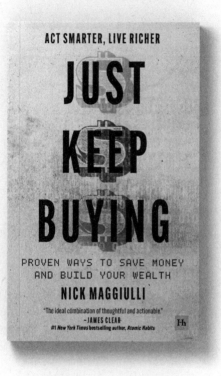

Just Keep Buying
Proven ways to save money and build your wealth
Nick Maggiulli

"The ideal combination of thoughtful and actionable."
—JAMES CLEAR, #1 *NEW YORK TIMES* BESTSELLING AUTHOR, *ATOMIC HABITS*

Available from all good book stores

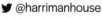